David Milch

MANCHESTER
1824

Manchester University Press

THE TELEVISION SERIES

series editors

JONATHAN BIGNELL
SARAH CARDWELL
STEVEN PEACOCK

already published

Paul Abbott BETH LOUISE JOHNSON

Alan Bennett KARA MCKECHNIE

Alan Clarke DAVE ROLINSON

Jimmy McGovern STEVE BLANDFORD

Andrew Davies SARAH CARDWELL

Tony Garnett STEPHEN LACEY

Trevor Griffiths JOHN TULLOCH

Troy Kennedy Martin LEZ COOKE

Terry Nation JONATHAN BIGNELL AND ANDREW O'DAY

Jimmy Perry and David Croft SIMON MORGAN-RUSSELL

Lynda La Plante JULIA HALLAM

Jack Rosenthal SUE VICE

Joss Whedon MATTHEW PATEMAN

JASON JACOBS

David Milch

Manchester University Press

Published by Manchester University Press
Altrincham Street, Manchester M1 7JA

www.manchesteruniversitypress.co.uk

British Library Cataloguing-in-Publication Data
A catalogue record for this book is available from the British Library

ISBN 978 0 7190 8343 3 hardback

First published 2020

Typeset in Scala by
Servis Filmsetting Ltd, Stockport, Cheshire
Printed in Great Britain
by TJ International Ltd, Padstow

To my parents
Jill Jacobs and John Jacobs

Contents

General editors' preface

Television is part of our everyday experience and is one of the most significant features of our cultural lives today. Yet its practitioners and its artistic and cultural achievements remain relatively unacknowledged. The books in this series aim to remedy this by addressing the work of major television writers and creators, and important and interesting genres of programme. Each volume provides an authoritative and accessible guide that focuses on either a particular practitioner's output or a body of related work, and assesses its contribution to television over the years. Books in the series give a carefully researched, historically based overview of the material addressed, and make a case for the importance of the work considered, by means of close textual analysis integrated with other materials. Many of the volumes draw on original sources, such as specially conducted interviews and archive material, and all of them list relevant bibliographic sources and provide full details of the programmes discussed.

In comparison with some related disciplines, Television Studies scholarship is still relatively young, and the series aims to contribute to this vigorous and evolving field. This series provides resources for critical thinking about television. While maintaining a clear focus on writers, creators and programmes themselves, the books in this series also take account of key critical concepts and theories in Television Studies. Each book is written from a particular critical or theoretical perspective, with reference to pertinent issues, and the approaches included in the series are varied and sometimes dissenting. Each author explicitly outlines the reasons for his or her particular focus, methodology or perspective. Readers are invited to think critically about the subject matter and approach covered in each book.

Although the series is addressed primarily to students and scholars of television, the books will also appeal to the many people who are interested in how television programmes have been commissioned, made and enjoyed. Since television has been so much a part of personal and public life in the twentieth and twenty-first centuries, we hope that the series will engage with, and sometimes challenge, a broad and diverse readership.

Sarah Cardwell
Jonathan Bignell
Steven Peacock

Acknowledgements

Thank you to Matthew Frost and Steven Peacock for inviting me to contribute to the Television Series and for suggesting that I write about David Milch. Matthew Frost deserves particular thanks for his patience and trust in me as the years went on. David Milch was generous, open and trusting in welcoming me to consult his materials on various shows, and for allowing me behind the scenes to observe his working life. Unless otherwise indicated, quotations are drawn from the archive of his personal documents, mostly transcripts of talks in the writers' room, or from personal interviews. As this book went into production the news broke that Milch had been diagnosed with Alzheimer's disease; he revealed this in an interview that took place on the set of the *Deadwood* movie.

Many thanks to Sarah Cardwell for providing careful, detailed and intelligent comments on the manuscript. Thanks also to Steven Peacock for his wonderful comments and support and sketches. Murray Pomerance made a crucial intervention late in the writing for which I am also grateful. Part of the research for this book was funded by the former Faculty of Arts at the University of Queensland. My friend Alison Taylor was a steadfast and reliable source of comfort when matters seemed at a loss, and other times as well. Thanks and love as always to my wife, Valerie Spall, and to my children, who grew up in the shadow of my writing this.

Introduction

> I've had to learn that people aren't just good or just bad, but people are many things.
>
> Paul Biegler (James Stewart), *Anatomy of a Murder* (dir. Preminger, 1959)

This book offers an account of David Milch's fiction realised in television drama, and will engage with literature, film and aspects of philosophy insofar as they are relevant. His work is obsessed with cycles of failure and redemption among unworthy, self-loathing souls whose thickened articulations lay claim to what William Faulkner called man's 'puny, inexhaustible voice, still talking'.[1] Milch's worlds gather the weak of mind and spirit, the unwashed, the unlovely and the unloved, into a marvellous world of talk that strives for the holy lucidity of social companionship. These 'poor, forked creatures', lacking the moral muscularity of heroes or the vision and foresight of prophets, resemble Beckett's narrators who must, can't, but will 'go on', returning again to another dawn, another struggle to persuade themselves, or simply (but this is their hardest task) *accept*, that they are human beings, too. That they belong in the world. And in this dogged persistence they endure, for the most part, and outlast amid the challenges of a world unfit to acknowledge their belonging as creatures, children, of God. Milch's vision is deeply religious, which is to say that without being associated with any formally organised religion, it is grounded in the revelation that redemption can be received by the most 'unworthy' (by their own lights) through their seeking out and participating in the daily sacrament of human sociality – conversation, argument, conflict: the full intensity of a pack of souls. Social and individual 'dysfunctionality' (so-called) forms the substrate and fuels the metabolism of his groups; its distortions provide the ground against which his figures seek their sustenance for action, companionship, reflection, violence and love.

Only in the mutual acceptance and acknowledgement of weakness can these motley crews realise their true essence; even then they know, or will discover, that this realisation is but an ephemeral sanctuary. Their journey from inferno to heaven is but a journey across a Möbius strip.

Hence, revelations, discoveries, sanctuaries are not end points or final judgements. They are destinations before refuel and take-off, a machine cycle of dirty–clean–dirty–clean in which every point of rest or defilement is a temporary stop around an axis, and each apparent stop leans forward, rocking. This instability-in-stability means that his characters never reach a destination that is settled without the prospect of unsettling, that there is no real rest untroubled by the shadows of what tomorrow or the next minute might deliver. Even at the family dinner table or the happy bar, fear and the future peek through a slit in the curtains. Milch's characters and, I believe, the writer himself, operate most effectively under such shadows and observation, however exhausting and chilling the experience. In a perceptive summary of Milch's work David Thorburn has observed:

> Do all truly compelling storytellers rehearse the same preoccupations – themes, obsessions – in every story they tell? Perhaps not all. But think of Dostoyevsky, Kafka, Conrad, Faulkner, the contemporary American novelist Robert Stone, Hitchcock, Orson Welles ... At the heart of every Milch story is a morally damaged protagonist who feels himself or herself to be beyond forgiveness ... Milch's need or drive to imagine such a character is so deep that this central figure, in almost all his stories, is doubled, tripled, and replicated even further in subsidiary characters ... In Milch's archetypal scene an egregious sinner, a murderer, an abject drunkard, a suicidal prostitute who thinks herself beyond redemption – this person commits an urgent act of sympathy and compassion. In their most compelling form [...] such passages test our own resources of irony and sympathy. The Swearengen who kills in mercy is not so different from the Swearengen who kills for business and could not even exist without that bleak and murderous history. Still, it's a moment of grace by and for the forgotten and the unredeemed.[2]

It is the medium of episodic television drama that allows this kind of repetition, cycling and rotation to fold and unfold around the pivot of Milch's preoccupations. In a form such as the novel or feature film there has to be an ending (even if the prospect of a sequel is held in view). It is significant that almost every one of Milch's television shows has either been cancelled (*Big Apple* [2001], *Deadwood* [2004–06], *John From Cincinnati* [2007], *Luck* [2012]) or has seen him depart before the finale (*NYPD Blue* [1993–2006]). Either he abandons the work or it is taken away from him. Like the drug addict, he quits or is deprived of his fix; but addictions do not end even when one stops using: they go on until one reaches another kind of settlement.

It is perhaps surprising that the populace of his fictional worlds is built from such fragile materials, individuals so bound up in private cycles of fall, grace, backsliding and fall again that to construct anything with them is to invest in a house of cards, so precarious is their connective tissue to the world. In the first season of *Deadwood*, Andy Cramed (Zach Grenier), croupier at the Bella Union brothel, contracts the plague (smallpox) and is tossed into the woods to die by his boss Cy Tolliver (Powers Boothe); nursed to health by a drunken Jane Cannary (Robin Weigert), he vanishes for several episodes before returning to the makeshift quarantined part of the town, where he gets into conversation with the Revd Smith (Ray McKinnon), who is busy dismantling the flimsy plague tents:

Smith: How are you Mister Cramed?
Cramed: I backslid in the other camps. I went to Gayville with the best of intentions and wound up at dice.
Smith: Oh yes.
Cramed: Went to Elizabethtown and wound up at dice.
Smith: Oh yes.
Cramed: Thought I'd try to work here where I'd been good but you're putting the tent down.
Smith: Ask God's help Mister Cramed, wherever you find yourself. He will show you the path.
Cramed: Will you help me pray?

Disappearing again, he returns in season two, now as the *Reverend* Cramed, and successfully leads the funeral address for William Bullock (although the camera shows us, alone, that in finishing the speech he slips slightly into a puddle, a typically Milchean alloy of baptism and Fall). And yet, in the final episode of that season, after marrying Alma Garret to Whitney Ellsworth, Cramed succumbs to the taunts of his former boss, and viciously stabs Tolliver in the belly. For Tolliver, smallpox and religion are the same – a plague; as he stabs him Cramed says, 'God will not be mocked', but the act itself is, of course, a mortal sin. And, as Thorburn rightly points out, Milch's dramas teem with people like this who cycle through a pattern of fall–redemption–fall. The cyclic, sometimes formulaic nature of an episodic medium has been recruited to Milch's primary artistic fix, the fall, ascent and fall again of each of us.

An aspect of the agony of this movement for his characters is the presence and their knowledge of a better or best self, either frontally in view or just glimpsed, so that they cannot thoroughly be and thrive in one continuous, consistent and coherent mode of being. That knowledge, however partial, of 'something deeper', something better that we can attain, is the fulcrum of their movement between crisis and salvation. E. B. Farnum (William Sanderson) makes this evident in a moment of self-reflection-cum-abuse when talking to his servant, Richardson, in *Deadwood*:

> It is no disloyalty to be a realist, Richardson, we are mortal. One hopes for the best. One perseveres. One re-evaluates constantly. One is an asshole if one doesn't. Loyalty expanded is not loyalty betrayed. I contemplate no disloyalty to Al Swearengen. I feel exposed. I don't like being weak, and I know that I am. I yearn to rely on a stronger will. I fear what I'm capable of in its absence. Whereas you, Richardson, know *nothing* of yourself. Are you shitting or going blind? Or on foot or horseback? You vile fucking lump! Bury that offal in the Shepherd's Pie.

Knowledge does not beget action here: having a sense of the depth of one's failings helps us little to escape them, and a contented life cannot be merely willed into existence by a will at war with itself, by a mind haunted by desires that are unwanted but ever-present, like the sheer inescapable fact of the wrong card dealt into one's hand.[3] One needs ferociously *not* to be the person one has to be, and the nature of redemption is accepted with a similar inkling of its impermanence.

Milch's characters are restless figures and yet rarely loners or wanderers as we might expect; instead they are always 'on the move' inside. Despite the occasional standout soliloquy, Milch is not so much interested in the musings of the solitary; rather his characters find or put themselves in the stormy climates of moods, tensions fuelled by the dense stretched bands of resentments and slights. In all of this, what we see is also not what we register, and what we hear are lies and half-truths from those desperately seeking the cleansing nourishment – equally, perhaps, the cloak of its mendacities – of the social. Without that prospect, there is the alternative of gorgeous narcotic self-annihilation: opium, heroin, booze, the shot-glass after shot-glass charge of the bet. The succour of that self-destructive habit pays *both* impish pipers – the drugs provide reason to live and the propellant for continual self-loathing; that is everything such souls need in order to steal some rest from the restlessness of the racket of viciously critical voices in their mind, from the itch of the body and its desires, and the temptations of the tongue to yap and lie.

It would also be a mistake to picture Milch's characters as merely divided against themselves. That would be to hold up a static, glazed portrait. The apposite sense of them is provided by Milch in his frequent use of a line from Herman Melville's poem 'The Conflict of Convictions': 'I know a wind in purpose strong– / It spins *against* the way it drives.'[4] This gives us that sense of them as a cluster of contrasting and intersecting forces in motion at speed and depth. And so, this book is about how these people come to be the way they are on screen for us and how their lives are stamped by the vitality of the performances that embody them as much as the stories in which they participate.

This book does not seek to answer *why* one man would be driven to write fiction about such characters or the stories they inhabit and vitalise, since it is impossible to know the secrets of another's heart. But I do want to account for why Milch's fiction takes the shape, themes, talk and associations that it does; why his characters speak and act in the way that they do and what this *means* for us as a picture of America and the world. Neither does the book seek to provide a comprehensive itemisation of everything Milch has worked on or contributed to during his long career in the industry. Rather, I want to point to pieces of his fiction that begin to help us most in finding our way through the darkness and light, the mottled difficulty of his drama.

Authorship and intention

There is no doubt some truth in the claim made by psychoanalytic theories that self-division occurs to all of us in early childhood, but I am not concerned here with cashing out the meaning of Milch's work by constant reference to an excavation of his biography. I am, however, vitally concerned with his *intention*. This matter – of attributing and establishing at least some sense of the meaning of a work via reference to the intention of its maker – has been contested for at least the past half century. I have no interest in a defence of this method, except to cite my allegiance to William Empson's comments on the anti-intentionalist New Critics, exemplified by the 'Wimsatt Law', who rejected any reference to authorial intention as a contamination of interpretation. As Empson had it, this meant avoiding 'a process which all persons not insane are using in all their social experience'.[5] In the Preface to his collection *Using Biography* Empson expands the point:

> the Wimsatt Law ... says that no reader can ever grasp the intention of an author. This paradox results from a great failure to grasp the whole situation. Any speaker, when a baby, wanted to understand what people meant, why mum was cross for example, and had enough partial access to go on trying; the effort is usually carried on into adult life, although

> not always into old age. Success, it may be argued, is never complete. But it is nearer completeness in a successful piece of literature than in any other use of language.[6]

Further on, Empson hardens his argument in a way that is directly relevant to Milch, who has been vocal in interviews and elsewhere about his work and what lies behind it:

> When an author is admitting the source of his interest in a subject, and thereby asking his reader to share in it, he will often want to keep the surface of his argument unbroken; perhaps to reassure one type of reader without disturbing another type. This leads to irony at once, and it is practically the only means for an author to break the Wimsatt Law, to tell some of his readers what he is not telling. Of course they may all know, with an enjoyable connivance, that he is only pretending to keep it from some of them.[7]

Milch has been voluble about many of his intentions, but that seems to me to satisfy only one kind or one part of the audience. The work itself, and the single and collective intelligence behind that work, *intends* meaning that is not translatable into words – otherwise he would have written it down in a novel, poem or essay in the first place. Hence, in putting a thin, porous piece of paper between the man and the work, between the biography and the industrial process that realises the shows he is responsible for, I am aiming for an account of artistic output that carries some sense of how and why the man and his work are married.

Neither do I believe that artworks are defined or confined by the time or conditions of their making: it is a unique aspect of cultural products that they can transcend such things (ever listen to and enjoy Mozart? Or Al Green?) It is a strange and continuing fact about much of humanities scholarship that such matters as authorship and the transcendent nature of artworks has been under-investigated, either for reasons of theoretical hygiene or, perhaps, because much of the writing on art before the twentieth century remains merely a target for thinly disguised mockery from those inhabiting a pose of enlightened social and historical awareness.

However, the nature of authorship, its authority and source of intention remains a central concern in my account of Milch's work. This is because Milch himself 'spins against the way he drives', and his unusual method of composition itself exemplifies that tension – refusing to write on paper, he speaks the words aloud to a person who promptly types them on to a large screen in front of the author. And although many other writers have dictated for various reasons (Henry James,

James Joyce, Rod Serling), in Milch's case the *publicness* of the act is as important as the fact that he speaks rather than inscribes the words he is responsible for. David Shields, a former student of Milch's creative writing class at Yale in the 1970s, gives a striking account of the early nature of this predilection:

> Both Milch and I liked to write in the new underground wing of the Cross-Campus Library, but I needed the complete isolation of an enclosed cubicle, whereas Milch would work on his stories and plays and screenplays at the table in the centre of the room, drinking coffee, overhearing conversation – surrounded by human activity. I allegorized and romanticized this difference: to me, writing was a revenge upon life, upon my life, whereas to Milch writing seemed to be part of life. He was the first intellectual I'd ever met who not only seemed to like life but who reveled in it – who, in Conrad's famous phrase, 'to the destructive element submit[ted]'.[8]

After the success of his television shows vaulted him into a mass media presence, Milch continued to cultivate a public persona that is loquaciously vocal about his past addictions and misdemeanours while enigmatically overlaying this apparent candour with misdirection and outright deception by omission. This is a man whose intentions are in plain sight, and their visibility provides a hiding place for their core drivers, even as he professes to confess them. One preliminary explanation for this is not quite the festival of exhibitionism that his long-term collaborator Steven Bochco describes here:

> David perfected what I call the Art of Performance Writing. He would lie on the floor, surrounded by his adoring followers, and dictate his scripts to a script typist at the computer. A monitor would be in front of David where he lay on the floor, and he would dictate, then re-write, then re-write again and again, all verbally, for the amusement and edification of his adoring audience. Personally, I couldn't watch it. It was a display of narcissism that I found impossible to be witness to. This was his paid audience.[9]

However, I suspect that this process is more about self-defence than narcissistic self-flattery. During a remarkable series of talks given during the 2007–08 Writers' Guild of America strike, Milch described to the audience the array of critical forces that inhabits him:

> Just so you know that this is not self-indulgent, I have an ordering voice which is working when I'm sleeping. And when I wake up *[imitates cruelly sarcastic mocking voice]*: 'Oh, he wakes. He wakes. What's he gonna? – oh, he – that's his idea of urinating! With the split stream. That's how he thinks coffee is supposed to be made! That's how he thinks the

> ignition of the car should be turned on.' By the time I'm on my way to work ... I wanna shoot up.[10]

Milch has also spoken of the 'Committee' in the head of *NYPD Blue*'s Andy Sipowicz, similarly critical and cruel, which regularly tempts Sipowicz to temper its volume through the dulling effects of booze. In contrast to both Shields's and Bochco's view, Milch seems to be recruiting supporting numbers in the room as a counterweight to an internal *Stasi* of hostile archaeopsychic voices. Northrop Frye captures a sense of the oppression of those voices, and the ('perhaps') potential for restoration that takes us out of the isolation:

> When we become intolerably oppressed by the mystery of human existence and by what seems the utter impotence of God to do or even care anything about human suffering, we enter the stage of Eliot's 'word in the desert', and hear all the rhetoric of the ideologues, expurgating, revising, setting straight, rationalizing, proclaiming the time of renovation. After that, perhaps, the terrifying and welcome voice may begin, annihilating everything we thought we knew, and restoring everything we have never lost.[11]

The fact of Milch's preference for public writing (for example, we see him doing this on the *Deadwood* DVD extra feature material) makes it much harder to credibly deny human agency and intention as central aspects in the creation of television art. During a visit to his offices in Santa Monica in the spring of 2011, I sat with Milch and watched him write a scene for *Luck*, heard the words he said and watched as they appeared on the large monitor in front of us. The champion jockey Julie Krone was in the room too, and I'd spent most of the day with her husband, the sports journalist Jay Hovdey, and another writer, in a pleasant writing office decked with books about racing history and photos of jockeys and horses, as they progressed other parts of the episode for Milch's final revision. I knew, of course, about his technique of writing without paper, giving voice and reaction to fictional human and animal entities that, somewhere, would be realised and embodied by real humans and animals, speaking and moving according to, in large part, the decisions, revisions, the words spoken by Milch. Our gazes were fixed on the big screen where the black marks of the evolving script appeared, were erased, and appeared again – Milch is a compulsive editor and reviser, ever seeking to sharpen the locutions under the vast pressure of the demands of the production schedule, not to mention his commitment to the integrity of the intuition that brought the first marks into view.

I was in the room less than an hour; about a year later I watched the same scene on screen as it was transmitted. Words with power. When you see a writer at work you see nothing but the sheer biological fact of a human being in a room speaking, writing, being there. He is both an expressive entity and just a man talking. But the event I was briefly part of did not come from nothing or nowhere. As Milch says of his approach:

> I have trained myself in such a way to say, works do not save me but by my works I show my faith. I'm so obsessive ... so I know I have such ambivalence toward order of any kind, I just gotta stay away from it. So I dictate. I know if I try and do an outline, if I separate my works from my faith to that extent, I'd say, 'You know what? Let's do an outline, but just let me just get under a bridge with some dope and a fifth of vodka and I'll be right back.' So, I don't do no outlines. I let faith govern my works.[12]

Proximity to the flesh and blood individual responsible for these works creates its own challenges. Nietzsche probably spent the happiest years of his life when staying with the Wagners at their lakeside house in Tribschen, but it made his radical break with the vision and achievements of the composer much harder later on. More importantly, even if we grant that a credible source for the collaborative intelligence behind film and television lies with a single individual, why should this matter, since part of the value of art lies in the critical and popular approbation that is accrued years and centuries later, far removed from knowledge of individual artistic process? So, the challenge in part of this book and its relationship to authorship is the fact of seeing Milch at work, reading the thousands of pages of transcribed thoughts, as well as the many script drafts, his interviews, lectures – the entire jumble of immediacies that still shadow the work as it is and will remain after both he and I have vanished from the universe.

Nonetheless, I want to claim (and I am hardly the first to do so) that television fiction is a capable and thrilling engine for the creation of works of genius (that it might also produce great works of art is another matter; as V. F. Perkins has noted, 'there are many works of genius that are not great works of art').[13] That claim rests on the assumption that Milch, the social and historical being, found a way to inhabit the tradition of American literature only by working in an industry where there exists inbuilt deniability for failure and mediocrity, hence salving or, at least, partially satisfying his deadly interior critics. As a professor of film and television studies I am used to hearing my colleagues in literature question the claims of achievement in television by pointing to budgets, industrial conditions, the need to satisfy various demographics – as if great works of literature emerge by fairy light in a market-free space for contemplation. But it is true that one can park the failures, lack of commitment and character at the feet of a vulgar industry, or audience, or the entire cultural architecture that is inhospitable to the judgements that allow us to assert a standard, or have the courage and certainty to say 'this is great'.[14] Hence this book is not an account of the historical and industrial contexts and conditions in which Milch found himself, and neither is it a biographical study of the man and his battle to express his vision in an industry that is hostage to mere ratings. For me, David Milch is an emblem of artistic opportunity that was both thwarted and realised under conditions neither stultifying nor limitless: it is an account of a genius reaching out through characters and their stories in a medium whose appetite for achievement was extended and expanded in the light of his energy, teaching and writing.[15]

Genius is a highly contested term because it implies a luminosity of natural talent mystically begotten on fortunate individuals. Milch is wary of the term, and fond of misquoting Ezra Pound's saying that for every individual who fails through lack of talent, a thousand fail through lack of character.[16] For Kant, '[g]enius is the talent ... that gives the rule to art':[17] there is no formula for it, since it is characterised chiefly by originality and, although works of genius are exemplary models, it cannot be taught. Paul Guyer claims that 'the beauty of a work of genius lies precisely in the way it goes beyond anything that could be mechanically derived from any conscious intention of the artist'.[18] But as noted above, the collaborative nature of television makes tracking even conscious intention problematic for many scholars and critics. The singularity and unity of a consciousness expressing and intending in a collaborative medium situated in a vastly mediated industry such as Hollywood might give most of us pause when asserting claims of genius. Bignell and O'Day argue that the 'notion of television authorship [is] a collaborative enterprise between different production personnel, rather than located solely in the agency of the creator and/or writer'.[19] In a more hostile mode, Jeremy Butler argues against the 'elitism' of aesthetic evaluation deriving from a 'debunked auteur theory' imported into television scholarship from film studies: 'Auteurs do exist in television', he claims, '... but their "vision" is not necessary to make a program good. Much like a medieval cathedral beautiful television may be the product of dozens of workers' efforts.'[20]

Butler makes the common error of mistaking the labour that goes into producing a finished product as equivalent to the idea, design and authority that gives such a product its final shape. There is a reason that the words 'author' and 'authority' are so intimately related. A key anxiety, related to a culture-wide failure to practise judgement, is that assertions of value that rely for their force on singular individual achievements are mystifications of the production process, and are therefore simply disguised assertions of what Butler (among many others in film, television and cultural studies) calls 'dominant culture norms'. Such objections seek to demystify the object in order to study it better. I rather want to see the mystery that is at the heart of great art and its authorship in order to understand its achievements better.[21] We should not be concerned, in our troubles about value, solely with great art or masterpieces: television fiction's episodic nature above all shows us that moments of wit, eloquence, economy and dramatic intelligence deserve our attention too. The instrumentalist and formalist uncovering or unmasking of authorship as sets of social and historically conditioned processes and practices effectively masks what is special and distinctive about human creativity and cultural value – that they have the potential to transcend their time and place and conditions of making. As Berys Gaut puts it, despite the efforts of formalism and cultural studies, authorship remains 'oddly mysterious and deeply elusive'.[22]

Milch's rich history of collaboration – with Steven Bochco, Ted Mann, Jeffrey Lewis, Anthony Yerkovitch, Bill Clark and Michael Mann, to name a few – certainly offers support for the hackneyed 'making a cathedral' sense of creation. To judge by the credits alone (which requires a misunderstanding of the legal and financial nature of acknowledgement in film and television), Milch was proportionately a minor contributor to the writing of *NYPD Blue*, *Deadwood*, *John From Cincinnati* and *Luck*. Why then insist on the putative genius David Milch when an examination of the works themselves might be a sufficient focus? The answer lies in the relation of authorship to authority: our analyses should privilege the person or persons who credibly have both sufficient and final control over the work we evaluate. Sufficient control displays itself not just in the artist's personal input into that work but also in the fact that he or she uses the talent of others, absorbing them into that work. What is important about television authorship is not a repeated recognition of the impure, alloyed nature of most creative work, but rather the location and evaluation of the achievement of the artist most responsible, who has the greatest authority over the direction of it, whose continued existence holds it together and without whom it would be hard to imagine. Even at this generalised level there is unevenness: David Milch and Steven Bochco created *NYPD Blue* but it is clear that the tone and content of the show owe much to Milch's thematic and obsessive interests. Yet when Milch left the show in 1997 it continued for five more seasons. Perhaps we should think of television authorship less as a democracy, where everybody should be counted, and more as a kind of monarchy where the head of state makes the ultimate decisions, and whose traditions may continue even after the sovereign has departed (whether by abdication or execution).

Milch and the American literary tradition

The biographical tracking of Chapter 1 is far from a voyage to the man's core, or his faith (as noted above – who can know for sure?), or an argument that Milch's characters are merely versions or outgrowths of himself.[23] Rather, as with great painters and film directors (such as the Renoirs), he is able to respond to the constant stream of reality by channelling its buzzing, busy and blooming data through a fairly fixed, if somewhat warped, prism of his understanding of how and why it works in the way that it does. It is certainly the case that Milch wished to become part of the tradition of American literature he so admired, but his commitment to the 'Big Game' became complicated by working in a medium associated with low culture, and he was accused by at least one member of the tradition of selling out his talent. Nonetheless, my claim is that his works do indeed belong in that tradition. How this was given the opportunity to form and flourish requires that we locate Milch in his time and place. He was born in Buffalo, New York State in 1945, in a comfortable setting (his father was a surgeon), before attending Yale to study literature, and gaining a Master of Fine Arts as a graduate of the Iowa Writers' Workshop under the tutelage of, among others, Richard Yates and Kurt Vonnegut. Publishing poetry in the 1970s, he also worked as a research assistant for Robert Penn Warren and Cleanth Brooks at Yale again.

Such a background points – does it not? – to a future career as a novelist: like Warren, John Cheever, Philip Roth and his contemporary Jane Smiley, he was a product of what Mark McGurl calls 'the Program Era'.[24] And others of his generation, notably genre fiction writers such as Stephen King, James Patterson, Kem Nunn as well as those somewhat snobbishly associated with the 'literary' end of the table – for example, Paul Auster, Richard Ford and Smiley again – all turned to the page as their primary form of output.

But Milch did not settle, as so many did, into the academic setting as a writer-in-residence; and although he was 'writing', very little emerged except for two published poems and a brief attempt at film-making (all footage apparently lost, it was described to me by Milch as 'interminable'). At the age of 37 Milch abruptly left the academic ecology of Yale in 1982 to write for a television show, *Hill Street Blues*. The reasons for this underpin Chapter 1, but as a teaser to that, let me briefly track how the suddenness of the shift from academia to Hollywood was not as abrupt as it may seem.

In 1980 Milch was research assistant (and contributed a lot of the text itself, if unacknowledged) to Professor R. W. B. Lewis for a book on the James family (mainly focusing on William, Alice and Henry). *The Jameses* is a turgid read which in any case was not completed until the late 1980s, but it had an esteemed publisher in Farrar, Straus and Giroux, and somehow Milch had found a way to pitch it to Merchant–Ivory Productions, a British company founded in the 1960s and looking to bolster a reputation as a maker of literature-based films (they had just released an adaptation of James's *The Europeans*). During the pitch Lewis was called out of the room; afterwards he told Milch that the call was from Milch's family, to say that his father was dead. He had shot himself in front of Milch's mother and brother. They had asked Lewis not to let their son know until the meeting was over. Even though we don't know the role that Milch proposed for himself, the meeting may indicate an early interest in screenwriting work.

Milch's life up to that point was less a continuous academic and artistic success than a blend of criminal activity, long-blocked attempts at creative writing and respectable academic assistance. Before and after the suicide his relationship with his father remained an enduring psychological pivot around which much of his work circles. Insofar as it is possible to extrapolate the man from the child, it is clear from later interviews given by Milch, including those for *Luck*, that this relationship continued to shape and deform his life even after Elmer Milch's death. And, in common with many other real and fictional narratives over the past two decades, Milch experienced sustained sexual abuse as a child, not from a family member, but from a friend of the family during summer camp in the Adirondack Mountains. He only remembered this during the writing of an episode of *NYPD Blue*. Parents, background, circumstances and education do not necessarily determine one's later life – young adults rebel, or seek what they did not have earlier, and many can transcend the lives into which they were born, however structurally difficult that is. Although for many artists the most interesting thing about their lives tends to be the art that they create, their pre-artistic life holds some interest for those of us concerned to track the meaning of their works.

These events in Milch's early life and his continuing preoccupation with his father help us understand, even if they do not explain or fully account for, his fiction. There we are propelled into worlds populated not only by the self-contested characters described above, but also those who are authority figures (and as well captured by their dissevered natures) – fathers, bosses, teachers, kind brutalisers and holy manipulators. In *Luck*, the ultimate authority of evil, Lucifer himself, seems embodied by the snake-like coiling of Mike Smythe (Michael Gambon).

Milch and network television

The success of *Hill Street Blues* (1981–87) – his first script for the show, 'Trial By Fury', won an Emmy – as the beginning of a radical shift in television fiction is well documented. But the collective setting for the writing of that fiction provided the very public sociality in which Milch could thrive, as well as the income that would allow him to continue his addictions (to gambling, alcohol and heroin among other things). Something in the very sociality of that writing, the necessity of competitive proximity to other writers, and the status of television as a medium of folk or popular art rather than capital-L Literature released his capacity as a highly productive screenwriter. This work also allowed the emergence of themes and concerns that were to recur throughout his career. Characters appear who embody in nascent forms the cyclic patterns described above, not least the characters of Detective Sal Benedetto and Lieutenant Norman Buntz, both played by Dennis Franz. Sergeant Mick Belker's (Bruce Weitz) relationship with his elderly father, who is suffering from dementia, resonates with Milch's life, but he also wrote across the entire range of the show's characters and interests. When *Hill Street Blues* was cancelled in 1987 Milch was in a strong position financially, but once again found it hard to find a stable relationship in the industry. He wrote a spin-off sitcom based around Franz's *Hill Street Blues* character, *Beverly Hills Buntz*, which was messed around by the network and cancelled after one season. Milch had some work as a script doctor (he had a reputation for writing well for black characters), on films such as *Crimson Tide* (1995) and *Bad Boys* (both 1995), but for several years he had no major ongoing projects until Steven Bochco reached out to him to develop the pilot for *NYPD Blue* in 1991. That show was one of the last transitional shows to emerge under the shadow of the ascendance of cable after the repeal of the fin-syn regulations.[25] It was a show about decline and fortitude anchored around one character whose own ebb and flow, success and recidivism stamped him into the history of American fictional icons – Detective Andy Sipowicz (played by Franz again). Milch found, then created, a medium within which his interests and writing could flourish.

Chapter 2 concentrates on the evolution of Sipowicz in *NYPD Blue*. Although Sipowicz has antecedents in Milch's first television writing for *Hill Street Blues*, it is in this show that we see a character develop across several seasons. Like many of Milch's most interesting protagonists, he is not a leader in an official sense (indeed, his promotion is the climax of the final episode of the show) – more of a 'groundling' trying to do the right thing under the pressure of increasingly bureaucratised authority. However, his natural leadership as a cop doing the job with integrity and intuition butts up against an equal proclivity towards self-loathing, addiction, resentment. Franz's realisation of Sipowicz is remarkable not just for its longevity, but for the way in which his performance allows the expression of an aspect little remarked on in writing about Milch: his somewhat grim sense of humour. In Sipowicz, Milch also settled on a writing method and mode of involvement in the production process that accommodated the demands of his nature to find both a salve for the commotion in his head, and a guide who could anchor him to reality – the latter being the highly decorated former NYPD detective Bill Clark, who advised and befriended Milch and supplied many of the early storylines for the show.

As my concentration on character indicates, I take Milch's primary achievement to be his success in telling stories *about* characters rather than fashioning complex plots with fancy conceptual or ontological loops that often appear more as cognitive puzzles to the audience. In his work, plots tend to be subordinate to the excavation and drilling into the alloyed natures of his characters. This is why Milch often draws on off-the-peg plots – crime stories, the historical West, the surf-noir novels of Kem Nunn, or the history of horseracing in South California – to provide a forward-moving narrative framework for that excavation. Even that first Emmy award-winning script for *Hill Street Blues* was based on a true event that Milch heard or read about in the newspaper. When he does try to improvise narrative structure, it is invariably the weakest aspect of the work (see *John From Cincinnati*). And this is why the fourth chapter concentrates on his use of popular genres as, in Stanley Cavell's terms, a *medium* by which or through which the work finds its expression.[26]

Milch's father was a successful surgeon in Buffalo, but his family background was strongly associated with organised crime. Aspects of Milch's own criminal activities and addictions draw something from the alloyed nature of his father's respectable position yet disreputable background; but this also helps account for Milch's early and sustained fascination over two decades with the crime genre and the strong attraction of matters of justice for television audiences. Importantly, it is in depicting the working lives of cops on the job that Milch invests the majority of his words (the bourgeoisie are conspicuous by their almost total absence from his oeuvre), and even *Deadwood* carries the figure of the conflicted cop in Seth Bullock (Timothy Olyphant). I believe this stems from an interest not so much in realism or social realism as some have claimed, but from the necessity in the face of ultimate stakes, such as incarceration or worse, to use stories to lie, deceive and reveal the truth. Milch is someone with a highly tuned capacity to detect such mendacity, counter it, and yet fall prey to the same self-deceptions.

Deadwood and later works

Chapter 3 explores how Milch's work began to move away from the police procedural genre after *NYPD Blue*, starting with *Brooklyn South* and *Big Apple*. The former is notable because it much more strongly encompasses the gradual shift to family melodrama in Milch's later work; the latter, his final 'cop show' to be made for television, is far more clearly beholden to a sense of strong religious feeling, to the extent that the advertising campaign for the show emphasised the figures of Adam and Eve against the background of the Tree of Knowledge and the Manhattan skyline. Finally, I present an account of *Deadwood* that locates it not as a pinnacle of achievement, but at least as Milch's most sustained chance to follow through and untangle a dense mix of stories and characters that, as Thorburn so rightly notes, repeat and echo and repeat again this cycle of fall and redemption. In some ways, that show has been flattered by its length (three twelve-episode seasons) and its abrupt cancellation, but it is nonetheless a remarkable example of consistent control that Milch was able to sustain within the industry for probably the last time in his career. *Deadwood* is clearly a member of the Western genre, having the typical concerns with settlement, civilisation, governance and the restlessness of violent men; it is, as I noted in the conclusion to my book on the series, a *prophecy*.[27] However, Milch's 'Western' appears more as a *destination* for humanity, a future in a post-apocalyptic world that is perversely set in the past (other shows, such as *Mad Men* [2007–15] and *Quarry* [2016], also use this conceit successfully). It imagines how human sociability might survive amid the mud, cum and violence of a world without law and order, where chaos and brutality hold the whip hand. And *Deadwood* brings into view much more emphatically the charismatic figure of the teacher in the form of Al Swearengen; as a corrupt, violently flawed and yet wise man, he is ultimately a symbol of unity, principle and order.

The figure of the wise man is repeated in subsequent works, *John From Cincinnati* and *Last of the Ninth*. *Last of the Ninth* was a show brought only to the pilot stage: a historical drama set in the Lindsay era of New York in 1972, during a period when cops were being assassinated on the street by members of the Black Liberation Army (BLA). The show focuses on the murders of Rocco Laurie and Gregory Forster, but crucially introduces the pairing of an older, wiser cop with a younger, former undercover one. This recaptures some of the energy of *NYPD Blue*'s most successful pairing of Sipowicz and Bobby Simone (Jimmy Smits), but it is a far darker account of a period during which Milch himself lived and peddled drugs to, among others, members of the BLA. At the same time, his co-writer for the show, Bill Clark, was working as an undercover cop, infiltrating the Young Patriots Organisation, which had strong, if transient, links to the Black Panthers.

It is as much a tragedy that this show was never picked up as it is that *Deadwood* and both of Milch's final shows, *John From Cincinnati* and *Luck*, were cancelled. Both shows feature strong elements of 'teaching': the bizarre sermonising of the central figure in the former, and the multiple characters (including two veteran horse trainers, an elderly crime boss and an older gambler) who take up the role of instruction as wise men in a world of young people unprepared to counter the evil and destruction that snakes through its metabolism in the latter. *John From Cincinnati* occupies a well-known American literary form, the jeremiad, and like *Deadwood* is an attempt at prophecy, with awkward elements of the supernatural brought in to unsettle what is, at its core, a very effective family melodrama. (As we shall see, Milch borrowed some of the 'it doesn't add up' approach that Stanley Kubrick had applied to his adaptation of *The Shining* [1980].) The show is obscure in some aspects of its plot but almost screamingly explicit in terms of its 'message'; it also suffered from significant production and casting problems. As with *Deadwood* it imagines the origins of human communication as intimately linked to a break, a fresh start, a new beginning and, hence, is strongly tied to the tradition of American literature and popular culture. Nonetheless, it remains one of the strangest and most compelling television shows ever produced.

Luck, by contrast, takes us back to Milch's early childhood excursions (at the age of five) when he was taken by his father and given money to bet on the races. As usual Milch was explicit about the origins and intentions behind the show in interviews preceding the premiere. There are other stories that Milch wanted to tell and that will never be produced, but what we are left with in *Luck* is both a testament to his enormous talent and a show that would release again the forces – productive and destructive – responsible for the making of this artist himself. He lost a lot of money betting on the horses during production, and afterwards was forced to sell his properties in Martha's Vineyard and Santa Monica.

Luck is a story about good and evil, and the comforts and strains of human community at the end of days. Put that way, in words, it seems banal. But this is why Milch speaks words that pass along the line of humanity from amanuensis to director to crew: he gives them up, so that they are free to create and animate the compelling worlds we see in his fiction. Rather than offer critical interpretations of the texts themselves, these final chapters draw on that speech in order to get inside how that happens, and why it matters.

Notes

1 William Faulkner, 'Banquet Speech', 10 December 1950, www.nobelprize.org/nobel_prizes/literature/laureates/1949/faulkner-speech.html (accessed 29 April 2019).

2 David Thorburn, 'David Milch's Depraved Saints', *in media res*, 27 April 2012, http://mediacommons.org/imr/2012/04/27/david-milchs-depraved-saints (accessed 29 April 2019).

3 For a discussion of the nature of volition turned against itself, see Harry Frankfurt, 'Identification and Wholeheartedness', in Ferdinand David Shoeman (ed.), *Responsibility, Character, and the Emotions: New Essays in Moral Psychology* (Cambridge: Cambridge University Press, 1987).

4 Douglas Robillard (ed.), *The Poems of Herman Melville* (Kent, OH: Kent State University Press, 2000), p. 55.

5 Quoted in Stefan Collini, *Common Reading* (New York: Oxford University Press, 2008), p. 106.

6 William Empson, *Using Biography* (Cambridge, MA: Harvard University Press, 1984), p. vii. Later in that book (p. 104) Empson notes 'a secondary ill-effect of the Wimsatt Law, which operates very often though not inevitably; the effort to ignore the author's Intention makes the critic impute to him some wrong Intention'.

7 Empson, *Using Biography*, pp. vii–viii.

8 David Shields, *Remote* (Madison, WI: University of Wisconsin Press, 2003 [1996]), p. 121.

9 Steven Bochco, *Truth Is a Total Defense* (self-published, 2016), p. 97.

10 www.youtube.com/watch?v=IPVzAts74EA&list=PLjPFoFkXTi17uaqGiHODG-2jiepZoYTQuJ (accessed 16 April 2018).

11 Northrop Frye, *Words with Power* (Toronto: University of Toronto Press, 2008), p. 265.

12 'The Idea of the Writer', www.youtube.com/watch?v=85FYtguoxEs (accessed 16 April 2018).

13 'Orson Welles: Interview with Victor F. Perkins', https://vimeo.com/29342070 (accessed 16 April 2018).

14 See Angus Kennedy, *Culture Wars* (Exeter: Imprint Academic, 2014).

15 For example, the writer of *True Detective* (2014, 2015, 2019), Nic Pizzolatto, gave

copies of *Deadwood* to the cast members of the first season; for the third season, Milch was credited as writer on one episode.

16 What Pound actually said is, 'More writers fail from lack of character than from lack of intelligence'; *A B C of Reading* (New York: New Directions, 2010), p. 193.

17 Immanuel Kant, *Critique of Judgement*, trans. Werner S. Pluhar (Indianapolis, IN: Hackett Publishing, 1987), p. 174.

18 Paul Guyer, *Kant* (New York: Routledge, 2007), p. 319.

19 Jonathan Bignell and Andrew O'Day, *Terry Nation* (Manchester: Manchester University Press, 2004), p. 6.

20 Jeremy Butler, *Television Style* (New York: Routledge, 2010), p. 18.

21 For a brilliant account of the centrality of mystery in any account of the arts, see Denis Donoghue, *Arts without Mystery* (London: BBC Books, 1983).

22 Berys Gaut, *A Philosophy of Cinematic Art* (Cambridge: Cambridge University Press, 2010), p. 98.

23 'Milch called [my] stories "tropisms," which when I looked it up in the dictionary turned out to mean an "involuntary orientation by an organism or one of its parts that involves turning or curving and is a positive or negative response to a source of stimulation."' Shields, *Remote*, p. 122.

24 Mark McGurl, *The Program Era: Postwar Fiction and the Rise of Creative Writing* (Cambridge, MA: Harvard University Press, 2011).

25 For an excellent account of this industrial context, including the repeal of fin-syn, see Jennifer Holt, 'Vertical Vision: Deregulation, Industrial Economy and Prime-Time Design', in Mark Jancovitch and James Lyons (eds), *Quality Popular Television* (London: British Film Institute, 2003).

26 See Stanley Cavell, 'The Fact of Television', in *Themes Out of School: Effects and Causes* (Chicago: University of Chicago Press, 1984).

27 Jason Jacobs, *Deadwood* (London: Palgrave/BFI, 2012).

Words

I

> Passion, and passion in its profoundest, is not a thing demanding a palatial stage whereon to play its part. Down among the groundlings, among the beggars and rakers of the garbage, profound passion is enacted. And the circumstances that provoke it, however, trivial or mean, are no measure of its power.
>
> Herman Melville, *Billy Budd, Sailor*[1]

In 1970 David Sanford Milch submitted two chapters from a novel as part of his Master of Fine Arts at the prestigious Iowa Writers' Workshop. The never-to-be-published novel was entitled *The Groundlings*, and the title was clearly inspired by this passage from Melville's last prose work, itself unpublished during his lifetime.[2] Here and since, Milch's writing has consistently engaged with the lives and passions of 'groundlings', a word originally denoting those so poor that they were located unseated in the pit of the theatre below the stage, and which has acquired the meaning of unsophisticated or uncritical readers. These are the low, cheap and often dirty creatures close to the ground whose lives undergo scrutiny in some of Milch's most compelling works such as *NYPD Blue*, *Deadwood*, *John From Cincinnati* and *Luck*. The latter show's most compelling characters are described in the script as The Degenerates – Marcus (Kevin Dunn), an irascible, wheelchair-bound, oxy-mask huffing worrier; Jerry (Jason Gedrick), a younger, hopped-up gambling genius; the kindly but dim-witted Renzo (Richie Coster); and the endlessly concupiscent Lonnie (Ian Hart) – who together allow us to participate in the profound highs and lows of the racetrack, and who threaten to steal the show altogether from its big star heavy-hitters Dustin Hoffman (Ace Bernstein) and Nick Nolte (Walter Smith). The Degenerates are characters for whom Milch has personal affection, and his dissertation was a signpost on his journey from a literary wonder boy and teacher in the 1960s and 1970s to a Hollywood television screenwriter and showrunner in the 1980s,

1990s and 2000s. Both forms of communication and expression are powered by words as the building blocks of character and story, and tracking Milch's engagement with both allows us to get a sense of his inheritance of and participation in the traditions of American literature.

When I first met Milch in 2010 he showed me a copy of one of the volumes of *American Literature: The Makers and the Making* that he kept in his office: flicking through its many double-columned pages he said, 'This is the tradition in which I see myself.' Perhaps one had to be there, because it was said with a characteristic sense of *submission* to something greater, rather than an egotistical carving out of artistic identity in the world. Milch's conception of himself in interviews, commentaries and workshops is explicitly tied to literature, especially his tutelage under the Southern poet and novelist whom he met at Yale, Robert Penn Warren. 'The people I write for are all dead', he has remarked, 'Twain, Melville, James.' The claim that Milch belongs in the pantheon of those artists who have captured the metabolism of American life and history in depth – Philip Roth, Cormac McCarthy, Nicholas Ray, Sam Peckinpah, Frank Capra, Robert Stone (some of them also carried the burden of early promise and floundered in the grip of addiction) – is not an attempt to elevate the status of either him or television through association with culturally validated and admired traditions. (What would be the point?) His fame and success have come exclusively from that despised emblem of commercialised vulgarity in the minds of most academics, teachers, critics and connoisseurs of literature – a slack-jawed, dribbling purveyor of all that is bent, distorting and beguiling: television, the medium for groundlings.

That this is an entirely false image of television, of art and of Milch's contribution to both can be demonstrated in the tracing of his gradual maturation during the 1960s and 1970s, so that we see the move to television not as the sacrificing of loftier ambitions – despite what others such as his teacher at Iowa, Richard Yates, told him – but rather a necessary honouring of his particular skills as a storyteller and writer that, through a peculiar set of circumstances, washed him up at the medium that seems perfectly adjusted in its mendacity and sociality to an artist of his talents. Any assessment of Milch is bound to be caught between the discipline of Literary Studies, which has little time for television (beyond the use of its literary adaptations to engage bored students, or gestures of dilettantism such as writing about *Mad Men* for the *Wall Street Journal*), and the younger discipline of Television Studies, which celebrates the medium as an emblem of folk culture and is suspicious of any claims to high art as defiling the medium's specificity. In the former's dim lights, the dramatic products of television are unworthy of attention because corrupted by collective, commercial and industrial imperatives that ineluctably distort the characteristic voice of the individual artist; whereas, for the lords and ladies of Television Studies, all claims of artistic integrity, intentionality and artistic achievement smack of the illegal border crossing of transcendent values from the pre-structuralist Stone Age of mystical, organic evaluative behaviour, and 'values' are not something we should associate with television at all.[3] In between, some of the finest works of art of the past decade vanish or are taken up only for the ways in which they reflect aspects of their social, cultural, industrial and other historical circumstances. In any case, the hygienic splitting of medium-specific works makes more sense in critical and reflective contexts than it does in practice: there are other forces in US literary culture and its institutions which shared a great deal with the mass entertainment industry. The story of Milch's early development as a writer outlined in what follows eschews both approaches, instead mixing biographical elements with a cultural history of American criticism and creative practice.

Elmer Milch

Milch was not born to a literary family, but he has a background that brims with events that resonate with his work. His relatives settled in the US after fleeing the European anti-Jewish pogroms at the turn of the twentieth century; his great grandmother on his mother's side witnessed the beheading of her husband by a Cossack. In *True Blue*, his account of the development of *NYPD Blue*, Milch gives an extraordinary account of the accident that befell his father, Elmer Milch, shortly after his marriage to Molly. Trained as a doctor, Milch Sr was recruited to a military medical unit during the Second World War; the night before he was due to go overseas in 1944 the jeep he was driving collided with an army truck, and in the accident his lower body was crushed. He was to spend the next year undergoing reconstructive surgery. The event had a lasting effect on Elmer: every three months or so thereafter 'he'd need to be catheterized to dilate his urinary passage, which was constricted by scar tissue', and he remained addicted to the strong narcotic painkillers taken during his recovery for the rest of his life.[4] This vivid image of recurrent scarring and the relief of narcotics all bound up with unspecified desire and the implication of deceit (on his father's reason for being in the jeep, Milch writes: 'the public version was that the base was sealed down because of the imminent troop embarkation and he'd taken the jeep to drive into town to call my mother and tell her goodbye'), like many of the autobiographical scenes in *True Blue*, has a script-like quality to it. The words are freighted with unstated implications that seem to require our further work as readers to fully activate or realise their deepest meaning, and they carry forward – as we shall see – to Milch's learning at Iowa.

Milch's mother was not allowed access to her badly injured husband for many months, but eventually she was permitted to spend time alone with him in his hospital room. In *True Blue*, when writing about himself, Milch often 'says' something powerful by simply not saying it, and hence opens a door for the reader: 'When he was released from the hospital, they left together to get Bob [Robert, his elder brother]. By this time, my mother was pregnant with me.'[5] This is a Milchean scene *par excellence*: a statement of his origins in which injury, pain, narcotics, institutional rules and law as much as desire and love are the prominent contextual components in the act of conception. The meaning stored in the sentence unpacks as something like: 'I came from this; this is my beginning.'

A young, recently married couple forced apart by a horrific accident ('his bladder could be visualised about four inches below his neck', according to Milch) on the eve of what was Elmer Milch's departure for an uncertain, potentially lethal wartime destination (one assumes it was the D-Day operation) are, finally, allowed to be in one another's company as he recovers to a state where one might judge that he is fit to be seen by his loved ones. One might wonder at the pseudo-public setting of the hospital bed, however privately arranged, and the potential for shame and secrecy that it held. What about its proximity to procedures and implements of care, recovery, agencies of pain and resources to salve, and their intermixing in an imagination that has remained in intimate thrall to his father's moods, persona and ultimate destiny? To what extent are we hostage to our parents' intentions, hopes and aspirations for us in the moments before, during and after our conception? One might take up the doubleness of Milch's conception from the kernel of a brutal trauma and painful recovery alongside the miracle of survival, the release and joy of reunion between young lovers forced to forgo sex (even if it were physically possible), where desire and love overcome pain and injury and damage. Or, in another mood, one's imagination might become susceptible to atavistic determinism, a temptation to deploy destiny as following the pathway of one's origins, cursed like Noah's son, Ham, to *know* (something – but what? In the biblical version the curse and its reasons are hardly straightforward or known in themselves.) But then, if that is so, this is part of a literary, almost mythic story of origin, included in a book capitalising on the success of a network TV show in the 1990s. Up until the sessions Milch recorded during the 2007–08 Writers' Guild of America strike, *True Blue* provides the most extensive autobiographical account of his background, offering a robustly candid and yet – seemingly impossibly – at the same time obstructed view. Sometimes we can hide anything and everything by putting it in plain sight.

As we shall see when we come to consider the role of New Criticism in American literary studies, the role of biography in accounting for artistic achievement has for a long time been under suspicion as a simplified version of cultural mediation; the art expresses the life, so understanding the life brings us closer to appreciating the nature of the work. However, Milch's background, and his father's, strike me as an important component in a larger picture in order to grasp some aspects of the significance of the lived experience of the young boy: of the deceit, despair, lies, doubleness and concealment of deeper motives and desires in the life of a father who so dominated but did not wholly define Milch's later artistic life. It is hard to overstate the resonance and power of his father's psychic authority.

Elmer Milch's boyhood was itself fractured by the unsettling behaviour of his parents and grandparents. His mother was the eldest of ten children, and as a grown man Elmer was therefore more or less the same age as his uncles. Her father was a bootlegger involved in the Jewish organised crime milieu that would culminate in Meyer Lansky's domination of clubs and casinos in Saratoga and then south across New York State. David Milch eventually met Lansky, thinking he might write his biography, but found him so unreliable that he 'couldn't even be honest about what time it was'. Of his great grandfather Milch said, 'probably the nicest thing about him was that he was a bootlegger'. Once, when the police showed up looking for a murder suspect, he blamed his own son, who had to flee the state and change his name. He later went on to run the Latin Quarter club in New York with Lou Walters (Barbara's father), where mob money would be laundered.

When the patriarch's wife died, he took his daughter and her husband with the young Elmer into his house, and may well have taken up with Elmer's mother – his daughter – in an incestuous relationship. Hence Elmer's early childhood was forged within this powerful melodramatic and criminal setting, with rival father figures and mortal stakes. Whatever was going on in the house, his father eventually attempted suicide by throwing himself off Niagara Falls in a barrel. Quite apart from living in this strange Sirkean domestic situation, Elmer's own seclusion from the illicit activities and forbidden pleasures of uncles of the same age no doubt caused inner friction as well, for

Elmer was also given a functional role in the extended family's destiny. Like Michael Corleone in *The Godfather*, the family planned to keep their youngest away from criminal activities and send him to college where he could acquire legitimate bourgeois status. As in that movie, in a setting of wise-guy shenanigans and illicit manoeuvring this must have felt like an intolerable constraint.

At the time Lansky ran 'the first and greatest carpet joint' (a hotel/casino outside the town with a restaurant attached) in Saratoga; it was called The Piping Rock and was located near the legendary racecourse.[6] During the summer holidays from medical college Elmer would work as a waiter in the restaurant there, but when one of his uncles ('Uncle Hutz') caught him playing pool at a nearby bar, he threw Elmer's companion through a first-floor window, breaking his neck and paralysing him for life. This violent spectacle reinforced the stakes of Elmer's role in the family in his own mind; according to David Milch, the racecourse in Saratoga 'was always associated in [his father's] mind with a lot of unresolved stuff', and after he qualified as a doctor, every August he would visit the track, where he had a box and was known as The Doc. Boyhood summers at the Saratoga track must have made the world of mobster activity seem vivid and tempting, and Elmer owed himself an annual taste. The burden of expectation, and the specifying of destiny, might have demanded a release, the carving out of a space where Elmer could be what he might have been had he not been elected to stand as the legitimate emblem of the family's embourgeoisement.

Elmer was to become a Chief of Surgery at Buffalo State Hospital, a 'clinical professor who conducted some of the early vascular experiments on dogs (some of the survivors became ... household pets) and later perfected several techniques in the gastrointestinal surgery which became his speciality'.[7] Less exaltedly, Elmer performed hernia operations on gangsters so that they could claim medical exemption from testifying at the Kefauver Senate hearings into organised crime in the early 1950s. They recovered at the Milch home, where the young boy experienced the diversity of visits not only from distant European relations displaced after the war, but also colourful figures from the mob.

Milch's childhood

That sense of the exotic, illicit world as having a truth, a groundedness in emotional reality and vitality that really moved people, contrasted with the outwardly bourgeois life of an esteemed surgeon; hence there was a conflict between outward appearance and inner truth. This was surely an important part of the highly potent emotional content transmitted to the young David Milch. He was born in March 1945, the younger of two boys; his brother Robert was always full of aspirational admiration for his father, reading fiction and comics in which heroic medics and benign scientists healed the world, wanting to emulate his dad's success as a man of science and medicine. Hence, that role had been taken once David arrived on the scene: what was left? Siblings almost always fight, mostly for play and attention, but also in order to carve out an identity that makes them special and distinctive in the eyes of their parents, teachers and guardians. David had to find the ground on which he could stand distinct as his father's son and, of course, there was another side to Elmer available to please. His father was astute and attentive enough to notice this early on.

At the age of five Milch was taken by his father to the box at the Saratoga racecourse. Recalling the event in later years in an interview promoting *Luck*, Milch mimicked Elmer's authoritative voice as he gave his son instructions on how to bet:

> Max the waiter will run your fucking bets for you. He's got fifty dollars. I don't want to see you betting more than five dollars on a fucking race. Do not let me see you fucking sneaking out here on your own![8]

Milch commented that the final line was delivered with a face that implied the full alterity of intention in contrast with overt meaning: 'My dad nourished hopes for me that had been denied him.' In Milch's later reflection on this moment, his father's adult-talk to his son who had no idea what was going on was something which, 'in the fullness of time ... if one accepts the grace of God which is constantly operative, it is possible to understand ... as a gesture of love'. As with art, there is no formula or map for the vast and ever-evolving nature of love between human beings, and the treatment of one's own children is often fraught with the complications and difficulties of love, its expression and suppression. Some of this is beyond control, no doubt, and Milch Sr's attempt to 'give' David a special part of his own sense of what he was denied as a child himself had no overt adult sanction or justification. So his shouting was as much, perhaps, to say to those around (whether they could hear or not), *this* is no sissy kid who won't know what time it is as a grown up. Of course, children are intensely sensitive to the doubleness of parental messages, the mismatch between the overt instructional content and the deeper, vastly more potent, psychological one. In these terms, 'Don't fucking sneak out here on your own!' *really* means 'My deepest self always craves to be here and you will win my love and admiration, despite the punishment I have to be seen to give by the conventional society I am part of, if you *do* sneak out here. Because that's what I always wanted to do at your age, don't you want to too?'

Later, in talks, Milch – as usual he is very candid about such things – would indicate that events such as these fostered in him as a child the illusion that we are only *known* by the figures who originate us. This meant integrating the idea

> that I'm a fucking shitbird and a degenerate – he must have figured that out before I knew it ... We want to love the organising sources in our lives, so that we are able to idealise the ordering forces and [...] that creates the sense of doubleness of being an outsider but [also] a tremendous yearning toward participation in order.[9]

The psychological layers that accrete around such powerfully convoluted parental messages require considerable ingenuity to decipher and operationalise for a child – to construct and master, as it were, the imaginative capacity to be one thing and yet seem convincingly to be something else, even to oneself. Eventually the adult Milch would find a way of sustaining his layered density of deception, self-deception and love productively and generatively in the entertainment industry, where illusion, doubleness and the exploitation of the shades and gradations between seeming and being are the regular everyday currency. That said, there are plenty of parents who no doubt performed similar acts that recruited their children into whatever psychological stage they were playing out. In the past, and certainly in Milch's past, extended families, networks of friends, neighbours, community associations and other forms of human solidarity diluted the direct impact of such parental forces; one wonders how Milch would have fared if growing up in the atomised world of children and adults in the twenty-first century.

While his parents holidayed at Saratoga in the August racing season, Robert and David were sent to Camp Paradox for Boys, a summer camp in the Adirondack Mountains, in a beautiful setting alongside the lake that gave it its name. An early brochure claims that the camp's aspiration was to develop each boy's 'physical, mental and moral well being, and to foster his self-reliance'. Former attendees included Nathanael West, Richard Rodgers and Lorenz Hart, and David and Myron Selznick. But at the age of six Milch experienced extreme homesickness, weeping at night and bedwetting. The counsellor assigned to ease his pangs (these were usually young men and women, sometimes college students) instead sexually abused him, 'for a considerable period of time ... and I thought he was the greatest guy in the world'. It is not clear whether the abuse was conducted by one person or more: at one stage Milch has mentioned that 'they' 'dressed him up like Sophie Tucker', although this may not have had anything to do with the paedophilic exploitation of a sad little boy. In his talks during the writers' strike, on the topic of how difficult it is for some artists to deal with industrial authority, Milch mentioned that he had experienced having 'authority figures do that' (ejaculate in his face). Bizarrely (that is, only for those who don't know the secrets of the secret), the counsellor/abuser was also a gambler and befriended Milch's parents, even securing an invitation to join them regularly in their box at the Saratoga track. This event is one of the constitutive traumas that Milch chose to make public, beginning with his lectures and workshops in the early part of the twenty-first century, indicating that he took such events to be decisive, if subsequently obscured. As an adult he did not remember that the abuse had happened at all until his fifties, when writing a story arc in *NYPD Blue* in the latter half of the 1990s.

Growing up in the Rust Belt city of Buffalo during the 1950s, Milch was a delinquent child. He was taken to the local police station at seven years old after stealing his mother's charity collection box and renting a boat on the local lake at Delaware Park, near Hallam Road where they lived, after the attendant noticed he was carrying a butcher's knife (for 'a lion hunt').[10] He would take drugs from his father's well-stocked medicine cabinet, consuming them without knowing what they were, and hence often wandered around in a dazed state, with uppers and downers working against one another. He regularly sneaked into the Saratoga racecourse, and at twelve was caught trying to sneak across the Canadian border en route to another track. He made best friends with another delinquent, a slightly younger boy named Almon, whom they called Judgy (his grandfather had been a judge) – '[we] paired up because we were troublemakers and shitbirds' – and a boy called Timmy Wright (a shortish boy also known as The Flying Wedge or The Stump).[11] They would hang out in all weathers near grocery stores, offering money to adults to buy them alcohol. Milch recounts how Judgy nearly died at fourteen because he could not stop drinking, and Milch was certainly drinking from a young age too.[12]

His relationship with Elmer continued to be difficult, emotionally and physically. In *True Blue* he recounts the story of joining his dad on a regular family trip to a local diner; somehow he'd made Elmer angry:

> It wasn't intentional, because I never tried to get my father mad my whole life. Maybe I'd been late getting home from playing with friends or somehow else loused up the process of our getting to the diner. Also, I'm sure he'd come home frustrated or upset about something from work so whatever I did was magnified as an irritant. My dad held the door as my brother and mother went into the diner. As I followed them

> inside, moving under his arm, he brought his fist down on the back of my neck. I was eight or nine, and besides the pain of being hit I couldn't understand what was going on. Nothing that happened through the rest of the meal explained it to me. My dad didn't give any indication the event had taken place except to sit with the muscles in his jaws working which was a sign he was upset. I didn't say anything either ... In one way this wasn't typical ... [but] he *was* always driven by things it was hard to understand, and which seemed to force him to live in a very narrow and specific way, and you didn't want to mess him up.[13]

In later interviews Milch claimed that when he was beaten as punishment for whatever misbehaviour, his father would subsequently weep out an apology: in Milch's phrase he would attempt to 'knock the resemblance out of him'.[14] Milch's recollection in *True Blue*, interwoven with what is basically an insider production account of the first two seasons of *NYPD Blue*, indicates that from a very early age he was, like many of us, confronted with the paradox or puzzle that actions, emotions and thinking don't add up neatly into a coherent, patterned story where meaning is clear and legible. However tidy and strict Elmer's habits and schedule, he did not control, perhaps did not even anticipate at that moment, the blow to his child's neck. And yet all these things remain as components of what the man did; in that sense, what he was.

Elmer's silence in the diner does not suggest, at that moment, a lively house full of talk, which is a notable feature of Milch's fictions; but along with Judgy there were other people in his childhood who supplied vitality. *Deadwood: Stories of the Black Hills*, the show's accompanying book released shortly after it was cancelled, contains and sometimes repeats some of the same autobiographical material as *True Blue*, including this portrait of a friendship:

> There was a guy I knew in the fifties [i.e. when Milch was child/teenager], a drunk whose shadow is cast on every one of the central male characters I write. He was the father of a friend of mine, and he wound up living in some ramshackle hut on the Niagara River. He was a drunk in a desperate but accessible way, as opposed to my own Dad, who had the same demons but was not so accessible. There was a hospitality in the exuberance of his language. Exaggeration didn't bother him. He felt it was of the essence.[15]

Milch also claimed that when he was young, 'my idea of fun was to go to the station or to bars and listen to people lie. I always thought there was something remarkable and uplifting about that.'[16] Having an ear for, or capacity to recognise, deceit and mendacity is one thing (particularly useful for cops), but finding it 'uplifting', in the way that young people might find music or religious devotion uplifting, is odd. One often feels deep, vicarious, humiliation or embarrassment on behalf of the deceitful person, whether or not they realise they have been rumbled by an observer or interlocutor.

The point is that these early experiences do not add up to, or provide a formula for, David Milch: Television Genius, since one can imagine many similar experiences in which the outcome would be quite different. However, learning what we now know about Milch does make his background flash alive with significance. I am trying to understand the formation of Milch's interests as the product of the sedimentation of past events that have thrown up certain habits and aesthetic preferences; to grasp the geology of his artistic identity. A key moment in his relationship with his father was being told that he could not help with whatever it was David needed ('he knew I was fucked up'). But, his father continued, he should find a guide who could. Despite the trouble Milch got into, his strong bourgeois family status, not least his mother's role as president of the Buffalo Board of Education and his father's position as clinical professor and Chief of Surgery at Buffalo General Hospital, ensured that he stayed out of jail and avoided a police record. He enrolled at Yale, majoring in African Studies, and it was here he found the mentor who was to dominate his development as an artist.

Yale and Robert Penn Warren

The stimulus for this was the death of Judgy in a car accident, an accident in which either the driver or Judgy had been drinking. Milch came back from Yale to attend the funeral but was 'drunk throughout'. Judgy's father, Jim, was banned from attending, possibly by a court order: I suspect he was the 'accessible drunk' who lived in the hut. Milch himself was drunk as he carried the coffin along with the pallbearers.

Back at Yale, as he recounts it, Milch began a process of atonement, imagining what it was like for the absent father, Jim: 'I wrote it out in scenes.' We can recognise these efforts as about 'groundlings', with Jim 'working as a bartender having a shitty day before being told over the phone of his son's death. It was the product also of feeling bad – disloyal for not going to see Jim; the story expanded to involve other people in Judgy's family.'[17] His recourse to words as the mode of atonement, as a patterning, ordering, even converting of the pain of the experience, may have prompted Milch to switch from African Studies to a Literature Major. This led to his meeting with his first 'guide' of his adulthood, the poet and novelist Robert Penn Warren, a professor at Yale who carried the distinction of having won the Pulitzer prize for both fiction and non-fiction. Milch had already read Warren's novels, and he first met him 'sober … as he walked toward his office in one of the residential colleges':

> I introduced myself and said I was trying to learn how to write. With what I came to learn was customary generosity, Mr. Warren said he'd be pleased to read the scenes about Judgy's family. The following Monday, in his office, Mr. Warren said I had a good deal to learn about structure, but the scenes I had written had a vein of real feeling and had lifted him up. He said he'd be happy to teach me.[18]

From this meeting onwards Warren was to be a decisive influence throughout the rest of Milch's artistic career.

Milch clearly admired Warren's teaching style, which in seminars would consist of him reflecting in detail about the work in question, eventually inviting comment from the students; he was described by one of his students as godlike, with 'such an aura of mastery about him, true wisdom'.[19] Perhaps it was this style that Milch was later to draw on and cultivate himself in writers' workshops at Yale and later in the writers' room in Hollywood. As the transcriptions of his conversations with writers on *Deadwood* and *John From Cincinnati* demonstrate, Milch became a fine raconteur and monologuist. As he talks, Milch often develops a theme that modulates characters and scenes, all refracted through vast, densely packed details of history, anthropology and literature, while remaining continuously subordinate to the overall demands of his artistic intuition and design. Certainly, he got some aspects of this from the way Warren taught; it is an approach to teaching that does not flatter students, eschewing even a formal Socratic pattern of asking for questions and comments, and investing faith in them as listeners and learners. Milch claims that he 'always sat in a corner, in thrall and saying almost nothing'. One imagines the father's voice as legislative at home, but liberatory at school. But that dominant voice, absorbing all silence, can also be the product of uncertainty and sensitivity to one's imagination of critical voices that would take flight in moments of hesitation and pause. It is therefore hard to overstate the importance of this meeting for Milch's conception of himself as a writer; nearly fifty years later he continued to cite and quote 'Mister Warren'.

By the early 1960s when Milch arrived at Yale, Warren was a senior figure in American letters, a Southern poet, novelist and critical thinker, heir to the mantle of William Faulkner (Leslie Fiedler describes him as his 'disciple'),[20] and his status as a major literary and critical figure was assured. In Fiedler's 1960 account of the mythic resonances of the great American novel he is described as 'a poet, critic, and pedagogue as a well as a novelist who has attempted the risky game of presenting to our largest audience the anti-Western in the guise of the Western, the anti-historical romance in the guise of that form itself'.[21] Had Warren been another kind of man and teacher the impromptu meeting might have turned out another way, but according to Milch's recollection, 'He could always see the best in people.'[22] Warren was interested in Milch not merely out of good manners or teacherly interest: the central character of his novel *Flood* (1964), Brad Tolliver, is a novelist with early promise who ends up becoming a screenwriter, and who in his 'cynicism, his smart-aleck cleverness, and the brusque coarseness of his speech' seems prophetic in his resemblance to Milch, even though Warren barely knew Milch at the time of writing the novel.[23] Whatever the case, a seed of fascination with this precocious young man was clearly available.

It is not clear why Milch found the courage to approach Warren, except the sense of impulsive forwardness that had powered his early delinquent behaviour; but it may have been the experience of the power of writing to handle the emotional materials of the past, and transform those subjective, stabbing, scatterings of sense and feeling into patterns that were at least legible and perhaps hinted at some kind of transformation, if not the beginning of atonement. In Warren he found a practising writer who was uniquely receptive to such thinking. That said, it is important not to conflate influence with a kind of crude cross-fertilisation. I am not claiming that Milch's achievement or success depended solely on his proximity to a literary tradition, but it is certainly true that Warren's conception of that tradition and the interpersonal wisdom they shared during long walks together (somewhat later in the 1970s) mattered very much to the young would-be writer. Joseph Millichap rightly claims that 'From 1965 to his death in 1989, Warren successively acted as Milch's teacher, mentor and colleague ... Warren's creative canon demonstrates a number of influences and intertextualities with Milch's diverse productions, providing insight into the literary contexts that make *Deadwood* high quality television.'[24] That said, neither *Deadwood* nor any other of Milch's works necessarily requires a literary context in order to appreciate its achievement or to designate it 'quality television' (a phrase that is rather like a claim for a brand of appliance or politician). Nor does the fact that Milch's work draws to some extent on traditionally literary concerns necessarily negate its distinctive qualities as television, because television is precisely a medium that can blend a wide spectrum of artistic traditions according to its trends, fashions and industrial needs.

We should not underestimate Warren's role as a kinder, less self-obstructive father figure whose guidance nourished Milch before and after his death; but they are different artists in the end, and citing correspondences between bits and pieces of their output as evidence of influence underplays Milch's achievements, and tends to conceive television as a mere relay for literary ideas. Indeed, Warren's influence on Milch is much more at the level of exemplar: he was a powerful, deeply humane and moral paternal figure, and a living example of a working artist who was approaching the peak of his powers at the time they first met. Because of this it is worth briefly situating Warren's literary significance and status when Milch met him at Yale.

Born in 1905 in Kentucky, Robert Penn Warren had, by the time he won the Pulitzer prize for his novel *All The King's Men* in 1945, established himself as a distinctive voice in the literary 'Southern Renaissance', one of a dozen people based at Vanderbilt University who were known as the Southern Agrarian movement (aka 'The Fugitives'), under the leadership of John Crowe Ransom. In broad terms this movement's identity was formed in the tension between asserting the provincial specificity of the South in their writing, and absorbing the international artistic trends exemplified by European modernism. The tension between the local and the national, as well as the particular and the universal, was played out and discussed in a variety of ways. In Warren's work it was transcended to some extent by a wider affinity with the nation as a whole; it is a tension captured by the beautiful reading voice we hear on recordings of his poetry readings: grounded in its Kentuckian twang but with content strongly influenced by the high modernism of T. S. Eliot. (As a student he was, like many others, an admirer of *The Waste Land* and memorised the entire work.) Millichap claims that Milch's writing, like Warren's literary preferences, enjoyed the juxtaposition of vulgarity with abstraction, and in this way both shared a strong attraction to the work of Herman Melville. As Millichap notes, for Warren, Melville was 'aiming at a style rich and yet shot through with realism and prosaism, sometimes casual and open and sometimes dense and intellectually weighted, fluid and various because following the contours of the subject or rather the contours of his own complex feelings about the subject'.[25]

Likewise both men shared a fascination with fathers and sons at odds, although Warren admired his gentle father, who was a school-teacher, as exemplified in his novel *The Cave*.[26] But the crucial lesson that Warren gifted to Milch was the idea of the transcendence of the ego and its demands, a theme that recurs throughout his poetry, fiction and other writings: 'Through the awareness of life's pathos and the pain of self-criticism man may escape the entrapment of his own ego and achieve a communion with his fellows and with nature', he wrote in

1955.[27] The influence of T. S. Eliot, in particular the meditations on time and its relationship to modernity in *Four Quartets* (see, for example 'Little Gidding', lines 85–9) was returned to again and again in his poetry. Harold Bloom, in his foreword to *The Collected Poems of Robert Penn Warren*, mentions how he had lunch with Warren in 1973 shortly after he had read Bloom's *The Anxiety of Influence: A Theory of Poetry*, in which Warren – a close friend of W. K. Wimsatt – 'emphasised his uncanny sense of recognising his own relation to his precursor, Eliot, in my descriptions of the agonistic relationship between strong poets and their inheritors'.[28]

While Milch did not have the same relation artistically to Warren, the impact of Eliot was passed on: in 2007, over lunch, one producer mentioned a man he knew who continued to be 'haunted by his past'. 'That's its job', quipped Milch, who went on to cite Warren's poem 'Homage to Theodore Dreiser', in which the poet characterises Dreiser's sense of history as 'the constable hand that clutches'.[29] This exchange prompted a comment from a female voice (I believe one of Milch's co-writers) who mentioned Eliot's preference for the word 'clutch' (see stanza two of *The Waste Land*). Milch's response was 'If I ever met him [Eliot] I'd punch him in the face.' 'But he was so good', protested the woman. 'Yeah, that's what I mean.' Eliot, Warren and Milch share a fascination with time as a central aspect of the mysterious dislocations afforded by modernity and the art produced within it, but only Milch worked in a medium in which episodic time is front and centre as an aspect of its fictional output.

The influence of Eliot continued to be felt in Warren's work (such as *You, Emperors and Others: Poems 1957–60* for which he won another Pulitzer and was duly elected to the American Academy of Arts and Letters), but by the time he met Milch he had mastered and absorbed the style of Eliot's high modernism, and his work was shifting to its final mature phase when Warren would write his best poems. He was also a social commentator, and in the winter of 1964, just shy of his sixtieth birthday, he was 'running around with shotguns' in Mississippi and Alabama interviewing African-American leaders of the Civil Rights Movement, including Martin Luther King and Malcolm X, as well as writers such as Ralph Ellison and James Baldwin, as research for his book, *Who Speaks For The Negro?*[30] Eliot's interest in time, transience and tradition is shared by Warren and Milch, and both would write extraordinary work that returned to the thematic core of Eliot's late poems.

To put it crudely, this is the paradox that has haunted civilisation for the past century and a half: how is meaning (the kind that guides an individual life, a society, a sense of purpose, which is to say transcendental meaning) possible without time (how can it be eternal in the way we value art as transcendent), when it is seemingly at the current moment impossible within our time? Eliot's last poems recuperate meaning of this kind by imagining himself back inside the little community, and its collective store of knowledge, at Little Gidding, a tiny location in England with a church and manor house. For a brief time in the early seventeenth century, under the leadership of a scholar called Nicholas Ferrar, its Christian community followed a monastic-like lifestyle, narrativising and harmonising the Gospels, with Ferrar risking heresy by avoiding the distinction in his service between the liturgy and the sermon. That sense of community formed and harmonised through narrative and the rituals of listening to speech is one that attracted both Eliot and, of course, Milch.[31]

Warren only taught one semester per year, so Milch would have been taught or at least attended lectures by Cleanth Brooks as well. Brooks and Warren in particular were central figures in the formation of American New Criticism, an approach that emphasises the textual unity and integrity of the literary work itself as the primary object of study. It stressed the centrality of close analysis of the work itself, eschewing didactic or biographical critical approaches. Long-term friends, Brooks and Warren had published *Understanding Poetry* in 1938, arguably one of the most influential literary textbooks of the twentieth century; it instructed generations of students and teachers on how to read poetry. Like Clement Greenberg's account of abstract art, it places an emphasis on form as the carrier of meaning; it admonishes those who see poems as containers of messages, or as mere stimuli for sensations. Instead the aim is to find and account for meaning that mitigates impressionistic readings, arguing instead that we should attend to the meaning-making mechanisms of the work itself. However, their approach is far less schematic than it appears at first glance, and is similar to the criticism of William Empson in its flexible and responsive admiration for the achievement of good art. Warren in particular was uncomfortable with the designation 'New Critic' and rejected the way the label had been taken up, arguing that it was not a system but 'intelligence, tact, discipline, honesty, sensitivity – those are the things we have to depend on, after all, to give us what we prize in criticism, the insight'.[32]

Warren and Brooks had worked together since the 1930s. When Warren was appointed professor in the English Department at Yale in 1961 it concentrated the two central figures in New Criticism at New Haven, both 'Southerners'.[33] But it also dated them to some extent, since neither was to participate in the revolution of poststructuralism (especially the work of Barthes, Foucault, Lacan and de Man) which would at the end of that decade make a decisive impact on the humanities, although the full devastation of this shift would not be felt until decades later.[34] Recalling his teaching in the early 1970s, shortly after meeting Derrida in Paris, Stanley Cavell wrote, 'the new criticism [...] famously understood to be represented at Yale by W.K. Wimsatt and Cleanth Brooks and Robert Penn Warren had no fight left in it to match the excitement and intensity of literary and philosophical interpretation of the new thing from Paris'.[35]

One aspect of New Criticism that may have attracted Milch, which is particularly evident in the work of Brooks, was its insistence on unity. This is an approach that sees literature as a connective tissue, or alternate resting place, between art and the atomised and alienated estrangement of human beings under the hostile material and psychological conditions of the world. For example, here is Warren discussing Hawthorne: 'The work of art is, for the alienated man, his crucial connection with that world beyond him.'[36] As Stefan Collini has noted, unity was the notion that binds the diversity of New Critical approaches, the sense that the work of art patterned and shaped those otherwise chaotic tensions and contradictions that the everyday world of modernity kept throwing up, in contrast to the fragmented, partial and utilitarian forms of modern and scientific knowledge. Within the critical diversity of those wholly or partially associated with New Criticism,

> one could ... speculate on the structural resemblances between, on the one hand, [T. S.] Eliot's implied ideal of 'the associated sensibility' or [I. A.] Richards's 'synaesthesia of conflicting impulses', and on the other, the Southern Agrarians' idea of 'the South' or [F. R.] Leavis's of 'the organic community'. They are all prized as forms of wholeness, the opposite of the partial, the fragmented, the specialized, the instrumental. Thus understood, even the most intricate New Critical teaching out of the play of ambiguity and paradox in long-familiar poems encodes a cultural argument. 'The well-wrought urn', the 'verbal icon' and the rest function as allegories of the overcoming of dividedness, all the more effective (and perhaps all the more ideological) for being immune to the kind of merely empirical counter-evidence that can always be cited against any historically located model.[37]

As Warren said in a later interview, there were 'many different kinds of animal under that [New Critical] tent'.[38] In practical terms this meant a stress on the complexities of form that have to hold in place – in tension – the diverse, paradoxical and ambiguous elements that make up the content of the work: 'The formal unity that is a fully realised work of literature (so the critical *patois* of the day tended to put it) functions to reproach the partial and the mechanical, and thus to trump the merely propositional language characteristic of both utilitarianism and science'; hence the shared stress on 'transcendent formal power'.[39]

Around the time Milch was at Yale, Brooks and Warren were working on an essay about how to write a critical paper; Brooks made notes upon and amendments to Warren's draft, largely concerning 'substantive' issues about the intentionality of the author, and in the accompanying letter says,

> There is one technical term I would have us walk around. You will see that I have qualified 'contextual' to make it plain that [it] is the social and historical and other such contexts that we have in mind, for 'contextual' has in certain quarters taken on a technical meaning: the insistence that the meaning of any part of [a] literary work must be examined in the light of the full literary context in which it operates. We mean *that* – our whole book is based on it – but our point (on the page [in] question) is to bring in a *larger* context.[40]

That said, Collini's insight that the critics inflated the unifying power of literature as a force against the shredding effects of modernity was a legacy that we see inherited by Milch in some of his greatest work, in particular *Deadwood* and *John From Cincinnati*, which are strongly occupied with the search for community, the commonness in diverse or outwardly antagonistic forces. One can detect in Milch's discussions a good deal of this sensibility, but his stress on unity was to have a radically different inflection, more mystical, one that tended to draw out, as well as socialise, the religious dimension of the aspiration to ontological wholeness. This proximity to the end years of New Criticism sets him apart somewhat from novelists such as Philip Roth, Don DeLillo, Paul Auster and J. M. Coetzee, who tended to, at least in their early works, thematise the formal problems (in particular with narration, and the nature of a 'character' as an ontological entity driving storytelling) associated with poststructuralist concerns.

Milch's second inheritance from Warren came later but was in its formative stages as he transferred to an English Literature Major. In 1963 Brooks and Warren formulated and embarked on a project of mapping American literature in what was to become the magisterial four-volume *American Literature: The Makers and the Making*. This was to be a survey, with lengthy extracts and critical commentary, of the entire range of American literary output. As Brooks describes it (in correspondence with Warren about his sample chapter),

> your long essay demonstrates how much can be woven together of biography and criticism – how much sense can be made of Hawthorne's career by discussing some texts rather fully and alluding to others and bringing in the relevant parts of his life as a man and as an artist – and how all this can be pointed toward the study of the history of American literature.[41]

By grasping the origins of American literary art and broadening considerably the putative limitations of New Criticism, the issue of modern alienation might be accounted for by tracking and quoting in intimate detail the myriad origins, trends and currents of mood, thought and feeling that constituted American literature. A new world, born on the right side of the Enlightenment, would in its literary expression hold the answer to how and why our current struggle with meaning (most shatteringly exemplified by Eliot's *The Waste Land*) evolved in the way it did. Their collaborator, Richard (Dick) W. B. Lewis, was an Americanist who was similarly concerned with the literary origins of American thought and philosophy; his first book, *The American Adam: Innocence, Tragedy and Tradition in the Nineteenth Century*, developed the concept of 'Adamism' – the idea of the pervasive figure of the new man that was a recurrent theme in American literature and popular fiction.

Emboldened by Warren's positive response to his first 'Judgy' stories, Milch brought along another chapter of what was now conceived of as a novel (eventually to become *The Groundlings*), in what he later described as 'a pure act of stupidity, selfishness, and juvenile behaviour', by turning up unexpectedly at Warren's family home:

> He read it, and it was good and he was very good about it. Then I said, 'You know, I don't know if I want to write anymore.' To make him really come out and say – who knows, whatever – because he'd already told me, 'No-one writes dialogue better than you.' Now, I've interrupted his dinner, he's been very gracious, and I say that, and he looks me in the eye and says, 'Understand, David. I don't give a shit who writes and who doesn't.' In other words, if you, David are soliciting from me, 'Oh you must, I ain't gonna say that, because that's up to you.'[42]

Of course, Milch did become a writer, and persevered with *The Groundlings* at the Iowa Writers' Workshop where he went after graduating Phi Beta Kappa from Yale. In so far as Milch was taking his father's advice and following a wise guide, it is hard to imagine a better one for someone in the early stages of conceiving himself as an artist.[43] Warren stimulated Milch to thrive and commit to a vital and lively, not to mention highly successful, region of American industry – its art and literature – and as the relationship deepened he would be regularly invited to Warren's home (sometimes other students enjoyed this privilege as well). For Milch, Warren 'had the gift of thinking the best of people, and that somehow made you be your best, or at least want to'.[44] Note the characteristic sting at the end of that sentence: it is part of the agony of many of Milch's characters that they know they have the capacity to be their 'best self' (in the sense of Cavell's version of moral perfectionism).

While Milch went on to win the Tinker prize for the highest achievement as an English senior,[45] such early rewards, not least Warren's praise, may well have prompted grand aspirations that were ripe for self-sabotage. Repeated enough, this kind of adulation encourages a mode of thinking which tends to put one always on guard against oneself. Some people are their own punishment, getting in the way of, or discriminating against, themselves. One is tempted to see the praise and success of Milch as a Wonder Boy of American Literature (Lillian Hellman, herself an unreliable judge of many things, was an early admirer) congealing into a burden of promise and expectation that eventually threatened to overwhelm his ability and motivation. Wanting to be your best can produce an ideal that is paralysing or crushing in its unattainable purity.

Iowa and after

That Milch's addiction to alcohol could be accommodated in the persona of the Great American Novelist was convenient: all of the major figures in American literature – Hemingway, Faulkner, Melville, Cheever, Fitzgerald to name a few – were drunks (the last had a drunken scuffle with Warren at one point). Warren himself drank, as did Milch's other teachers, and Richard Yates, who taught Milch at Iowa, was a chronic alcoholic. It was part of being in the Big Game of Literature, one that was to continue well into the century, with Stephen King and Bret Easton Ellis, for example, quite open about their willing seduction by alcohol and other narcotics. Despite this calling card, Milch would take the invitation to its fullest expression. He was inspired to become a writer, not an academic, and on Warren's recommendation received a teaching fellowship at the University of Iowa where he was also enrolled in the famous Iowa Writers' Workshop. That workshop, spawning many like it across US universities in the post-war period, was equally formative in Milch's later working practices. It was part of what Mark McGurl has characterised as the 'overwhelming problem for post-war American fiction ... how to adapt modernist principles of writing, developed in the late nineteenth and early twentieth centuries well outside the academy, to a literary field increasingly dominated by bureaucratic institutions of higher education'.[46] The establishment of degree-granting entities such as the Iowa Writers' Workshop was part of a 'new hospitality to self-expressive creativity on the part of progressive-minded universities' and was a component of the 'increasingly direct orientation of higher education to the values of the market'.[47] Few US writers before the war had bothered to attend university at all: Twain, Melville, Hemingway had at best glancing involvement, and those who did attend, such as Henry James, did not see that time as in any way preparatory for their writing career.

The overriding approach when Milch was there was 'show not tell', which stabilised a set of literary values around the formal organisation of point of view, reinforcing the sense of Iowa as an 'aesthetic institution': 'you write what you know by showing how you tell'.[48] This was emblematised by textbooks such as *Understanding Fiction* (1943, rewritten 1959), which 'embodied much the same conception of literary value as the workshop, and circulated through the system of higher education, introducing the elitist discourse of literary modernism to the self-same social masses it typically held in contempt'.[49] Brooks and Warren's *Understanding Fiction* was 'undoubtedly the most important of post-war fiction textbooks', and Warren represented the 'large-scale intrusion of practitioner-critics ... into the domain of literary scholars' which began in the 1930s. In this context New Criticism became a means to theorise and promote the centrality of the artist to the appreciation of the literary: 'The New Criticism put the point of view of the artist at the very centre of post-war literary studies, where the New Critical textbook served as an aid to understanding and potentially emulating his "creative process".'

The paradox is, of course, that while New Criticism avoided the mere biographical as a source and origin of textual meaning, it replaced that source with a higher if more abstract category of the master of narrational control: the literary artist. The flesh and blood behind it was far less relevant, or even tangible, than the materials and the work itself. In 2008 in his introductory talk to interns working in his office at the Red Board production company in Santa Monica, we can hear Milch echo this idea:

> Maybe it would be a kinda left-handed way to get at about these writing exercises by talking about the fucking mess on the floor of this office. Every place that I work winds up exactly the same. And I think that the reason for it, is that I feel like I do everything wrong. So I would rather not try to pick it up, because it's evidence of failure. I'd rather disavow any

> connection with these words until I have an immediate need for them, because the collateral associations with these words – the personal, private associations that I have with them – which are: 'I wrote them. I don't keep a clean place. I'm not well-organised' – I try to minimise what could be called the *fanciful* associations, the private associations with these expressions of the processes of my imagination. In order to keep those processes separate from my felt sense of my personality [...] Before you met me you knew that I was a writer. A writer writes. Encountering me in the flesh really has nothing to do with my work. My work exists separately from the physical being of flesh and blood who generates it. Similarly, the personality construct which moved me to begin to write, and to continue writing, really has no proper, primary connection with your experience of the work itself. Now, our culture tries to attach all sorts of biographical connections and so on, but in fact in its pure form, the work [is a] work of the imagination.[50]

We can see in this the wider context in which Warren may well have been receptive to a student arriving at his digs with chapters from a novel. It was part of a sense of a nation-wide critical project that would stimulate students of literature to attempt to craft their own creative responses to the world, while subtracting themselves from it and in doing so negating the alienated, fragmented accumulation that made up the individual's 'personality construct'.

McGurl's account of the post-war intertwining of higher education institutions and literary creativity argues that the idea of disciplining desire, the work and effort of creative self-tutoring, was central for Iowa scholar-practitioners such as Flannery O'Connor. Discipline became for her 'a kind of religion', and we can see Milch's later work ethic being modulated by his sense of the discipline of behavioural reinforcement through habit. The formation of writing discipline was the meat and potatoes of creative writing teaching in US higher education during the 1960s, and that self-control was exemplified in the handling of narrative point of view, largely by hiding it in plain view. This cleaved to another characteristic of writing programmes: the suppression in prose of authorial presence so that the form – the larger structural design and significance of the patterning of storytelling – was left to do its work, so that the 'Jamesian narrative poetics favoured and codified in the New Criticism, is considered the cardinal formal sin of pre-modernist narration: authorial intrusion'.[51]

Here we can see the tension built into the tutoring of individual voice within a small group setting, with all its attendant rituals of public scrutiny, evaluation and, one imagines, ritualised humiliation, where being able to distance oneself from the work – 'the materials' as Milch tends to refer to his plans, characters and stories – was equally a means to insulate the self from its own hurt. What is striking is how close this model of group criticism and shared creative exchange is to that of the writers' room that is characteristic of television production as it developed later on, especially during the multi-narrative, multi-character shows of the 1980s and afterwards. For the television industry represented another highly formalised institution of creative production.[52] In both creative writing qualifications and television fiction, an external force creates discipline: in television fiction it is the industrial pressures of the cycle of episodic production that requires multiple writers; at Iowa and similar workshops it was the formalised requirement to produce creative material in order to receive a qualification. As Blake Bailey characterised Iowa, 'The workshop was composed of a hundred or so carefully selected graduate writers who prided themselves on being part of a bohemian community of writers.'[53] It embodied a certain counter-cultural quality – there was pot-smoking, sexual promiscuity and, of course, drinking. This theatricalised sense of membership at the margins was rapidly becoming a mainstream activity, and resistance to conformity, far from being opposed to institutional values, was becoming enshrined as part of what such institutions were, in fact, in the market to produce. This rhymes with John Thornton Caldwell's account of the Los Angeles production industry as thriving on a conformist sense of diverse difference, with every creative establishing their sense of being beyond the putatively stifling norms of industrial production in a way that was absolutely shared by the vast majority of its participants.[54]

And in another parallel with Hollywood, the counter-cultural identity at Iowa was freighted with some interpersonal nastiness: according to Bailey it was a 'snake pit of internecine strife between poets and fiction writers, traditionalists and experimentalists, the talented and the not-so-talented, the drunk and the not-so-drunk, the faculty and the administrators'.[55] In this context the discovery and tutoring of individual voice was frequently hostage to waves and currents of mood, prejudice and personal enmity. Once a week on a Friday afternoon, workshop sessions were held where the fifteen or so students in the group exchanged their fiction by reading aloud to one another. These writing efforts were subsequently discussed, 'often viciously'.[56] This was part of the lesson that transcending the narcissistic desires that prompted the personal, authorial voice to intrude into the text was necessary unless one wanted to cop a verbal beating.

Milch warmed to this site of conflict. Richard Yates, who arrived at Iowa in 1964 to teach at the workshop, used a method whereby he would talk to the class about his enthusiasms for particular work, drawing on textual quotations for evidence of his evaluative claims. Bailey's lively account of Yates's mostly miserable time there contains a snapshot of the young Milch as a 'bright young thing'. Yates disliked Milch largely because of his status as a privileged, prize-winning Yale graduate who, thanks to Warren, already had a teaching fellowship (this was not at the workshop itself but elsewhere at the university, where he taught composition to members of the university's prestigious basketball team). Yates hated the condescending sneering that this status conferred on his student, especially during those Friday afternoon sessions when other writers were criticised under Milch's deadly critical spotlight. 'Milch was a slasher in workshops. He was part of a new wave of Ivy League students at Iowa; some of these students were contemptuous about Iowa's casual non-academic milieu. Milch thought Yates was a joke – too nonprofessional, stumbling and shy. Too conversational.'[57] In his biography of Warren, Joseph Blotner describes his laid-back, seemingly casual teaching mode, but by contrast, Milch's aggressive declarative mode seemed designed to do harm. In any case the fetishisation of youthful literary ability that had its roots in the Romantic conception of talent made Milch the target of Yates's (himself a young hotshot) contempt. In a bar one evening after a Friday session, Yates 'let himself go' in Milch's presence: 'He went to Yale! He graduated first in his class! Warren said he had an ear for dialogue that rivals Hemingway! And here he is twenty-one years old...'[58] Milch, who described himself at the time as an 'unfinished spirit', remembers the speech as a 'devastating encapsulation of everything pretentious and self-important',[59] but despite his father's occupation, Milch's background was certainly not that of a classic Ivy Leaguer, especially given that Yale's restriction on the admission of Jews had only been relaxed in 1960. Milch's impish behaviour was less a product of privilege, and probably, if we are generous, akin to the agonistic relations between current and former 'Wonder Boys' that Bloom's *Anxiety of Influence* tries to theorise across much longer stretches of time.[60]

Apart from the completion of two chapters of *The Groundlings*, there are three aspects to Milch's time at Iowa that seem pertinent. The first is the absorption of the small group ethic – a mode of teaching and evaluating creative output developed at Iowa but later taken up at Stanford and elsewhere. The subordination of the self to the art, and the knowledge as one wrote that one might be crucified in public when it was read on Friday, favoured the articulate exhibitionist and charismatic performer, because the moment of critique rather than the moment of writing was verbal and immediate and could harvest the response of a present audience, rather than the written word that was vulnerable only to the spotlight and magnitude of private auto-critical voices. Secondly, Milch's early gift for dialogue was a signal of his facility for screen-based or performed fiction rather than densely crafted descriptive prose, and this was nurtured by his evidently deadly verbal pyrotechnics. As signalled above, in the later phase of his career Milch adapted the Iowa model of literary internship at his production company in Santa Monica, and was providing lectures and workshops at universities in the US and Europe.

Finally, Iowa allowed Milch to continue his non-discriminatory consumption of narcotics and pursuit of gambling. The circumstances of his arrival at Iowa could not have been more benign: apart from the tutoring work, he was provided with accommodation in a basement apartment at the house of the classicist and theatre scholar Peter Arnott, who used puppets in order to restage, revivify and theorise the spatial aspects of Greek theatre.[61] But, drinking heavily and somewhat baffled by the puppets decorating Arnott's home on his return from nightly benders, Milch soon ended up in the city at the Hotel Jefferson, living off a credit card and pursuing a dissolute lifestyle. As he later recalled,

> [t]he whole idea about being a writer was how well did you hold your liquor and write. It was a given that you were supposed to be drunk because Hemingway was a drunk, Faulkner was a drunk, Fitzgerald was a drunk, all my teachers were drunks; Richard Yates – big drunk. Kurt Vonnegut tremendous, tremendous consumer of cannabis. And I was an alcoholic anyway.[62]

Within a year Milch had begun occasionally sleeping on the streets. He had sold his 'novel' on the basis of a writing sample and some no doubt fine recommendations from Warren, Hellman and others (presumably the same chapters of *The Groundlings* that he eventually submitted for his Iowa MFA, and perhaps similar to the ones he had shown to Warren). But he had sold it to a number of different publishers, effectively meaning that it could not be published at all. Nonetheless he graduated from Iowa successfully. In 2011 I asked Milch how much the burden of expectation had affected his writing at that time: he agreed it was paralysing. At some point during the next decade he spent a year typing out the same twelve pages of fiction, word for word, punctuation for punctuation, day after day. Little wonder that one discovery arising from that ghastly blockage was his aversion to writing words on paper; quite a shock for an aspirant novelist hunting the Big Game of American Literature. And there is no doubt that this is what Milch was aiming for, even back in the days of his first stint at Yale in Warren's classes and company. Ted Mann, Milch's writing collaborator on *Deadwood* and *John From Cincinnati*, told me of a conversation they had outside the lot after a day shooting an episode of *NYPD Blue* in the 1990s, when Milch claimed he could have been in the Big Game, but had failed. Mann reminded Milch of it later when they were writing *Deadwood*:

> It was a sad thing and when you're on a genre cop show it doesn't readily transcend the limits of its form ... we were walking across [the *Deadwood* set] and I said fifteen years ago you said to me that you'd felt that you'd kinda missed your promise ... and I think maybe you have, maybe we didn't think it was possible then ... and I think you've gone some portion of the way to realising it. And he looked at me and he said, 'I think so too'. That was the show that made it clear to him. The medium was capable of supporting it and the audience could support it, if you could deliver it. The story was always in Hollywood was that you can't do that kind of thing ... but if you are a master of your craft it is your responsibility to package your material...[63]

No longer a college student, the end of the 1960s meant Milch was eligible for the draft, and with the introduction in 1969 of a lottery system he drew a low number and was almost certain of being called up for combat duty in Vietnam. However, like many other educated children of the bourgeoisie, he had options. He was enrolled back at Yale, this time in the Law School where he was a contemporary of Hillary Rodham, Bill Clinton and Clarence Thomas. This period of the late 1960s and early 1970s was one when his delinquent behaviour dominated any creative apprenticeship, and he was involved in several dangerous criminal activities. Many of these became fodder for later recounting, as stories and parables about his peculiarity as an artist as a young man.

His time at Yale Law was a portrait of untutored recklessness and crazy disregard for risk, even by the standards of the Phi Delta Kappa fraternity whose members included Bob Woodward and George W. Bush (who was president of that fraternity). He took LSD for ninety days in a row. In his most infamous story, his friend at the time, Bobby 'Uptight' Greenlee (later a performer in the acid band Root Boy Slim), asked him to apartment-sit while he returned to Chicago to try to save his marriage. While alone there Milch discovered a Civil War sabre and set about destroying Bobby's clothes and furniture in a scene that is eerily similar to one in Warren's final novel, *A Place to Come To* (1979). The narrator, Jed Tewksbury, recounts his father's drunken behaviour:

> some nights he would forget to eat, and hell might break loose in Alabama, like the night he took down off the wall above the fireplace

> the Confederate saber his old granddad had used to fight Yankees, and started screaming *yip-hee!* – which he took to be the Rebel yell – and rising in imaginary stirrups and damning and son-a-bitching the Blue-Bellies and waving the rusty old blade around and performing hideous carnage in that place of the slaughter.[64]

Milch, still under the influence of acid, discovered a shotgun in Bobby's ruined apartment which he assembled and took outside, where he began 'shooting out every godamn [street]light on Whitney Avenue'. The police soon arrived in a patrol car, which he shot at from a distance. Fortunately he was far enough away to avoid immediate detection, but other forces would reveal his hand:

> I stash my shotgun under a car, I mail my shotgun shells, I go running up to the cops and say, 'Jesus Christ somebody is bullshit back there!' So they say, 'We know, we got the report, get out of the area...' So I get about fifty feet. Now, the dramatic inadequacy of reality sets in. So I say, 'You dumb Dego bastards! It was me!'[65]

There is some truth in the assertion that the 'dramatic inadequacy of reality', a sharper-bladed version of Thoreau's 'quiet desperation', was a strong presence during these years in Milch's late twenties and early thirties. Given that he had fired in the direction of the patrol car (his aim thankfully adjusted by the drugs), he was fortunate to have lesser charges applied, but nonetheless he was a felon, and ineligible to continue Law at Yale.

What Milch did next is unclear. It was probably around this time that he became a heroin addict. In the early 1970s he was involved in drug dealing (to, among others, Eldridge Cleaver, one of the leaders of the Black Panther Party) and the large-scale manufacture of LSD. This was a business interest he acquired after meeting by chance an old college friend, Floyd, at Grand Central Station (perhaps he was begging for money there). Floyd had made vast amounts of cash selling LSD wholesale, and through this connection Milch would wind up in Mexico, and would eventually be imprisoned there. It was a very dangerous time: much later on, after the success of *Deadwood*, Milch talked about some of the events of this time, such as running his mouth off during deals when there was a loaded shotgun to his head, and shooting incidents (in shops, in his friends' car); the Panthers called him 'the craziest white cat' they knew. While he was making acid in Cuernavaca, his chemist died of peritonitis, partly because of the mistaken treatment that the chemist's girlfriend Yum-Yum had provided in the form of an enema. Given the circumstances and setting, Milch decided to bury the body. Before he pushed the corpse into the grave, he took out the chemist's ID, on the off chance that he might have relatives who might like to know that he was gone. Milch looked at the card and saw himself: it was Milch's own ID that he had sold illegally six months before. One does not have to be of a literary mind to feel the symbolic resonance and moment of such an event, the sense that one has become capable of anything, absorbed into a world beyond one's control, a figure alien to oneself, who smiles back, grimly mocking.

However, events that have no meaning sometimes seem to scream at us that they do. ('Coincidence is God's way of staying anonymous' is a saying that reveals this craving for order.) It may be that the way Milch has subsequently related such stories to an audience has given them a literary quality, although he certainly did not think of that dimension at the time.[66] Whether it was this event alone or, more likely, the accumulation of other things, Milch eventually took up the opportunity to return to Yale to work as a research assistant for Warren, Brooks and Lewis on their epic *American Literature: The Makers and the Making* project. While Milch's habits continued, they had less risk than the Mexico adventures, and Yale offered the added benefit of afternoon walks where he could listen to and discourse with Warren.

By 1970 Milch had submitted the first two chapters of his novel *The Groundlings* as the dissertation part of his MFA at Iowa. Coming in at thirty-six pages, double-spaced, it is a tight but potent piece of work. It should be no surprise given the title and Milch's background that elements of his later work are evident here. The supervisor was John Leggett and the thesis committee consisted of William Price Fox and Richard Yates, the latter in one of his last duties before he was kicked out of Iowa. The chapters included seem to be the novel's first ones (they are numbered one and two), although they could feasibly belong, together, later on in an episodic series of 'scenes'.

The Groundlings

The novel begins with a character called Torch being met by his slightly injured brother, Mark, at an airport. It transpires that there has been a family tragedy: their other brother Judgy has died in a car accident. The funeral has taken place, but Mark blames himself for Judgy's death, which may have been suicide. This and the next chapter are dominated by dialogue between these two characters. The first is mostly set in the men's toilet at the airport, the second taking place during the car journey back home, and finishing as they arrive there. The writing is taut and descriptive, with events, gestures and actions conveyed with an impassive restraint that is suggestive of a larger unspecified symbolic dimension. This is the first paragraph:

> On his release from Customs Torch went to the airport barber shop and gave the shoeshine boy fifty cents to get him a clean towel. He took it to the men's room, where he stripped to the waist and washed his hands, his face, and the upper part of his torso. When he was done he dried himself and combed his hair, then put his shirt back on, staring at his reflection in the mirror above the sink. After a moment, he turned, draped the towel over a coat-hook, and went out to the waiting room.[67]

This describes the actions of a person and implies an interior life ('staring at his reflection') but never specifies or clarifies or allows us access to that life at all. It is a good example of the narrational control that emphasises to the reader the limits of their view; this is an impersonal style, what McGurl calls an 'amalgam of intimacy and distance embedded in third person limited narration'.[68] The prose is camera-like, recording only surface events – as if they are directions given to an actor.

Torch meets his brother Mark, who has a fresh laceration on his head, but we are never told how this happened. This puts in plain sight a conversation that must have happened between them that we did not see and is not mentioned. Warren was not wrong about Milch's facility for dialogue (he was 25 when this was submitted for examination) as most of what follows is dialogue based, with only stage directions – asterisks (cf. *The Great Gatsby*, one of Yates's favourite novels)[69] – to denote the passing of time. The fluency of the dialogue is in contrast, at first, to the strangely directed prose which seems awkwardly concerned with getting objects and people from one place to another. Nonetheless these objects begin to accrue meaning as they are used as props – the towel that Torch gives his brother is the one he had 'gotten from the barber shop' and which Mark later uses to dry his face as he seems to defrost and become less passive. And in this gesture we see the familiar mechanism of modernist narration that embeds mythic narratives at depth in ordinary settings – in this case, perhaps, the cloth that St Veronica used to wipe the tears and sweat from Christ's face as he endured his journey to Calvary.

This is clearly one of the 'scenes' about the death and its aftermath of his childhood friend Judgy, in a car crash outside Ithaca, that Milch wrote after he came back from the funeral, and probably the first he showed to Warren at Yale. As Milch noted in *True Blue*, 'Throughout the next weeks I imagined other people in Judgy's family, writing scenes about each of them when they found out he's been killed.'[70]

This story is set not when Torch or Milch find out about the crash, but several days, maybe even weeks later. The fact that it is this story and no other suggests that the earliest work Milch produced was still being worked on as long as five years afterwards. This is the first hint of the obsessive revisionism that was to characterise most of Milch's later writing practice, one that produced radical solutions in order to offset its non-productive consequences. It is surprising that Milch did not change Judgy's name or the setting of the story in Buffalo.[71] Indeed, throughout it is strikingly frank in its autobiographical candour: Judgy is 'Judgy', David becomes 'Mark' and 'Torch' (perhaps Milch's brother, Robert) is little more than the spotlight of Milch's own conscience shining back on himself. Milch doubles himself and puts a key traumatic experience centre stage. In a move that he was to continue in Hollywood, Milch appears to play by the rules, hiding the presence of authorial narration in the form of the prose, and yet there he is. David Shields recounts how reading *The Groundlings* years after being taught by Milch, he recognised the strategy:

> The two phrases Milch had used most often in class were 'strategy of indirection,' which meant it should take the reader forever to figure out what was happening, since life was difficult, and 'content tests form,' which meant that since life was difficult it should take the reader forever to figure out what was happening. It took me forever to figure out what was happening in *The Groundlings*, but it had an undeniable narcotic pull, probably because there is so much Milch in it...[72]

Once Mark gets talking and the back story begins to flow, the dialogue acquires momentum and bite. It becomes clear that Mark's narcissistic self-loathing is a means for him to remain central to the concerns of the events around him. By blaming himself for Judgy's death he acquires a role in the drama in contrast to the one his brother ascribes to him. 'Oh that's right Torch', says Mark. 'Stay above it all. You stay in the regions of immaculation. Don't get involved with the shit-bird. Stay away from the mind-fucker.' What the mind-fucking 'shit-bird' Mark does is to undermine the hidden social, personal and familial rules of ordinary life. The powerful spotlight of his social intellect effectively drains others: 'Oh sure Torch', he tells his brother, 'I'm a really swell guy. All I've got to do is stay away from people, so I don't fuck their minds. All I've got to do is restrict myself to paper-work.'

Mark blames himself for Judgy's death because he convinced his mother to get a court order removing his abusive father from the house. But the prose is highly resistant to functionally revealing much in the way of back story, so dominated is the telling of it by the lens of Mark's dialogue. We get hints about his odd behaviour which similarly elide interior motivation or narrational content ('Mark was staring at the snow which covered the spot where he had knelt'); in this sense our attention has nowhere to go except to consider form and overall patterns. This focuses our attention on the authenticity and deceit around this trauma and Mark's articulate sense of his inadequacy and destructiveness as a human being. It shades sometimes into adolescent grief, but it also contains quite developed aspects of Milchean dialogue in its dense locutions that mix formal and archaic speech. And it homes in on the precision and chaotic power of an intellect uncertain of its secure footing in the world yet sharpening its blade on the raw flesh of reality. 'Well this is really refreshing, Torch', says Mark, 'it's nice to see you evince a little morbidity.' 'Evince' is too academic a word for our early sense of the character we have known up to now, and the idea of morbidity takes a while to settle into; and yet the line flows brilliantly as an emblem of Mark's attempt to be loving and sarcastic in a way that falls short of, while evoking, his unspecified talent at 'mind-fucking'. Mark is interested in the protocols, practices and anthropology of the funeral he attended (like Milch, he was drunk), and when goaded into recounting what he calls his 'abominations', Mark describes his manipulation of a girl, Carol: 'I manage to impute a motive to her visit which, as long as we're being charitable, we'll say that it might not have existed.' He describes picking up a hitchhiker on the way to the airport who he convinces has killed his own father 'by indirection': 'So I catalysed it. I got him to see the connection.' The first chapter ends with them pulling off the highway.

The next resumes with them talking in the now parked car. Mark is convinced that Judgy (in a gesture reminiscent of a famous scene in *The Great Gatsby*) 'grabbed the wheel' of the car before it crashed and caused the accident that killed him. The issue or debate between the brothers is the extent to which Mark is reading symbolic meaning into an event that he has limited knowledge of – as Torch puts it, 'Some stupid bullshit car wreck. Something that doesn't mean anything.' This in turn reflects back on the availability to the reader of similarly explanatory and clarifying matter. We are then alerted to the status of actions, gestures and objects as having 'catalysing' symbolic weight that, equally, might make us the victims of a 'mind-fucking' (including, one cannot help but think, Yates himself). We might well wonder whether we are making connections that cannot be sufficiently sustained by the materials we are given. Hence while it uses real events that clearly had personal resonance for Milch, it equally displays both a 'New Critical' sensibility of holding ambiguities in tension, and an

'Iowan' flavour that subordinates personal voice to the discipline of form, anonymising point of view so completely that we are drawn to the procedure as an aesthetic technique. The writing plays its hand very closely and eschews any description of interiority: 'Mark was silent. Torch watched him for a moment.' Milch would later describe this technique as 'opening the door for the audience', that is, creating situations whose meanings seem undefined, allowing the reader to fill this space with themselves, and then manipulating their more intimate involvement.

The repeated use of objects, actions and gestures means that they are recruited to a patterning that is like Mark's 'compulsion to have some moral relation to every move that's made in this vale of tears'. Since descriptions and attribution of inner life come mostly from what the characters say, the narrative process is largely apprehensible in the organisation and stylisation of dialogue. This does give some of the longer passages a script-like quality, but this is subsumed under the more prominent moral questions that are raised by the conversation between the two of them. As Torch tells Mark, 'the natural impulse is to ... interpret something like this', which includes self-deceit and mendacity, which may be 'congenial, you know, to your ... inclinations'. The two ellipses, which are in the original, naturalistically denote hesitation, small moments when thought may occur. But they also signal a pause or space that prompts the reader to reflect on *their* own process of meaning attribution. Milch takes this particularly private event – the death of his close friend, the traumatic thing that prompted him to write and show his writing to Warren – and makes it part of a modernist tradition and aesthetic: the search for meaning in forms of contemporary representation.

The issue – what caused the crash that killed Judgy – is indeterminable (we cannot make a reliable judgement about it) because those who were there may well be lying about what happened for their own purposes, and even if they are not lying this still does not settle the matter for good. As Torchy points out, 'perhaps he was farting around or something' or 'the steering went out of whack'. Ultimately, according to Torch, the reason it happened doesn't matter, except 'You can't act like it's true, or say anything about it, because it'll kill Mum.' So there is a pragmatic dimension to meaning and acting. More than this, Mark is unsure of his own motivation: 'I don't know what I meant to do. I can't tell.' Milch may be saying that language cannot be used as a tool to get at what drives and nor can we use it to divine or define possible reasons with any clarity or make them legible to ourselves or others. Mark seems convinced that their mother had to take out a court order banning his father from the house, a move that folds in the fact that Judgy's father Jim was excluded from his son's funeral. Real content from the real world is recruited into this epistemological impasse, giving the writing a personal aesthetic kick for the writer, but leaving the reader ultimately 'stuck' in a prison house of un-meaning.

As the discussion progresses Torch elaborates a (William) Jamesian version of pragmatism – that whatever the ambiguities of intention, what matters is the cashed-out value of subsequent actions. For him, Mark is simply taking the easy way out by blaming himself, and enjoying the buzz of its dramatic value:

> Okay, so now you decide because you're ambivalent you're guilty, and then you fasten on Judgy dying and say you were responsible for it, because it's the most dramatic metaphor for guilt that's available. But not because, you know, of anything that's got peas, corn or tomatoes to do with Judge. And that gives you, I mean now you not only have a moral stance toward Dad getting kicked out, but you've also got one toward this thing. You now have a defined relationship to the death too. You have killed your brother. So now you don't have to reconcile yourself to the fact a dude you took bike trips with is dead, or try to find something in that to live with. You've got a posture ready-made, something easy and convenient and dramatic.

There are two distinctively Milchean aspects to this speech, quite apart from its moral complexity and length. The first is the sense that we attribute meaning for self-centred, self-loathing but ultimately redeemable reasons, many of them to do with finding the security, familiarity and comfort of self-hatred. The second is the sheer relentless tone of Torch's analysis – it is a quite devastating exposure of Mark's position and he is reduced to feeble attempts to stop his brother going on. Mark's self-disgust has a physical dimension as well in this subhuman soliloquy:

> That's what it is. That's what I can't stand. I hate all the openings, all the wholes. I hate my breath and I hate my shit and I hate what comes out of cunts. I can't stand ... I hate the smell of stale piss in my pants. I hate ... And that's what I'd be. I'd be bare naked, all holes and stink.

This and the 'dramatic inadequacy of reality', self-dramatising, contempt and loathing helps Mark to find 'a place to come to'. Torch tells him towards the end of the chapter to go to sleep and 'let the world do its own spinning' (a line echoed by E. B. Farnum's advice to Al Swearengen in *Deadwood*). They get back on the road, cross the border into the US (apparently the airport was in Canada – another ellipsis) and arrive at their parents' home.

After his sleep Mark seems to be in a different state: the world and its objects have taken on a luminosity and simplicity, as if washed clean again. 'Amazing', he says as he looks at the house; he picks up a rubbish bin lid that has fallen off, then puts it back on the ground, saying, 'Thus rejecting the doctrine of unearned significance, M. Lytle strode briskly...' What does this literary gesture mean for us or for Mark? That he is cheerful again, that things can be reset or left at will? That it is all garbage, left to drift in the open? Mark becomes a literary relay at the end, commenting on his own responses: '"La, sir. No post-mortems." Mark feigned a flourish. "And choosing to disregard that unfortunate declaration, he took to his bed."' Sleep again promises another dawn, a new day, a new beginning, the core of the American Dream.

The Groundlings strikes a familiar note for viewers of *Deadwood*: the mixture of long, soliloquy-like speeches in which characters reveal, as they conceal, their inner lives in sideways gestures of speech and comment, in particular aspects of their putative guilt, loathing and their own fantasised power over others. The conversation that Mark conducts with his attentive, sensible interlocutor might be one between Joanie Stubbs and Charlie Utter, or Ace Bernstein and Gus Dimitriou. Equally, the back and forth between them is also reminiscent of the writing 'exercises' that Milch asked his workshop participants and interns to complete as stage one of his 'habit formation' training process: two voices (A and B) arguing out a dramatic position with each another. Among the synecdochal objects and actions is Mark's continuing thirst; after being seemingly convinced by Torch's pragmatism before falling asleep in the car, he says, 'God, I'm really thirsty.' When they get home in the last few lines of the chapter he finds sustenance by drinking a little water at the kitchen sink. Spiritual thirst and nourishment seem to be the issue here. Torch frequently characterises Mark as 'pissing and moaning' and there is a lot of 'pissing', whereas Torch's ablutions are regular and methodical: chapter 1 begins with him washing and chapter 2 ends with him washing before sleep (as in many *Deadwood* episodes, the chapter ends when the characters lose consciousness for the night). Mark is looking for a purity of motive, clear as water, one that can close the seemingly implacable distance of doubleness in perception and intention, the discrepancy between the world's outer and his inner. The mirroring of the past in the present – the conversation about a car wreck takes place in a car – and the sense that actions and behaviour in the present are a mechanism for purifying that pain of the past is an insight already embedded here.

Warren, Melville and the makers of literature

Once the dissertation had been passed, and Milch had finished his drug-manufacturing stint, he returned to Yale as a research assistant for Warren, Brooks and Lewis, as well as doing some teaching, including creative writing. It was a relatively stable period, although David Shields's description of him indicates that he still had one foot in the world of addiction, high risk, and did little by way of writing:

> Milch looked like he'd never been released from *Rebel Without A Cause*: he wore tennis shoes, blue jeans, a pack of Marlboros rolled into the sleeve of his white T-shirt, and a permanent smirk. The only person I've ever known who could convey genuine menace in a classroom, he paced back and forth, chain-smoked, lectured non-stop without notes, rarely allowed anyone to say anything, insisted that we call him "Mr. Milch," addressed us – with pseudo-politeness – as "Mr." or "Miss," and asked questions that somehow were impossible to answer without sounding either feeble-minded or overscrupulous.[73]

But proximity to Warren, to his house, family, work and conversation, sustained Milch's artistic nourishment even if he was not himself productive, and *The Groundlings* itself, despite its brevity, is strongly influenced by some of Warren's mature poetry, which he was writing by the time he taught his final semester at Yale in 1973. This suggests that Milch continued contact with him even during his escapades in the drug trade. Harold Bloom describes the poetry's 'prophetic style, resonating like a new Isaiah', and places Warren alongside Melville as 'formidable exiles from our dominant Emersonian tradition'.[74]

Two of Warren's poems from this period in particular had a continuing grip on Milch's later work. Warren's mature phase coincided with his working on the *American Literature* books with Brooks and Lewis. That four-volume survey was a vast, ambitious task, and the writing process was necessarily collaborative: 'We all read everything, then one person would write up a given section and the others would re-write the first draft to their heart's desire – a continuing process.'[75] If we follow Bloom's periodisation, Warren's mature phase begins with the publication *Or Else – Poem/Poems 1968–1974*, poems not planned as a group but which subsequently emerged as a sequence. That collection includes 'I Am Dreaming of a White Christmas: The Natural History of a Vision', first published in *The Atlantic Monthly* in December 1973, which concludes with the line Milch often used as one of his key creative slogans.[76] The poem is based on a dream in which the poet comes upon the skeletons of his dead mother and father in an attic, amid the brown and yellow dust of past detritus and abandoned but preserved tokens of family history. They are seated figures who stare at him without eyes; around them the debris of Christmas past is scattered, wrapping paper and a ribbon, 'ripped long ago from some package of joy', but now like a 'fuse that failed'. There is a denuded Christmas tree with three unwrapped presents beneath it. Abruptly the poet's vision shifts to Times Square in the present, late evening, and the vivid urban reality of men emerging from porn cinemas with 'their drawers drying stiff at the crotch' (an image that could live comfortably in the world of *Deadwood*), where cars 'plunge' down Broadway and a 'dago' cop on a horse is 'as beautiful as a law of chemistry'. Then he is transported to the peak of the Nez Perce mountain in Wyoming and it begins to snow (hence the poem's title).

The poem's final stanza bundles up these diverse images into a resonant package:

> All items listed above belong in the world
> In which all things are continuous,
> And are parts of the original dream which,
> I am now trying to discover the logic of. This
> Is the process whereby pain of the past in its pastness
> May be converted into the future tense
> Of joy.[77]

An important caution in these lines is the word 'may': the 'process' may be writing a poem, writing anything, making some other form of art, or any other kind of effort. It offers the possibility of solace, not its guarantee. This was congruent with Milch's own experience of writing out the Judgy events in *The Groundlings*; this 'process' of making art might have been experienced as a directly purifying mechanism, where the availability of the present, like the arc of dawn light, transforms the apparently fixed nature of what has gone before, reinterpreting and readjusting the sedimented pressure of historical time and its accumulated pain in the present. That meant transforming it through the process of making art into something separate from the maker and the making: like a gift, it becomes portable, part of a gesture that seeks to elicit pleasure, or joy. But the balm did not last, nor did it spur Milch to write more. Warren's poem anticipates the false version of this 'process', of mistaking in some of the pleasing immediacies of the present a transformative force that is, in fact, as impotent as the process of drying semen on cloth. There is a concern in the poem with seeing and not seeing this immediacy – the dynamic sublime of snow falling on a 7,000-foot peak in the Teton Range is a doubled image of glacial and immediate transience. The snow and the poem's title are evocative of the classic Bing Crosby song as, it seems, a warning to the future about the historical forces ranged against the subsequent longevity and adhesion of artistic materials forged in the present. Anything or nothing might become relevant, could end up beneath the Christmas tree wrapped, as it were, as a work of art in the years to come.

The second poem that has proved influential for Milch is Warren's 'Homage to Theodore Dreiser'. Dreiser was a naturalistic novelist whose *Sister Carrie* and *An American Tragedy* were bestselling accounts of the cultural eruptions of desire around the coming of urban modernity in America at the turn of the twentieth century. Warren was interested in the doubleness and paradox of Dreiser who was, in Milch's words, a great storyteller but a terrible writer and 'one of the greatest shitbirds who ever walked the earth'. For Milch the poem raised in a particularly poignant form the question of the relationship between life and art. Dreiser's doubleness included the split between his often simple prose style and the organisation of his content: 'the rhythmic organisation of his materials, the vibrance which is the life of fictional illusion, the tension among elements, and the mutual interpenetration in meaning of part and whole which gives us the sense of prenatural fulfilment'.[78] Blotner notes Warren's affinity with Dreiser as one 'with a religious temperament but without religious faith', a sense of 'personal unfitness' with wretched personal qualities but ferocious energy and ambition.[79] The same can be said of Milch, although his faith in God seems, on most occasions, far stronger than either Warren's, Dreiser's or Melville's (who Hawthorne famously described as a man who could neither accept God nor rest content in his disbelief).[80]

The poem articulates a sordid physical repugnance at Dreiser's body and desires – his nasty, greedy aspiration to the shiny world of commodities that is set against the rarefied and delicate spirit of the writer. It seems, in the light of Milch's screen characters, a fundamental dialectic of character formation that he was to take up and evolve: 'Born with one hand in his pants and one in the till/ He knows that the filth of self, to be loved must be clad in glory.'[81] And this is a dialectic of the human born and forged in the world of emergent urban modernity where the sensual pleasures of status and consumption were absorbing obsessions of the body and mind. 'Nothing could help nothing, not reading Veblen or even Freud, for/ The world is a great ass propped high on pillows, the cunt/ Winks.'[82] It would be reductive to say that Milch merely adopted the analysis of this poem as a creative credo (it was published in the *New York Review of Books* in 1971), but the idea of discovering the finest art in apparently antagonistic forces, where the two ways of being in the world – of having a physicalised, desiring self, a shitbird, and a life as an artist – that these two might cooperate in the life of a human being was at the very least significant to a man now approaching his thirties.

He's no philosopher
His only gift is to enact
All that his deepest self abhors
And learn, in his self-contemptive distress,
The secret worth
Of all our human worthlessness.[83]

We can see in *The Groundlings*, particularly in Mark's 'self-contemplative distress', a feeling towards work that would, like Warren's, explore the relation between life, as a physical concrete desiring and grounded experience that one might recoil from, and the art that this same stinking creature was capable of creating.

While Milch continued to 'write' in his ever-moving but never-forward way, what he describes as his 'major education' continued as he worked as chief research assistant for Warren, Brooks and Lewis as they wrote *American Literature: The Makers and the Making* (he also assisted on the revised editions of *Understanding Fiction*). The multi-volume textbook has sections on particular writers including commentary and large extracts of their writing. This was collaborative work but, according to Brooks, 'though each always submitted his own work to the other two for suggestions, additions or cuts and a general cosmetic treatment, nearly all the introductions are substantially from one pen'.[84]

Lewis did the section on Melville's novels, while Warren dealt with his poetry, a development of his introduction to the *Selected Poems of Herman Melville*. For Warren, it was the Civil War that gave Melville 'the kind of big, athletic overmastering subject he always needed for his best work'.[85] As Blotner notes, much of Warren's writing on Melville was relevant to his own work; but it also touches on aspects of Milch's subsequent persona and interests, for he, too, seemed to thrive with topics and settings that reached into the deepest questions of American history and modernity. In his Civil War poems, Warren claims that Melville saw that

> there is a doubleness in things. Such doubleness lies in history too. Man is doomed to exert will to control events, but even when he seems to act effectively, the process in which his will operates may be only a mask for a secret process of which he has suspected nothing.[86]

In this respect Warren's admiration for the line in Melville's 'The Conflict of Convictions', 'I know a wind in purpose strong– / It spins *against* the way it drives', is clear in his notes on the text where he compares it to the doubleness in 'Misgivings' ('With shouts the torrents down the gorges go,/ And storms are formed behind the storms we feel').[87] Warren takes the spinning 'against the way it drives' notion to refer to historical movement, a 'brilliant metaphor' that captures the historical forces, the 'spinning necessity', which characterises the metabolism of human history.[88] The war also provided an opportunity for Melville to counter 'the stultifying effects of self-pity and self-absorption' which could be 'sublimated to the national tragedy'.[89] Warren describes his various 'self-divisions' and relates Melville's natural scepticism and yearning for religious certitude to his 'sexual tensions'. According to Warren, his use of 'precise, realistic detail' is 'played against more conventional poetic elements [... a] stylistic system of counterpointing' which puts those details such as the 'cartridge in the mouth' of a dead Confederate soldier in the woods – a prosaic line – against the lyricism of the rest of the poem.[90] The alloyed nature of the result was Melville's way of getting at and going beyond the illusion and doubleness that seemed to characterise his view of the world; it produced an odd kind of stoicism 'at once self-assertive and self-denying'.[91]

These precise observations and description of Melville's modes of thinking about the world and his place in it are reasonable ones to apply to Milch's own behaviour and output later on as an artist. It is not that Warren, as it were, somehow taught Milch to conduct himself and think of fiction as Melville did (since he certainly was nowhere near writing an epic masterpiece at the age of thirty), but rather that Warren recognised in Milch, perhaps very quickly, an affinity that he could see with his own interest in writers such as Dreiser and Melville. Anyone who has met or heard Milch can immediately perceive two things – an immense generosity of manners and attention and yet, too, and at the same time, a depth of shadow or veil that is unsettling, sometimes appearing as incredible verbal adeptness and intelligence, other times as a ferocious awareness and domination of the very atmosphere around him. Part of this is linked to what is most surprising if one has only seen him speak in public: a chronic shyness, covered by dazzling acts of wit, humour and talk; there it is as a substrate, peeping and blinking anxiously through the performative veil. This mixture of almost reckless boldness, acute shyness and signs of literary gifts formed perhaps a magnetic attractor for a poet of Warren's stature, a man in his late fifties only recently exposed (he was appointed at Yale in 1961) to working among and teaching the ever-young throng of undergraduate campus culture.

Milch's early penchant for listening to strangers lie indicates not just a thirst for the thrill of seeing deceit in action, but also a knowledge that a deeper truth lies in the lie. Any child can see that, but parsing it, finding its place, function and reason in the world is a far harder task. And the self-denying yet assertive trait is particularly evident as an aspect of Milch's showmanship that combines realistic candour about his dissolute earlier life with a lyrical, therapeutically inflected sense of the efforts he made to transcend it. As with good manners, showing the wound, the damage in public is a misdirection that can hide a far uglier (or, equally, happier) truth. Milch is fond of quoting Melville's poem 'The College Colonel' (1864), in which a returning war hero acknowledges the sense of a truth in the annihilation of battle that accounts for the 'alloy' of feeling he experiences during the home town celebrations. Those celebrations seem false but not in the sense of opposing the truth; as Warren says of the poem:

> [w]e cannot be too schematic about such polarities as we have been discussing. One pair shades into another. One pole does not cancel out its opposite. All belong to the complex texture of life as lived, to the density and equivocalness of experience. But to live in any full sense demands the effort to comprehend this complexity of texture, this density and equivocalness of experience, and yet not forfeit the ability to act. The man who 'sees through it', but who, at the same time, can act, who has a sense of the tragedy of the human plight, that is the hero for Melville.[92]

He goes on to contrast Melville with Walt Whitman, who tried to absorb life into his work without sharpening its conflictual nature, whereas 'for Melville, the poetry lies in a conflict of values, an inner conflict, and that is what he feels driven, ultimately to deal with'.[93] Comparing the two via Santayana's claim about Whitman's 'fuzziness', Warren then points to Melville's attempt to grasp life through 'first principles', a dialectic, a fundamental desire to see antagonisms and yet posit unity not through the absorption of conflict but rather through stoically facing up to those antagonisms: 'The streak of mysticism in Melville was at war with his ferocious appetite to know. He was a mystic who hated mysticism.'[94]

Warren's account of Melville puts the latter far closer to Milch than most critics allow: they both share an attraction to antagonism and doubleness and the desire to penetrate the surface of such conflict in order to see unity. At the same time there is a suspicion of that unity, so the process begins again, this time with the new, deeper surface of the object that needs to be broken open until its wholeness is allowed to shine before breaking. Melville was also attractive to both Warren and Milch because of his interest in narratives involving father–son quests.

Moby Dick is in part about Ishmael's evolution as a man 'who seeks a way into the world, and an understanding of the world, by seeking a father', and Melville's long epic poem *Clarel* (which Warren sees as a precursor to Eliot's *Waste Land*) has a similar structuring idea.[95] However, it is Melville's astonishing final prose work, *Billy Budd, Sailor*, that exemplifies the most extraordinary fusion of the two concerns – the father–son quest, and the penetration of the detail of appearance in order to find the transcendent mystery beneath. This short novel, set in a period of authoritarian naval policing, concerns the events leading to the trial and execution of a handsome young sailor. He has no awareness of how shiningly handsome he is, or how he 'lifts all boats' by merely walking among the crew. His only 'flaw' is a tendency to stutter; in Melville's words:

> Billy was a striking instance that the arch interferer, the envious marplot of Eden, still has more or less to do with every human consignment to this planet of Earth. In every case, one way or another he is sure to slip in his little card, as much as to remind us – I too have a hand here.[96]

Inordinately popular, Billy is resented by the first officer, Claggett, and called to the Captain's cabin on a misdemeanour confected by him. The Captain is called Vere, and his nickname is 'Starry', which indicates that he looks for the truth in the cosmic realm rather than attending to the immediate details at hand. Vere asks Billy to explain, but, frustrated by the questioning and confused by the injustice of the lie, Billy stutters and strikes out, killing Claggett with one blow. Vere knows full well that Billy was set up, and that Claggett was an evil man; nonetheless he has to hang Billy for the crime.

For Warren, *Billy Budd* is a meditation on father–son (Vere–Billy) reconciliation; in earlier drafts Billy was an older man, but in revision between 1886 and 1887 he was changed to a beautiful boy-man. This was twenty years after Melville's older son, Malcolm, had committed suicide on 5 December 1866 at the age of 17 by shooting himself in the head with a pistol. Warren speculates whether Melville in the story was taking into account his own father's failure, his own late 'failure' as a successful prose novelist and poet, as well as the deaths of his young sons, not only Malcolm but Stanwix, who died at the age of 35 in 1886. After discovering that his myopia would prevent him from becoming a dentist, as he wanted, Stanwix tried a number of jobs including the wholesale business and mining (in, of all places, Deadwood).[97] This tragic binding by death between father and son was, of course, resonant with Milch, whose difficult and obsessive father had his own father attempt suicide and was later to kill himself.

For Melville, *Billy Budd*, while coloured by these personal hurts, was an attempt to test out the truth of ideas, to 'see the deep relation of personality and ideas':

> Ideas are not merely to be judged abstractly as true of false; in one sense the personal tone, the quality of the commitment a person has to an idea and the depth and richness of his experience of an idea, are related to the 'truth: of an idea'.[98]

In other words, an abstract inner world *has* to have some manifestation in the outer one, and that can only be exhibited or detected in the way a person holds that idea, cleaves to it and operationalises it in his or her own behaviour. But such matters are inflected with external contextual accidents that impinge. For Billy, fate is an aspect of his speech, since his profound stutter contributes to his impulsive lashing out and killing of Claggett. The stutter indicates to the narrator that Satan 'too had a hand here'; Milch stuttered as a child and was called 'Duddy'. Such associations are not nothing for those who veer in the shadow of knowing about them. For however meaningless and trivial, they are lures and baits towards finding truth in the mistaken way that Melville warns us about. Certainly Milch would have been drawn privately, as much as he was as a researcher, to Warren's meditations on the Vere–Billy relationship.

The characters meet again near the end of the tale, just before Billy's execution, in a scene behind a locked door to which the reader is not given access: perhaps here the son finds the father. According to Warren, 'Is this the dream of the reconciling end of the search for the father that Melville, the son, never found in life?'[99] By putting the efforts of individual men against the canvas of history one can see 'man's vision of his role – in history, in relation to other men, and in self-definition – that offers the possibility of transcendence',[100] so that such transcendence is not negated or qualified by the tough details of reality but 'made possible by it – that is, by redemptive recognition, in the harsh fact, of the human bond'.[101] Only by the pressure of history and personal pain is man 'routed' into a knowledge of his fate, and into whatever triumph, however limited and qualified, is possible in it. (In a lengthy footnote, Warren replies to objections to his reading based on the fact that Melville was simply an 'unnatural' father, which concludes, after quoting from several touching letters that he sent to his children: 'Nothing is simple.')[102]

Milch described to Warren's biographer the intense model of an artist that Warren was for him. Working on *American Literature* he would complete biographical sketches of the authors, and then '[w]e would work during the morning, but the early afternoons were saved for his poetry, and then late in the afternoon we would take long walks and that was a terrific time'. For Milch this period in the early 1970s constituted 'some of my happiest memories', and researching the anthology was important in other ways too: 'it's always seemed to me that I never really got an education until I began to do that work for them'.[103] But Warren's discipline and talent as a mature artist would have made a daunting model even for an outwardly confident young talent like Milch. According to Blotner, Milch regarded his later capacity for spiritual preparation before writing as the key insight learned during the time that he and Warren worked and talked together:

> It gave Milch 'the opportunity of seeing someone like Mr. Warren, who had been able to fashion a coherent life, and whose commitment to art and to a way of being made sense, but was so extraordinarily human and inspiriting.' He admired the poetry and what seemed to him 'a unified sense of composition. It was a sense of a physical readying of the spirit to receive the poem; it's a process of breathing, and it's what I think makes his best and later poetry so almost visceral an experience to read.' Warren told him a story. Friedrich August von Kekulé, working toward a theory of the constitution of benzene, dreamed of a snake swallowing its tail. It was a visual model for his closed-chain theory that led to much of modern organic chemistry. A friend remarked that Kekulé was lucky to understand a complicated problem through a dream. But, Warren observed, there would have been no important result without his scientific training. And he quoted Louis Pasteur: 'The dream can come only to the prepared spirit.' David felt that Warren's whole mode of living was bent toward that end, toward that kind of harmony. He saw the poetry as 'an expression of a unified state of being which really is, for Mr. Warren, as close to an exalted state as someone who hasn't God can get.'[104]

Again we get the juxtaposition between the physical and the spiritual – the sense that physical exercise, the repetition of certain kinds of preparedness, results in the availability to something, mystically speaking, larger – unity. But a 'prepared spirit' requires time and effort (Warren worked seven days a week, twelve hours a day and regularly exercised). Milch worked hard too, and the correspondence between Cleanth Brooks and Warren testifies to his painstaking diligence and thoroughness – he was quickly found to be invaluable to the project. So, for example, he took the gigantic typescript of *American Literature: The Makers and the Making* to St Martin's Press in New York in 1971, Xeroxed, dated and collated materials, made suggestions, provided notes and revisions, and was first in mind (there was a lot of competition) when they needed research assistance for their many other projects.[105] The only problem, apart from a brief stay in hospital because of melanoma treatment, was a complaint from Robert Bly about Milch addressing him as 'Mister Bly' (a problem because Bly was a professor – 'the shit-heel', wrote Warren).

American Literature: The Makers and the Making was a monumental achievement. As R. W. B. Lewis later noted, 'it expanded far beyond a New Criticism survey of the chief texts in question ... into something like a full-scale account of American cultural history'.[106] He describes how the project gradually began to absorb and incorporate non-literary elements of popular culture (there is actually a section called 'Literature of the non-literary world'), which eventually involved travel writing, political writing, nature writing, Native American oratory and intellectual history. It was a massive undertaking that occupied and clearly taxed the three distinguished scholars and their chief assistant for nearly a decade. Milch, working at the core of this process, was probably at least as intimate with the entire work as any of the individual contributors. He had an editorial presence too. Much of Milch's subsequent reference to American literature and intellectual history takes its coordinates from this awesome mapping of national writing. As an education in the theory and practice of the ways in which others had tried to symbolically grasp the meaning of America and American life it was no doubt one of the best any aspiring writer could imagine.

It was also an emphatically collaborative and social process, as Lewis recalls: 'We met and talked for an afternoon or for two and three days at a time – at the Brookses' home in Northford, at the Warrens' home in Vermont, at Calhoun college at Yale.'[107] These critical meetings meant that Milch was used to the open discussion of writers and scholars, writing about writing and the wider national culture. At that time (unlike this time), to be at the heart of an American Ivy League campus was to be at the core of a commanding view of the history, metabolism and culture of the nation. There was, despite the reputation of New Criticism, no hygienic disavowal of mass culture, and Milch adopted certain specific prejudices from Brooks and Warren – such as their dislike of the New England Transcendentalists such as Emerson (especially his anchoring of life around abstractions and 'higher powers', although, as we shall see, Milch finds himself remarkably close to this kind of thinking in later life). One has the sense of each essay on each writer pushing the others in a competitive desire to get at the kernel of the work under scrutiny; this includes the 'folk' material as well. The commentary on the song 'John Henry', for example, demonstrates extraordinary research in its assessment of the history of railroad construction, of technology, and the steel-driver contests in Tennessee in the 1870s. As Lewis says, the contributors did not all think the same about literature, but 'delighted in their differences'.

'Stay in action'

But somehow, alongside this tutelage and education, Milch continued his other pursuits: he continued his use of heroin, which probably saved him from the alcohol-related deaths of some of his friends. He was also deepening his knowledge and experience of horseracing. As we have seen, his writing output ran into a repetitive block during this time. He began work on the narrative that was to eventually become *Luck* thirty years later, but by his own account he became impossibly blocked on an image of hands dealing money at a counter. This obsessional behaviour, a blocking around the process of creating output, was to result in some radical experimentation when he later became a screenwriter. Milch would certainly have known of Hollywood's uneasy relationship with literary heroes such as Fitzgerald and Faulkner, as well as from his contacts at Iowa. However, a certain intimacy between the two industries was well established by the 1970s. By 1976 Warren's novel *A Place to Come To* had been optioned by Hollywood and was being adapted by Robert Redford and Julian Barry. In fact Milch made (what he described to me as) an 'interminable' experimental film shot outside New Haven, a student film shown publicly once but never since released. What he did publish were two poems in prestigious journals, *The Atlantic Monthly* and *The Southern Review*. The by-line in the latter, from July 1975, suggests that Milch was busy writing during this time: 'He has written poetry, fiction, stage plays, and screen plays, and since 1971 has taught creative writing at Yale University.'[108]

The Southern Review poem is of particular interest because of its resonance with Milch's television fiction. It is called 'The Men at Haskell Levine's', and the subtitle, 'from *Gambling in Buffalo*', suggests that it is a part of a larger work based, as with *The Groundlings*, in Milch's home town. It is in four parts and is a psychological study of small town gambling habits. The first part of the poem presents a paradox: that men spend their days playing cards when the most they might win is forty dollars, far less than they would accept as a wage for an everyday job. Their dreams of winter 'away from the cold, in Florida' could never be financed even if they won every day of the week. And yet there they are: 'How are we to explain the conduct of these men?' the poet asks. As is familiar in Milch's work, we begin with an almost anthropological or sociological puzzle: for example, in *NYPD Blue* the question is something like, 'How can we reconcile our felt need for justice with the demands of the lives of the policemen who have to enforce it?'; or, in *Deadwood*, 'How can we improvise a society using only base components?'

In its second part the poem seems to arrive at a provisional answer by looking at behaviour in detail: it draws on specialist knowledge of gambling offered as expert insight into the human soul. For the gambler, winning is not always a priority – they may pass or stay in a hand for strategic or superstitious ('against his better judgement ... to bait his hook') reasons. But fundamentally they want to 'stay in action'. What does that mean? Does it relate to Melville's sense of living in paradoxes and yet acting? Because they want to 'stay in action', Haskell Levine's is the cheapest place that provides the longest experience (the poem, in a parody of *Walden*, lists the costs of taking a bus and gaining admission to the racecourse at Batavia Downs). Hence the discovery of the poem is that 'action' is gaining constant access 'to that state of felt engagement by one who has made a choice important for his fate', and playing cards is simply the cheapest way to stay in this state for the longest time.

The poem wants to convince us that there is a truth behind seemingly degenerate, wasteful activities. Being-in-action ties the gambler to a region of proximity to life unavailable (at those prices) elsewhere. Like Warren's 'Homage to Theodore Dreiser', it is a study of the strangeness of human life where the deepest felt aspirations live alongside profound destitution of spirit and body. The puzzle is where the interest in 'action' comes from; it is intensified as the poem concludes by the prospect of death and destitution, but these do not prompt the interest. We become comfortable with our necessary pathologies, we like the familiarity of our illness, the poem seems to say; but it offers no answers as to the origins of such feelings.

Whatever else Milch was doing teaching at Yale, he was clearly not on an academic tenure track, but he did develop a reputation. It is worth returning to David Shields's vivid account of the rock-star status that Milch had accrued by the mid-1970s now that we have seen him in the context of the comfort and sustenance of Warren, Brooks and Lewis's projects:

> Friends at Yale kept telling me about a creative writing teacher named David Milch. He had written speeches for Watergate felon Maurice Stans and songs for the Allman Brothers; he was an alcoholic; he was a compulsive gambler; he had written and discarded three novels of a projected four book series that R. W. B. Lewis and Robert Penn Warren thought possessed genius; he had been or still was a heroin addict and had served time in a Mexican jail for possession; he was kicked out of

> Yale Law School for shooting out the lights on a cop car. Who knew how much of it was true? Who cared? I enrolled in Yale's summer session: I wanted him to show me not only how to write but how to live.[109]

Shields's subsequent account, mixing admiration and resentment, paints Milch as a motorcycle-riding rebel, menacing his classes with the authority of sheer intellect. He taught Conrad, Faulkner, James and Twain; he was 'a macho pedant', 'a Jewish cowboy'.[110] After Yale, Shields enrolled at the Iowa Writers' Workshop.[111]

Milch may have been contemplating a career in screenwriting before he began work on *Hill Street Blues* in 1982. In the early 1970s, apart from his research duties for Brooks and Warren, he assisted R. W. B. Lewis on his biography of Edith Wharton, which won the Pulitzer prize for non-fiction in 1975. Milch is credited in its acknowledgements as a sine qua non for checking facts, procuring books and Xeroxing materials. Lewis goes on: 'As grateful as I am for all that, I owe Mr. Milch even more for the wealth of suggestions he made out of his extensive literary, psychological, medical and legal knowledge.'[112] David Thorburn has suggested that Milch may have contributed a lot more than that; one thing for certain is that the researcher discovered a key piece of information in Wharton's archive – left conspicuously in a place where a diligent scholar would discover it. This was a fragment of a story called 'Beatrice Palmato', a pornographic account of father–daughter incest (partly echoed in an *NYPD Blue* episode, 'Simone Says'). Milch had to plant the fragment in such a way that it would be noticed by Lewis, since he realised that just saying 'look what you missed' would be potentially personally injurious in a number of ways.

The Milch–Lewis collaboration was to take another step in 1979. Lewis's book *The Jameses: A Family Narrative* was finally published in 1991 but, as its acknowledgements attest, Milch had originally conceived the project as a ten-part television mini-series (this was a period when mini-series such as *Roots*, *Centennial* and *Holocaust* had prominence and popularity on network television). Milch was writing the scripts. He and Lewis pitched the idea to the National Endowment for the Arts funding, and Merchant–Ivory Productions were on board to produce it. Speaking on stage to David Thorburn in 2006 at MIT, Milch recounts what happened during the pitch when Lewis was suddenly called out of the room:

> describing the kind of torment some souls are exposed to, my dad was the only child of the eldest of ten children. And her name was ... Sapowicz ... several of his uncles were his contemporaries, and one was even younger than he was. They were all in the rackets. But because he

was the next generation he had to go to college and he became a very prominent surgeon and a professor of surgery ... But he was always drawn to – he was very frustrated by his professional identity ... In August he would always take us up to Saratoga racetrack where all of his family would congregate ... So very complicated relation between learning he was a very well recognised surgeon and this other darker part of his personality. His identity as a physician was the sort of civilising aspect ... you know my dad was a narcotic addict, he was an alcoholic, all the stuff that I became ... Towards the end of his life, my brother who had also become a surgeon and idolized my dad the same way I did, took over my father's care. And my dad would engage in self-mutilation and all sorts of unpleasant things. And, in his tormented mind because his sense of self was so associated with his professional identity as a physician, he became convinced that since my brother had become the caregiver of the family, my brother was having sexual relations with my mother. And took his life in front of them. To punish them for that. And then his last words were, 'Don't tell David 'til he's done with his pitch.'[113]

Elmer Milch's confusion that Robert was having sex with Mollie no doubt had some historical resonance with his own father's experience. He took professional competition personally and would pick open his operation sutures, a self-mutilation that culminated in his aggressive suicide, designed to establish a legacy so horrific that it could not be erased.[114] This final theatrical gesture, an attempt to stamp one's mark on the future via gruesome self-destruction, was the playing out of a harmartic script that took all of Milch's ingenuity and dedication to his art to transcend. Milch went on to tell Thorburn and his MIT audience: 'I am a very happy and grateful person ... the future is constantly in the process of interpreting the meaning of the past.' His brother became an internationally renowned hospice surgeon as a result, improving care for dying patients in ways that negated the sour intent of the father's self-annihilation. Milch uses this as a practical example, outside of art, of the way life can purify the dark weight of events in the past. It is not clear if Elmer's suicide (reported in his obituary as death from pneumonia) was the reason Milch did not go ahead with the mini-series, but in any case, it did not happen.

The story of Milch's leaving academia for Los Angeles is not a simple one of the transplantation of an unworldly scholar (or 'professor', a status often incorrectly attributed to him) into the ferocious milieu of a notoriously cut-throat and dangerous industry. It was three years later in 1982 before Milch moved there, and, as we have seen, he had already written screenplays and pitched at least one television series; this was hardly his first foray into the mass entertainment industry. It was changes to that industry that contributed to the circumstances that led to Milch's employment on *Hill Street Blues*. With his father dead and a happy marriage to documentary film-maker Rita Stern, a graduate of Yale, Milch was facing the prospect of heading into his late thirties with no stable or viable career. What he did have was an extraordinary combination of experience at the edges as well as the centre of American culture, and a deep commitment to somehow finding a place where the words that assailed and compelled him within the traditions he admired could achieve balance with the degeneracy of the desires that haunted and blocked them.

Notes

1 Herman Melville, *Billy Budd, Sailor* (Harmondsworth: Penguin, 1985), p. 356.
2 According to Andrew Delbanco, the manuscript had been stored in a 'tin bread box'. *Melville: His World and Work* (London: Picador, 2006), p. 290.
3 See, for example, Karen Lury, 'A Response to John Corner', *Screen* 48.3 (2007).
4 David Milch and Bill Clark, *True Blue: The Real Stories Behind NYPD Blue*, rev. edn (New York: Avon Books, 1997), p. 143
5 Milch and Clark, *True Blue*, p. 143.
6 Edward Hotaling, *They're Off: Horseracing at Saratoga* (Syracuse, NY: Syracuse University Press, 1995).
7 Milch and Clark, *True Blue*, p. 140.
8 Writers' Guild of America talk 2007.
9 'The Idea of the Writer', www.youtube.com/watch?v=85FytguoxEs (accessed 16 April 2018).
10 Philip Nyhui, 'David Milch's DEADWOOD: More acclaim for a Buffalo Native', *Buffalo Spree: The Magazine of Western New York*, Jan–Feb 2005, www.buffalospree.com/buffalospreemagazine/archives/2005_0102/010205milch.html (accessed 23 November 2016).
11 Milch and Clark, *True Blue*, p. 242.
12 Milch and Clark, *True Blue*, p. 243
13 Milch and Clark, *True Blue*, p. 137.
14 In *True Blue* (p. 137) Milch claims he was only hit three times by his father.
15 David Milch, *Deadwood: Tales of the Black Hills* (New York: Bloomsbury, 2006), p. 17.
16 Milch, *Deadwood: Tales of the Black Hills*, p. 17.
17 Unless otherwise indicated, quotations from David Milch are drawn from the archive of his personal documents, mostly transcripts of talks in the writers' room, held at his Red Board production company offices in Santa Monica, or from interviews with the author.
18 Milch and Clark, *True Blue*, pp. 245–6.
19 Joseph Blotner, *Robert Penn Warren* (New York: Random House, 1997), p. 381.
20 Leslie Fiedler, *Love and Death in the American Novel*, rev. edn (New York: Stein and Day, 1966), p. 331.
21 Fiedler, *Love and Death*, p. 409.
22 Blotner, *Robert Penn Warren*, p. 346.
23 Blotner, *Robert Penn Warren*, p. 351.

24 Joseph Millichap, 'Robert Penn Warren, David Milch and the Literary Contexts of *Deadwood*', in David Lavery (ed.), *Reading Deadwood: A Western to Swear By* (London: I. B. Tauris, 2006), p. 183.
25 Millichap, 'Robert Penn Warren, David Milch and the Literary Contexts of *Deadwood*', p. 186.
26 Blotner, *Robert Penn Warren*, p. 325.
27 Quoted in Blotner, *Robert Penn Warren*, p. 325, from Warren, 'Knowledge and the Self-Image of Man', *Southern Review* 62 (1955), pp. 6, 25.
28 Harold Bloom, 'Foreword', in John Burt (ed.), *The Collected Poems of Robert Penn Warren* (Baton Rouge, LA: Louisiana State University Press, 1998), p. xxiv.
29 Robert Penn Warren, 'Homage to Theodore Dreiser', in Burt (ed.), *Collected Poems of Robert Penn Warren*, p. 295.
30 Blotner, *Robert Penn Warren*, p. 361.
31 See A. L. Maycock, *Nicholas Ferrar of Little Gidding* (Grand Rapids, MI: William B. Eerdmans, 1980 [1938]). For an account of Rilke and Eliot's different response, see Roger Scruton, *Gentle Regrets* (London: Bloomsbury, 2006).
32 Blotner, *Robert Penn Warren*, p. 317.
33 James A. Grimshaw, Jr (ed.), *Cleanth Brooks and Robert Penn Warren: A Literary Correspondence* (Columbia, MO: University of Missouri Press, 1998), p. 243.
34 See Christopher Ricks, 'Literary Principles as Against Theory', in *Essays in Appreciation* (Oxford: Clarendon Press, 1996).
35 Stanley Cavell, *Little Did I Know* (Stanford, CA: Stanford University Press, 2010), p. 451.
36 Cleanth Brooks, R. W. B. Lewis and Robert Penn Warren, *American Literature: The Makers and the Making, Book B, 1826–1861* (New York: St. Martin's Press, 1973), p. 459.
37 Stefan Collini, *Common Reading* (Oxford: Oxford University Press, 2008), p. 263.
38 Warren in Gloria L. Cronin and Ben Siegel (eds), *Conversations with Robert Penn Warren* (Jackson, MI: University of Mississippi Press, 2005), p. 246.
39 Collini, *Common Reading*, p. 262.
40 Grimshaw (ed.), *Cleanth Brooks and Robert Penn Warren*, p. 270.
41 Grimshaw (ed.), *Cleanth Brooks and Robert Penn Warren*, pp. 261–2.
42 Mark Singer, 'The Misfit: How David Milch got from "NYPD Blue" to "Deadwood" by way of an Epistle of St. Paul', *The New Yorker*, 14 February 2005.
43 'As a model he was crucially important'; Singer, 'The Misfit'.
44 Blotner, *Robert Penn Warren*, p. 381.
45 The prize was named after a former professor of English at Yale, Chauncey Brewster Tinker, who was a strong opponent of New Criticism.
46 Mark McGurl, *The Program Era: Postwar Fiction and the Rise of Creative Writing* (Cambridge, MA: Harvard University Press, 2009), p. x.
47 McGurl, 'Response to Batuman', www.markmcgurl.com (accessed 9 February 2012).
48 McGurl, 'Response to Batuman', p. 148.
49 McGurl, 'Response to Batuman', p. 133.
50 Recorded 19 November 2008.
51 McGurl, *Program Era*, p. 141. See also George Toles's essay on Willa Cather which revisits this proscriptive aesthetic rule; 'Dipping into Omniscience with Willa Cather: Authorial Knowledge as Love', in Susan Wolf and Christopher Grau (eds), *Understanding Love: Philosophy, Film, and Fiction* (Oxford: Oxford University Press, 2014).
52 See Brett Martin's account of the formation and diversity of the television

writers' room, in *Difficult Men: Behind the Scenes of a Creative Revolution: From The Sopranos and The Wire to Mad Men and Breaking Bad* (London: Penguin, 2014).

53 Blake Bailey, *A Tragic Honesty: The Life and Work of Richard Yates* (New York: Picador, 2003), p. 321.

54 John Caldwell, *Production Culture* (Durham, NC: Duke University Press, 2008).

55 Bailey, *A Tragic Honesty*, p. 321.

56 Bailey, *A Tragic Honesty*, p. 328.

57 Bailey, *A Tragic Honesty*, p. 331.

58 Bailey, *A Tragic Honesty*, p. 332.

59 Bailey, *A Tragic Honesty*, p. 331.

60 Yates went to Hollywood and wrote scripts for Roger Corman, as well as a rewrite on *The Bridge at Remagen* (1969).

61 See the cover photograph for Peter Arnott's book, *Public Performance in the Greek Theatre* (Abingdon: Routledge, 1991) for a sense of how his puppets were deployed.

62 WGA talk, 2007.

63 Interview with Ted Mann, February 2010.

64 Robert Penn Warren, *A Place to Come To* (New York: Random House, 1977), p. 4.

65 'The Idea of the Writer', www.youtube.com/watch?v=kwTIGqOkokc (accessed 3 June 2019).

66 I raised this possibility – that at the time he may have seen the literary quality of the coincidence – over lunch with Milch in 2011: 'I certainly did not think that' was his patient response.

67 David Milch, 'Two Chapters from *The Groundlings*', MFA thesis, University of Iowa, May 1970.

68 McGurl, 'Response to Batuman', p. 141.

69 See Bailey, *A Tragic Honesty*, pp. 108–9.

70 Milch and Clark, *True Blue*, p. 245.

71 Neither did he change Torch's name; Torch himself turned up to a Milch reading at the Penn State Writers' Workshop in 2010.

72 David Shields, *Remote* (Madison, WI: University of Wisconsin Press, 2003 [1996]), p. 123.

73 Shields, *Remote*, p. 120.

74 Bloom, 'Foreword', pp. xxv, xxvi.

75 Warren, *Conversations*, p. 235.

76 Burt (ed.), *Collected Poems of Robert Penn Warren*, pp. 275–81.

77 Burt (ed.), *Collected Poems of Robert Penn Warren*, p. 281. When quoting this Milch tends to insert a 'the' before 'pain' in the penultimate line.

78 Blotner, *Robert Penn Warren*, p. 401.

79 Blotner, *Robert Penn Warren*, p. 401.

80 Sacvan Bercovitch, *The American Jeremiad* (Madison, WI: University of Wisconsin Press, 1978), p. 191.

81 Burt (ed.), *Collected Poems of Robert Penn Warren*, p. 295.

82 Burt (ed.), *Collected Poems of Robert Penn Warren*, p. 296.

83 Burt (ed.), *Collected Poems of Robert Penn Warren*, p. 297.

84 Blotner, *Robert Penn Warren*, p. 388.

85 Robert Penn Warren, 'Introduction', in *Selected Poems of Herman Melville* (Boston, MA: David R. Godine, 2004), p. 11.

86 Warren, 'Introduction', p. 18.

87 Douglas Robillard (ed.), *The Poems of Herman Melville* (Kent, OH: Kent State University Press, 2000), p. 53.

88 Warren, 'Introduction', p. 353.
89 Warren, 'Introduction', p. 9.
90 Warren, 'Introduction', pp. 15–16.
91 Warren, 'Introduction', p. 20.
92 Warren, 'Introduction', p. 22.
93 Warren, 'Introduction', p. 27.
94 Warren, 'Introduction', p. 31.
95 Warren, 'Introduction', p. 38.
96 Melville, *Billy Budd*, pp. 331–2.
97 Delbanco, *Melville: His World and Work*, p. 296.
98 Warren, 'Introduction', p. 45.
99 Warren, 'Introduction', p. 63.
100 Warren, 'Introduction', p. 69.
101 Warren, 'Introduction', p. 69.
102 Warren, 'Introduction', p. 82 n. 29.
103 Blotner, *Robert Penn Warren*, p. 392.
104 Blotner, *Robert Penn Warren*, pp. 392–3. This is an adaptation of Pasteur's *Dans les champs de l'observation le hasard ne favorise que les esprits préparés*, more often translated as 'chance favours the prepared mind'.
105 He also worked on revised versions of *Understanding Poetry*, *Understanding Fiction*, *Modern Rhetoric* and *An Approach to Literature*.
106 R. W. B. Lewis, 'Afterword', in Grimshaw (ed.), *Cleanth Brooks and Robert Penn Warren*, p. 419.
107 Lewis, 'Afterword', p. 420.
108 David Milch, 'The Men at Haskell Levine's', *The Southern Review* 11.3 (July 1975), p. 599.
109 Shields, *Remote*, pp. 119–20.
110 Shields, *Remote*, p. 121.
111 For the record, Shields misreads Milch's dissertation, despite claiming that he 'pored over every line'; for example, he assumes that Mark blames himself for his *father's* death rather than Judgy's.
112 R. W. B. Lewis, *Edith Wharton* (New York: Fromm International Publishing, 1993), p. 573. Milch was 30 at the time.
113 David Milch interviewed by David Thorburn at MIT, 2006, www.youtube.com/watch?v=MDTVIP8bvE8 (accessed 23 April 2018).
114 Cy Tolliver (Powers Boothe) unpicks his stitched stab wound towards the end of season three of *Deadwood*.

Character 2

> [T]he structure of a good story places its characters in an environment most congenial to their discovery of their deepest natures. Now and then ... it lets them cook ...
>
> David Milch[1]

Milch began writing for television in the final decades of the twentieth century, growing up and reaching maturity in a post-war period characterised by what Hannah Arendt described as a radical weakening of authority, in a civilisation unable to find coherent unity or meaning in the modernity it had established.[2] The modern world that Milch inhabited was gradually turning away from the attractions of risk, courage, chance and embrace of uncertain outcomes that had propelled and underpinned the early formation and expansion of the United States. Milch's family background, his childhood, his early friendships and education and his subsequent manoeuvring between being a reckless para-criminal and a tweed-jacket-wearing research assistant to a Pulitzer prize-winning poet and professor at Yale confounds any line between the authority of inherited convention and the courage to strike out uniquely as an individual force. Much great American literature is, of course, concerned with this theme: the best, *The Great Gatsby*, precisely realises, albeit briefly, the dazzling sunshine of what achieving that dream might mean, as well as the dark underpinnings necessary to bring it about.

This was a point in history when television fiction was undergoing transformation, and Milch's involvement sprang from his association with a former Yale room-mate, Jeffrey Lewis. The show most emblematic of this transformation was Steven Bochco and Michael Kozoll's creation *Hill Street Blues*. Bochco was Milch's contemporary and had been writing for television since his early twenties on prime-time detective shows such as *Ironside*, *Columbo* and *McMillan and Wife* for Universal Television. He moved to the top boutique independent production company MTM Enterprises which, under the leadership of its founder Grant Tinker, had forged an identity as a 'writers' company and included legendary figures such as James L. Brooks and Allan Burns.[3] In 1981 when Tinker became CEO of NBC – then running last of the three major networks in the ratings – he and the outgoing CEO Fred Silverman reached out to Bochco and Kozoll and offered them *carte blanche* to develop a cop show for the network. The pair initially wanted to do a hotel-based workplace ensemble drama, but the executives, including the head of entertainment Brandon Tartikoff, convinced them to develop a cop show:

> Silverman was looking for a series that combined the interpersonal dynamics of David Gerber's *Police Story* and the ethnically humorous misadventures of Danny Arnold's *Barney Miller* along with the vérité stylistics of the soon-to-be released theatrical film *Fort Apache, The Bronx* (1981).[4]

Bochco and Kozoll agreed on condition that 'you leave us alone to do whatever we want', a freedom that allowed them to experiment without second guessing the network's response.

It was Bochco who came up with the framing conceit that the duration of an episode would encompass one working day, beginning with the police roll call – the sergeant assigning jobs to the beat cops – and inserting (or 'telescoping') upcoming story topics within episodes. This Aristotelian discipline was partly enabled by the more radical decision not to resolve individual storylines within one episode (although in the second season each episode did include one resolved story). It is difficult to overestimate the industrial, critical and aesthetic impact of this show despite the fact that it never rated highly. As John Caldwell says,

> *Hill Street Blues* stands as a self-made, and pre-meditated stylistic breakthrough. The series proved influential both for writer-producers and for director-cinematographers. In the years since it aired, the show and its producer, Steven Bochco, have taken on an almost mythological stature for how great television art can happen again and prosper...[5]

Caldwell argues that the show was modelled on Susan and Alan Raymond's 1976 low-budget, independent video *Police Tapes*, 'extrapolating that improvised vérité look for 35mm feature quality cameras'.[6] Artistically, *Hill Street Blues* was one of the most distinctive cultural products to emerge in America during the 1980s: it radically transformed the look and ambition of television fiction production and raised the bar on what might be achieved in a mainstream network show. Bochco himself was a benign but tough industry and artistic presence – in the middle of the second season he shut his production company down in order to compel better writing. He inserted blackouts before and after the commercial breaks in each episode to insulate the show from the toxicity of advertising. While overall ratings were low, for the first time 'quality demographics' became important, with advertisers such as American Express and Mercedes finding the audience it harvested attractive. (According to Bochco, it was 'the first time I heard the concept of demographics'.)[7]

Bochco was also able to assemble a production team and cast to his liking: Greg Hoblit (director) and Mike Post (music) were to become essential members of his team; the visual look of the show was evocative, as was the musical design. Visually, it recruited the now tired 'documentary' look, sometimes using lightweight, hand-held Arriflex rather than studio cameras; aurally it allowed cross-talking and a boosting of ambient noise. As the show became iconic, what Bochco calls the show's thematic promise was played out: this was a 'world of consequence' where the span of the show over time allowed the tracking of the impact of action and reaction across weeks, rather than minutes within a single episode. Multiple storylines, with many characters, thickened the *mise-en-scène* and the soundtrack so that *Hill Street Blues* had a sense of a deeper fabric of meaning and a vitality to the frame and its off-screen space. As Bochco put it, 'It busted the rules of television, it created a language.' This was the first time melodrama and tragedy had been mixed with such rapid, abrupt alternations in tone. By using a large ensemble cast and several narrative storylines the show established what was to become a conventional mode for many US dramas over the next two decades. The alternation in tone between comic, serious, tragic, melodramatic, sometimes juxtaposed and intersecting was, too, to become a familiar mode evident even in shows as late as *The West Wing*.

But none of this industrial and artistic change had anything to do with Milch: he had never even heard of the show until he visited Hollywood in 1982. This itself was the result of an unforeseen event: while *Hill Street Blues*'s first season was aired in January 1981 and its second later that same year, a Writers' Guild of America strike meant that that show was desperate for scripts if it was to meet its production targets for the third season in the autumn. Jeffrey Lewis, now working as a writer/producer on the show, recommended Milch to Bochco. As David Bianculli aptly puts it, 'Milch had rolled the dice – a natural reaction given his gambling nature – left Yale and joined Bochco's *Hill Street* staff and got his first script writing assignment.'[8] Bochco claims that he 'was always attracted to playwrights, journalists, novelists, lawyers – in short, anyone who'd actually had a life outside the hothouse of our inbred industry. I figured I could always teach them the form of television writing. It wasn't rocket science.'[9] This is how he describes their first meeting:

> Fat Dave, as he referred to himself, presented as a typical college professor: eye glasses, somewhat overweight, tweed jacket, shirt and tie, khakis – almost a cliché of the college professor. David was deferential, but clearly bright, and creatively, we were immediately attracted to one another. Our first meeting was very productive. David had an idea for a script about a nun who was raped and murdered.[10]

The idea had been prompted by Milch reading about a case of a sexually assaulted nun in the *New York Post*: many of Milch's stories, in this show and *NYPD Blue*, adapted real news events as plot stimulants. The script led to the 1982 third season opener, entitled 'Trial By Fury'. It won Milch an Emmy in the 1983 awards for Most Outstanding Writing for a Drama Series, as well as the Humanitas prize. Milch's success in winning the Emmy for his first television script mirrored the early praise that he had won from Warren for his first attempt at writing about Judgy's death twenty years earlier at Yale. The gift or luck of success before one really knows what one is doing can be a blight on developing talent, especially when an intelligent man is constantly trying to discover what he did right in order to succeed in a state of what must have seemed like raw naivety. Milch claims that he was such a neophyte screenwriter that he did not understand the meaning of 'INT' and 'EXT' on the sample scripts he'd been given and sprinkled the designations at random over his own first draft.

It was Bochco who had the idea of counterpointing the story of the rape and killing of a nun, which generates enormous publicity and threatens a mob attack on the police station, with the killing of a Hispanic bodega owner gunned down in a robbery. That killing is largely ignored, considered by the cops as a routine consequence of one's unlucky circumstances or inheritance. This structure gives the episode its peculiar and compelling moral tension: 'what we come to realize is that the bodega murder will go unsolved, and that is the price of catching the killer of the nun. The kind of systemic cynicism that the two stories, side-by-side, exposed dramatically made the hour terrific, conceptually.'[11] Milch went away and rewrote the script with this new idea and other notes Bochco had given him; according to the latter it was 'one of the best scripts I'd ever read', and Milch was optioned for the rest of the season.[12] At 37, he now had a regular paying job (the salary was so colossal that he thought his first pay cheque had been miscalculated at a month's rather than a week's wage). He was also working in an environment where the writing was necessarily open to scrutiny, comment, revision and criticism; it had an immediate audience, and he could finally reconcile ambition with inclination.

Bochco was another significant guide for Milch to follow, even though the two were contemporaries. Bochco not only gave Milch the break, but also tutored him in the art of world building on screen. However, he was never an artistic guide in the way Warren was, and Bochco himself admits that it was a difficult but deep relationship.[13] Thanks to him, though, Milch found himself in a crucible of writing and he learned the craft quickly. The writers' room was a story-generating machine, but it became a happier place once Milch had joined; as Bochco recalled:

> Seven days a week you just carried in your head hundreds of stories, dozens of characters ... Boy that was hard, you know every day you just sort of dread cranking it up again because it was so exhausting and so relentless. I think finally you know when Fat Dave came into our lives – David Milch – it never got easier – but at least with David in our world, he is such a lunatic, he is so crazy that we started to laugh, I mean we laughed more in those years than I've ever laughed before or since, David was just nuts ... There was a sort of collective consciousness of the show that we had custody of. It was a show that had a memory. What we would do is we would all sit in a room and we'd hammer out these stories ... and then figure out what the structure was and then you'd say to Michael [Kozoll] here you write this one, this is really up your alley, David you write this one ... and I'll write this one ... and then everybody would give me their pieces and I'll put the pieces together and fix the overlaps ... or David would do it, we'd take turns taking ultimate responsibility. We developed a lot of systems and they worked.[14]

'Trial By Fury' is an extraordinary episode even by the high standards of *Hill Street Blues*. The story begins with the rape and mutilation of a white nun by two black men who are quickly arrested and taken to the station. Captain Furillo (Daniel J. Travanti), disgusted by the assault (which quickly becomes a murder after the victim dies in hospital), is told by the Assistant District Attorney that there is not enough evidence to convict the suspects: only a confession from them will secure that. (Most *NYPD Blue* episodes hinge around this truth – as the cops see it, without a written confession justice is almost impossible.) Milch did not present this story from the newspapers just because of its sensational content: by placing it in a context whereby the police *know* they have the men responsible but cannot do anything without those men volunteering a confession (which would be irrational for men prepared to commit such an act in the first place), the abstract notion of justice is given stark concrete particularity. Ezra Pound said (reviewing Eliot's first book of poetry): 'Art does not avoid universals, it strikes at them all the harder in that it strikes through particulars.'[15] The universal abstraction 'Justice', and what is at stake in that concept, becomes real through the handling of these particulars.

Outside the station an angry mob demands frontier justice and Furillo, against the advice of the District Attorney Joyce Davenport (Victoria Hamel) – who is also having an affair with him – releases the suspects, knowing full well that they will be torn apart outside. As these events take place the show's typical threading of narrative arcs casts this main one into relief. There is a lighthearted but also sordid depiction of a cuckolded husband with his head jammed between the toilet bowl and the bathtub following a fight with his wife's lover; and there is the Hispanic mother of the murdered bodega owner pleading for justice, even though without witnesses or evidence the cops can do nothing about it. These apparently subsidiary issues are funnelled into Furillo's fury (like the cuckold, he is jammed between two immovable objects: only destructive violence – a hammer to the toilet bowl, a risky release of known killers to a mob – can break the impasse), and our understanding as an audience of what is at stake is modelled by his repugnance as we discover the extent of the atrocity committed on the nun's body. But Milch turns the screw further by recruiting the ideologically potent image of black men raping not just a white woman, but a white virgin, calling up precisely the deepest fears of violent miscegenation. (For an example, compare the climax of D. W. Griffith's *Birth of a Nation* [1915], in which the white father holds a gun to his virgin daughter's head in order to execute her before, the film implies, the black mob invade his house to rape her and the Nation.)[16] Furillo's impasse echoes the situation facing David Sumner (Dustin Hoffman) at the end of *Straw Dogs* (1971), whereby an individual is faced with a moral choice whose urgent immediacy leaves little time for reflection. Furillo knows that the bureaucratic protections afforded the accused mean they have to be released, but that doing so will endanger their lives. He uses that to his advantage in order, effectively, to force their confession. But whereas *Straw Dogs* poses urgent feelings of injustice in a remote setting and in ways that recruit but frustrate audience demands for clarity, 'Trial By Fury' situates the matter within the working institutions of the law in a busy urban location.[17] It is not simply because the nun is white that the case gets the attention it does; the episode implies that the cops are well aware of the inequity in the allocation of their energies to that high-profile case, when compared to that of the murdered bodega owner. There is no room for the kind of heroic initiative (however morally complex) that we see Sumner deliver to his home invaders. Our attachments to the events are dispersed *across* a range of characters and viewpoints, settling here and there on one or the other, obstructing a settled view of them.

Milch's background as both deviant and Ivy League tutor seems at first far away from the gritty matters of a run-down police station. But he finds in *Hill Street Blues* a solution to the disparate forces of his 'unfinished spirit'. Unlike the idiosyncratic and ethnically inflected cop shows and buddy cop genres that preceded it (such as *Banacek, Kojak, Starsky and Hutch*), this show allowed Milch a range of 'entry points' into various characters and their running story arcs. It also allowed him to recruit one of Warren's central themes, the ineluctable bond between time and storytelling, in order to fashion a pattern that might endlessly defer resolution. The traditions of television held that in fictional worlds, drama finds resolution or at least 'rest'. Furillo's decision to use the power of the mob – the surrogate audience – in order to force the confession is troubling because it clashes with our expectation that some third way will be found to avoid being confronted with anarchy outside a police station. It clashes also with the putative realism that underpins the genre. The issue is crystallised in the doubleness we feel as we see the nun's death threaten to tear apart the order of law; as Furillo puts it in his final confrontation with Davenport: 'This is the kind of crime that tears a city apart, Joyce. It brings out what's savage in thousands of people. It has to be dealt with very quickly.' This is contrasted with the relative indifference to the 'ordinary', unsensational killing of a store owner. This is not merely a structural tension or a piece of social comment. It is internalised in Furillo too: at the end, challenged by Davenport that he has merely used 'the oldest excuse in the world. The end justifies the means', she leaves and he hears that there is no likely suspect for the 'Rodriguez robbery-homicide'. He leaves the station for his church, where he asks his priest for atonement. This is the ending, but it is not a resolution: Furillo spins against the way he drives.

Milch's good fortune in finding a place on the staff of *Hill Street Blues* and excelling there was to set a pattern for the next twenty years of his life. Almost exclusively (apart from some script doctoring on Hollywood features) he worked on television crime shows, mostly police-based ensemble dramas. That allowed him to return, in different inflections of that setting, to the issue of the relationship between individuals with 'unfinished spirits' and the working communities in which they have to find a place. In one interpretation of Melville's poem 'The Conflict of Convictions', it is the wind of history that 'spins *against* the way it drives'; this sense of forward propulsion whose energy is generated by forces acting against it captures not only the biographical oddity of Milch's career up to this point, but also the recurring inner conflicts of the characters he was to create when he had the opportunity to do so. They embody what the philosopher Harry Frankfurt has eloquently called 'second-order volitions' – the desire to stop drinking, shooting up, gambling, smoking, eating – whatever – fighting against the compulsion to do those very things.[18] At the heart of the matter is the strange way human beings move through the world wanting to want what they don't want, and not wanting to want what they do want. Hence lying is not a social form of deception, play or performance, but merely a conventional expression of a direct contradiction at the heart of the character's metabolism. Whether morally complex or simple, they are canted sideways, not ripening ciphers waiting to reveal an inner depth. For Plato the nature of character is living behind a mask, a deceit, a fantasy of unity and completion sent to solve the real congealed messiness of human affairs. In Milch's world this is entirely reversed: what faces us in his characters is the congealed messiness oozing across a fragmented surface, and somewhere beneath that lies the peace of unity and completion, if only transiently visible or experienced.

Central to that doubled 'facingness' is the way his characters talk. This is evident from the first scene of 'Trial By Fury', the roll call pre-title sequence which began every episode. It is early morning (7.04 a.m. according to a caption) and desk sergeant Phil Esterhaus (Michael Conrad) stands at a lectern and tells his audience of just-woken, burger-snacking beat cops about the power of language.[19] The cops are diverse: young, old, uniformed, plain-clothes, black, white, Hispanic, who relish the ornate character of the sergeant's oratory as much as their junk food breakfast. Esterhaus is a tall, greying, solid man whose voice and face carry the tracks of uniformed experience on the street, now incorporated into the authoritative wisdom he broadcasts to his younger flock. Behind Esterhaus, completing our sense of him as a pedagogue, is a chalkboard covered with lists of words such as 'dang', 'drat' and 'shoot'. Reading from his notes he begins to cover the list of jobs, priorities, warnings and commanding orders the cops need to be aware of before venturing out on to the mean streets. Of course, he is delivering these things to us too, like a menu or chapter breakdown of topics, situations and themes that will arise during our time with the episode. For example:

> We also begin with an operation at the Alice Street bus terminal concerning the commercial activities of gay gentlemen of pleasure in the

> depot men's room ... In this regard I call your attention to the currently voguish 'brown bag' manoeuver in which one of the two cavaleros sharing a men's room stall stands with his feet on a shopping bag, thus convincing passing law enforcement agents it has only a single and legitimate tenant.

He carries the audience with us, as the hand-held 'floating' camera captures reactions, responses, eating, and as his speech picks its path along the events imagined and implied. He concludes: 'Would that we could address our problems of urban blight and inflation as resourcefully as we satisfy our passions.' Conrad gives this line just enough understatement to imply a half-amused recognition that it is a thought that has moved across his thinking many times during a long career.

Esterhaus's next item concerns a memo from Chief Daniels about police profanity 'in our dealings with the civilian populace'. He returns to the lectern so that the blackboard is in view behind him, gripping its edges: one is reminded of Father Mapple's 'mild voice of unassuming authority' in *Moby Dick*. Indeed, it becomes a pulpit as Esterhaus clasps his hands in front of him, interlocking his fingers, his eyes downward as he speaks. He illustrates the issue at stake by recounting a complaint from an elderly woman who had called for police assistance about her stolen car. The uniformed officer responding to her call was 'so accustomed to certain patterns of speech, that on arriving at the scene cheerfully enquired – and I quote – "so what the bleep's wrong with your car ma'am?"' His audience falls about laughing – but Esterhaus *says* 'bleep' not 'fuck', even though the cops respond as if he had said that. We might be slightly confused at this moment – is Esterhaus censoring himself, or is the show, knowing it cannot allow *itself* that profanity, and hence bringing that doubleness to our attention, asking us to believe that he did say 'fuck' even though he did not? Esterhaus proposes that they try to use the substitutes written on the board behind him so that 'with time and usage' they will become second nature. He is asking them to get into the habits of network television by substituting absurdly inoffensive words for those that routinely lubricate everyday language, so that 'your recourse to obscenity will then become fresh and vital when you encounter situations and individuals for whom only obscenity will suffice'.

So, we have a scene about the moderation and control of language, one that has necessarily hit the limits of network television's permitted expressiveness. This is what I mean by Milch's 'facing' us with language, in the manner that art scholar Michael Fried and philosopher Robert Pippin have described when discussing the shift from 'absorption', in which the represented human subject appears both unaware and unconcerned that they are being looked at, to a modernist form in which the audience is directly confronted with the gaze or the attention of the subject and yet is at a loss to conceive what that 'face' or, in this case, talk actually adds up to.[20] It is perhaps mere coincidence that this scene and these topics were part of the script that Milch was assigned to write: but he did rewrite it, so at some level the words are his. But like Esterhaus, they are his and yet under conditions of control and higher authority.

It is worth remembering, in the context of a book focusing on one individual, V. F. Perkins's observation that

> In the factory-like conditions of film-making the notion of the director as a sole creator, uniquely responsible for a picture's qualities, defects, impact and meaning, must be approached with at least some caution. Because it is a collective enterprise, film-making involves many separate personalities, distinct and sometimes conflicting intentions, varying abilities and imperfect control. A movie cannot be fully and uniquely one man's creation.[21]

Perkins, on hearing that I was writing a book on Milch, asked why he had never directed. At the time I didn't have an answer (beyond the crass observation that Milch disliked handling technology); now, however, there is at least one suggestion. For Milch, writing was not simply the preparation of a script for subsequent realisation on screen by another creative crew. Milch wanted the words themselves to be etched visually, to draw attention to themselves as what it is that characters are made of. Which is to say that what they *do*, for the most part, is speak, and they *are what they do*. This is what I mean by the peculiar way Milch's characters 'face us' with words, in a visual and aural medium that allows us to calibrate those words against the performances that realise their vitality. This is why, in something mostly unremarked in writing on Milch, most of his characters move about so little on screen while they talk. Many of them stand still and deliver their lines, rather like Esterhaus at his pulpit. For all the ways in which Milch has been incorporated into the later Golden (or for some 'Platinum') age of television drama, his use of action, 'cinematic' or otherwise, is relatively limited. He is quite a 'theatrical' writer in the sense of 'staging' speaking in front of us. We tend to overlook this because the content of his characters' speech is so unusual and tends to knock us off balance (for example, it is very difficult to transcribe his dialogue because he often reverses or switches the usual order of words). The key opportunity he needed next, once he was embedded in the industry, was the means to create a character of his own who could speak in a voice he invented.

The industrial shifts in which he found himself over the next decade allowed him to do this.

Dennis Franz: Benedetto to Sipowicz

No doubt Milch's early experiences in academia – whether in the group workshops of Iowa or the collective collation of writing for the volumes of *American Literature* – might have found an echo in at least some part of the production machine of industrial mass entertainment. *Hill Street Blues* is often discussed in terms of the effect of shifting industrial forces rather than as an aesthetic object that emerged from an artistic as well as a corporate milieu, part of the tendency in television and cultural studies to erase human agency, particularly that of talented artists. According to Blake Bailey, Kurt Vonnegut 'wryly observed' to Richard Yates that *Hill Street Blues* was 'a very important work of art'.[22] This literary snobbery towards mass culture was, to some extent, a product of envy. More than any other show *Hill Street Blues* demonstrated a complex and deep canvas of drama, especially concerning the modulation of multiple characters and storylines over the long timespan of a 22-episode season. In fact *Hill Street Blues* attracted much critical approbation from Joyce Carol Oates and Leslie Fiedler.[23] It was no doubt comforting for writers like Yates to assume and tell Milch (as he regularly did) that he had sold out – and Milch himself might have wondered whether he might ever again have a shot at the Big Game of American Letters, despite the fact that most novelists, then and now, earn a large part of their income from writing treatments, adaptations and script fixes for Hollywood. To suggest, as Milch has, that television is a 'fallen medium' implies that it once occupied a more elevated position, but it also allows one to imagine one's own integrity and distinction down among the groundlings where the weight of expectation may be lower. A medium cannot be fallen, like a person or a society or an empire: television is no more fallen than books are. It is possible that some of Iowa's thinking about medium specificity and the value of limitations – what McGurl calls its 'Limitations Theology' where possibility and limitation are equivalents – stuck as part of Milch's thinking, although in his later years he claimed not to be interested in medium specificity at all.[24]

The external demands of network television with its rapid production schedule (*Hill Street Blues* averaged 20–22 episodes a season, with two 'seasons' in its first year), and the demands of a growing family (Milch was to have three children with Rita Stern: Ben, Elizabeth and Olivia), meant that Milch could abdicate responsibility for aspirations to 'art' or the Big Game, and use his handsome salary to fund his continuing addictions. There is an interview with Milch from the early 1980s about his work on the show, and the journalist makes the point that he met Milch at breakfast at 7 a.m. But what the article does not say is that far from being an ambitious early riser, Milch had spent the night gambling in Las Vegas and had just flown back, a habit he repeated during his working week. He would later remark to friends that if his wife hadn't heard from him by 9 p.m., the question was not so much 'Where is David?', but 'What State is he in?' Drugs, guns, booze, women, gambling: once Milch returned home after he had been 'on a run' (as he called it) and burned his clothes in his back yard so his wife could not detect the range of activities annealed on them.[25] And having been a 'professor' at Yale he had the perfect means to impress an industry always anxious about and eager to prove its cultural credentials.

When Bochco was fired from the show in 1985, Milch and Jeffrey Lewis took over as executive producers for its final two seasons. The costs of the show had, in the view of the company, got out of control and Bochco would not compromise.[26] Its emphasis shifted, even if its formula of multi-story, ensemble performance remained intact: Esterhaus's emblem of paternal care, captured in the final line of the roll call segment – 'Be careful out there' – was adjusted to 'Let's do it to them before they do it to us.' When the show ended in 1989, Milch received considerable financial compensation – reportedly 18 million dollars. But there were more important outcomes to Milch's involvement: he had established a good reputation in the industry as a screenwriter and producer; this was leavened by recognition of his volatility, another index for what might pass as creative genius, rather than mere awkwardness. Indeed, his impulsive identity was emerging as a perfect fit for an industry that craved individual, idiosyncratic artists who depended on intangibles such as aura, artistic temperament and literary inheritance. Secondly, he had in a very short time learned the ways of the industry at the helm of one of the most innovative and complex dramas of its time, in a genre which was precisely about the struggle to maintain order in the face of chaos. *Hill Street Blues* also gave Milch the opportunity to work with Dennis Franz. It was this actor who allowed him to create his first distinct television character, and it was in this show that Milch began to craft something approaching the Andy Sipowicz who dominated *NYPD Blue* a few years later.

Many of the great movie performances rest on the participation of the reality of the actor in more than body alone: in television that opportunity is extended and transformed because both entities, character and actor, grow into one another in ways that can feed a good writer's imagination and evolve and deepen an actor's inhabiting of the character. These features are further focused by the opportunity provided by streaming services to watch episodes one after another instead of separated by a week: it radically transforms how we experience older network shows, in particular *Hill Street Blues* and *NYPD Blue*.[27] This kind of character becomes a medium, something, in Cavell's words,

> through which or by means of which something specific gets done or said in particular ways. It provides, one might say, particular ways to get through to someone, to make sense; in art they are forms, like forms of speech. To discover ways of making sense is always a matter of the relation of an artist to his art, each discovering the other.[28]

In television, unlike film, the actor cannot predict, has no special knowledge of, the final destiny or events that will fully fill out a self. But this was precisely the kind of fragmented uncertainty that Milch was looking for: an unfinished spirit, trying to make sense of this in a generic fiction with its own conventions.

Franz was born in a working-class family in Illinois, a few months before Milch; unlike the latter he was drafted and served in Vietnam for nearly a year (a past recruited to Sipowicz's back story). He worked several times with Robert Altman and was part of Brian de Palma's regular ensemble during the 1970s (five parts), with his sleaziest role undoubtedly that of the extortionist voyeur photographer Manny Karp in *Blow Out* (1981). He played in a Chicago theatre production of a play called *Cops* alongside Joe Mantegna where he began the study of police behaviour that would inform his subsequent roles:

> for research we would find places that Chicago's finest would go to eat, to drink, I would observe them on the street and try to get an understanding of their behaviour ... see if there was anything I could understand or relate to ... from then on I played like 28 cops – Sipowicz was number 28 ... along the way I began really observing law enforcement, seeing police officers and seeing if there was any similarities amongst them, and one of the similarities I seemed to see, they have a great awareness of where they are, in a room, in a surrounding, their eyes are always searching, they know things behind them, in front of them and they keep their eye out ... They are – I felt always looking for ... they don't expect the best in people, they have a little bit of that opposite feeling. I tried to manipulate those into the various characters to different degrees ... I tried to incorporate some of those traits into the characters.[29]

Hence, although he appears as a 'type' of cop – overweight, balding, a kind of a 'jobsworth' or gauleiter wonderfully captured in his performance in *Die Hard 2* (1990) – each type is inflected to a different degree: they are not simply the same thing repeated, even if that helps with casting and long-term work. Franz had discovered a resource that was career-enabling, and his discovery by Milch led to one of the most resonant television characters of the twentieth century.[30] This unheroic physical type implied corruption (it's worth comparing the size of Franz to Milch himself during the 1980s and 1990s; they are quite similar and the moniker 'Fat Dave', at that time, made sense),[31] as well as the prioritisation of one's own pleasure above duty.

Franz's first role in *Hill Street Blues* was as Detective Sal Benedetto, a corrupt plain-clothes cop working in narcotics. Even in the fractured world of *Hill Street Blues* the cops were rescuers and healers: they confronted the loose, unregulated ambiguities and challenges with a mixture of courage and recklessness. Benedetto, by contrast, appears to thrive among the lowlife, among the groundlings. He is a knows-better, smart-alec, sharp-tongued operator. When we see him approach the door of a bar he pauses to lift his overcoat with both hands above his collar as if resetting his character and preparing an entrance. He swaggers in a way that overestimates self-possession in contrast to his rat-like appearance, what Delmore Schwartz in his famous poem calls 'the withness of the body'.[32] Franz pulls this off with ease. But the wise-guy knowingness of Benedetto leaves the audience with little pleasure except in the expectation of his comeuppance. The contrast is with Cavell's notion of how Hollywood movies interpreted Baudelaire's description of the Dandy as a type:

> The feature of the 'hidden fire' is essential. Our conviction in the strength of the hero depends upon our conviction in the strength and purity of character he has formed to keep his fires banked ... He does not *know* he will succeed; what he knows is himself, his readiness. The private hero must be a hero of privacy.[33]

In contrast, the string-vested, pot-bellied sweatiness of Franz's character is a kind of oven for a pot roast of cowardly juices, and his only self-knowledge is the necessity of avoiding danger or hard work. Privacy exists only as a cloak for corrupt practice. The problem with Benedetto is that he is a small-time operator, hardly spinning against the way he drives, just against the system of honour and codes that constrains his illicit transactions. He fights with his colleagues and seems indifferent to the accumulated effluence of crime and tragedy surrounding them; put more crudely, he is not one of the tribe. *Their* community, although often fractious, is captured beautifully in the title sequence as squad cars drive around a wintry urban landscape in what could be New York, Chicago (or Buffalo – the location is never specified), interspersed with freeze-frame shots of the central actors. They are a troupe, and Benedetto does not fit; when he talks to Furillo the actors manage to establish a physical sense that they belong somehow to a different species, and indeed he is compared by others to invertebrate life ('The guy is a snail; he leaves a trail of slime everywhere he goes'; [to Benedetto] 'Why don't you call me when you get your oil changed?')[34] Franz as Benedetto infects and disrupts the frame, which means he is both compelling and yet offsets too much the already canted formula that the show was known for. In this respect he seems like some of the degenerate characters from Erskine Caldwell's novels who 'live in a civilization which not only failed to civilize but has contaminated and distorted what is natural'.[35] This was not a view that *Hill Street Blues* or the network could countenance (ironically, three decades later it was the hegemonic view of much network and cable television fiction); and Milch was no doubt unhappy at the way the individuality expressed by the characters gradually formed into types who were forced into interaction by the setting and the format, the 'house style'. He would have known of the comment made by Brooks (or Warren or Lewis) about Steinbeck in *American Literature: The Makers and the Making* that:

> What may be needed, both for society and for art, is not unity, which dissolves individuals within it, but community, which is a sharing among distinct human persons. What may be needed is not group-men but companions.[36]

Franz's later character, Lieutenant Norman Buntz, has the impish, mischievous wit of Benedetto but not the hard-core corruption. George Toles, in an essay on the criticism of Pauline Kael, has written that a 'star persona is usually about an edge, where two somewhat incongruous or divergent tendencies are palatably and mysteriously brought together'.[37] Rather than form a unity that erases the seam between the two, it can mean that the edges of each are frequently in view, not sharply defined but, as in Conrad's description of Marlow's storytelling technique, 'a glow that brings out the haze'.[38] Toles goes on to remark that while most critics are 'beholden (often unconsciously) to ideals of unity and balance in a work of art', Kael conversely saw the strength of the movie medium in its unruliness, a 'gravitation to disorder' which is 'ill-disposed to evenness and fair proportion'.[39] Franz's 'edges' don't come together but grate as marked exhibits in his presentation of both Benedetto and Buntz; in the former case, the cockiness of the playground bully who is not brave or heroic enough to inflict violence centre stage – in the car park after the school bell – but snipes from a safe vantage point with put-downs and wisecracks, while unable to hide the resentment he carries about his lot, doomed to stay on the perimeter of the social world and its comforts. This would merely be pathos if Franz did not bring to it a sensibility that is anemone-like in its multi-tentacles, ever-waving to capture the slights, moods and hostility of others (in that sea creature's anatomy the mouth also acts as an anus).

Benedetto is finally killed off after being exposed by his key competitor in the squad, J. D. LaRue, a wide boy himself but blessed with chiselled good looks and dress sense, and that innate sense of honour to the police community, however poorly expressed, that is shared by the rest of the squad. In a bizarre siege ending in a bank vault, Benedetto, threatening to detonate an explosive, is confronted by a police robot, the 'TK460'; we see his final monologue relayed by the camera on this device: 'What's the good word, Captain? A good cop is a straight cop is an honest cop is a happy cop. Well you can take a high colonic. I'm proud of what I did, I lived real good.' Benedetto blows himself up, and we get a lingering shot of LaRue watching the aftermath on the monitor.[40] Benedetto's final gesture in releasing his hostage and his pathetic attack on a robot contrasts with Furillo's brutal comment to Davenport following his death: 'He won't be missed.' Part of the irony of the script is that a running issue has been the delay in the arrival of the police payroll; shortly after the suicide we hear it has arrived – the industry has paid us off for what we did, and Benedetto was too toxic to last more than five episodes before being killed off by it. But Franz as Benedetto had allowed Milch to explore what a character could achieve as a tonal contrast in an ensemble drama, much as Milch himself carried a crazy, impish reputation in the writers' room. Franz returned for nearly seventy episodes as Norman Buntz, the name evoking a more regular as well as ethnic flavour. But Benedetto was Milch's first attempt to realise and see through the narrative career of a character in his first season on the show in 1983.

Franz was brought back as Buntz two years later, but adjusted for longevity. According to Milch,

> I felt *Hill Street Blues* presented a sanitized view of police work, based on my own experiences. The first character I introduced was Sal Benedetto, a bad cop who I felt realistically represented one aspect of policing. In one episode he robbed a bank and when they sent in a robot after him, he ended up beating the robot with his fists. He's a Luddite, he hates technology and anything modern. They made me kill him off. Later, when I was in charge of the show I brought him back as Norman Buntz ... Buntz is a cop who is very uncomfortable in his own skin...[41]

Introduced in the fifth season (after a brief appearance in the fourth), Buntz maintained many of Benedetto's qualities without being a mortal threat to the moral integrity of the community as a whole: 'We figured that with a name like Buntz he'd have to be a pretty tough guy because he'd have to fight to defend his name...' Buntz 'had a chip on his shoulder', Franz says. 'I was a mutt – my clothes, my name, and I learned to embrace that.'[42]

NYPD Blue: first season

When *Hill Street Blues* reached its final episode in May 1987, Milch and Jeffrey Lewis attempted a spin-off dramedy in which Buntz had quit the force and joined with his former snitch, Sid (Peter Jurasik), as private detectives in California: *Beverly Hills Buntz*. Milch had already earned over 18 million dollars as executive producer once *Hill Street Blues* went into syndication, so the fact that the new show ran into difficulties from the start (three pilots were shot, the final attempt recruiting Oscar winner Hal Ashby to direct), while disappointing, was not career terminating. It ran for one season of thirteen episodes, although only nine were broadcast. Milch and Franz did not work together again until *NYPD Blue* in 1993. Bochco by this point had had mixed success with a string of shows such as *Hooperman, Cop Rock, Doogie Howser MD* and *LA Law*, some of which Milch had worked on, but never with the kind of long-term commitment he brought to the squad-based cop show. For all the plaudits he had accrued even at this point, Bochco was never really a 'writer's writer' – although he had written many scripts, he was more in the way Horace Newcomb and Robert S. Alley put it, a dominant and innovative player in 'the producer's medium'.[43] But this network-dominated medium was already changing again by the turn of the decade. The US depression of 1990–91 had heralded the cheaper genre of reality television that used non-copyrighted, non-unionised footage to fill airtime; the rise of subscription cable and the lack of restraint on its content meant that the limits and constraints on 'adult' content were vanishing. More than that, Bochco had no lasting bitterness towards Milch, despite him and Jeffrey Lewis taking over *Hill Street Blues* as executive producers. As he puts it:

> Given our friendship and our close working ties, I felt betrayed by both of them. I knew I could forgive David. He's a self-described sociopath. He actually said that to me, once. He's just not capable of the kind of

> integrity that I think most of us would feel compelled to act upon. It would be like being angry with someone for having blue eyes. It's not their fault. There's nothing they can do about it.[44]

By 1991 Bochco's success, especially with *Doogie Howser* and *LA Law*, was in serious trouble: the visionaries in network planning could not foresee a future for one-hour television dramas (this was the point when shows as contrasting as *Dallas* and *Twin Peaks* were axed). As Bochco puts it:

> In 1991 the bottom had pretty much dropped out of the one-hour drama business, replaced by much cheaper to produce news magazine hours. The last bona fide network hit has been my own *LA Law* in 1986. The lack of subsequent one-hour hits had two very immediate consequences: new one-hours were floundering in the ratings, and syndication revenues for one-hour series had become anaemic at best. Plus, cable programming with its lax to non-existent censorship, was eating broadcast TV's dramas for lunch.[45]

It was Bochco's idea to compete with the latter by developing a one-hour drama with 'adult sexuality (nudity in other words)' and a 'more liberal use of the kind of "street language" we were all familiar with in our normal lives'. He pitched it to Bob Iger of ABC, and after approval he reached out to Milch. Upon leaving MTM after the cancellation of *Hill Street Blues*, Milch had picked up a two-year contract with Paramount (this included a period when he worked on some feature scripts – all uncredited, except for the TV movie *Home Free* [1988] and a spin-off feature from the short-lived TV show he created, *Capital News*). At this point he also made his first attempt to get sober and drug free ('dry but not sober'), which left him suicidally depressed for several months. Milch had written episodes for some of Bochco's other projects, including *LA Law* and *Civil Wars*. But the promise of a cop show, and one that might offer him more control as co-creator, was clearly a good prospect.

According to Bochco, Milch's initial script was poor, in the sense that it simply addressed the wrong topic: an undercover cop 'who'd infiltrated one of the Mafia families in New York, and he wanted to do a show about wiretapping, mobsters, etc.'[46] Milch was to pursue this idea later on in *Big Apple* (2001) and *Last of the Ninth* (2008) (the former was cancelled after only eight episodes, the latter was made into a pilot but not picked up by its network). Bochco was already having problems with the very notion of a more explicit kind of show from the industry that he was persuading to fund it, and the premiere was delayed by a year when Southern affiliates got wind of the intention and threatened not to air it.

This hiatus allowed Milch more time to research, and by chance he met a journalist, Michael Daly (suggested by a long-term friend, the investigative journalist and writer Jimmy Breslin), who recommended that he meet Bill Clark, a NYPD detective who at the time was already legendary as one of the most decorated in the city. After joining the force in 1969, he earned his gold detective shield in 1972; like Franz he had served in Vietnam in the infantry and as a scout dog handler. Even more attractive, given Milch's obsession at the time, Clark had served as an undercover cop for two years, infiltrating leftist militant groups posing as a disaffected Vietnam grunt who had been radicalised by the brutality he had witnessed. This is adopted as a back story in *NYPD Blue* for Sipowicz (revealed in season four), when he talks about coming back from Vietnam and being recruited as an undercover cop. He infiltrated the Young Patriots Organisation ('it's like the women's auxiliary unit for the Black Panthers', Sipowicz says: 'Then I'd work my cover job. Then drink.') Clark had also gained distinction for operations against the Gambino Mafia family, which was again congruent with Milch's, though not Bochco's, interests.

Clark brought an entire lived experience into Milch's view, from the history of policing to how to hold a gun, how a badge is worn, what the politics and the job really entail. He also brought a moral attitude: 'In court', he told Milch,

> if you're testifying and you're looking for justice it's really serious stuff. And the District Attorneys seem to be doodling as if it's a sport. They'll come out the courtroom during recess and want to talk to you about sports or something ... it seems like we're the only ones who really care and that's what the show tries to show repeatedly. So many other people try to victimize the victims and we're about the only ones who do the right thing for them.[47]

After Bochco and Warren, Clark now occupied the role of guide, this time into a world of courage and heroism in the face of evil and degeneracy. Clark was streetwise but courageous – he would never let his colleagues bust into a room of suspects before him, in case one of his squad was hurt. Milch's madcap and dangerous feats were driven by something else, but he was also at home with the 'groundlings' and, like Clark, 'lifted all boats' when he came into the room. Milch spent many months talking to Clark, who was still working full time as a homicide detective. Their joint authorship of *True Blue* means that it alternates between Milch's and Clark's autobiographical sections and their description of the production process of *NYPD Blue*. It reads like an account of a partnership. If Warren was a father figure, Clark was more of a big brother as well as a protector for Milch in an industry in which he did not get along with executives.[48]

By staying close to Clark, Milch for the first time was doing research on a grand scale for his own creative interests. He later said, 'The focusing is on the moral fibre of these men and women who do police work, that's at the heart of this show. How they live with themselves in choosing this profession.'[49] In *Hill Street Blues* this multi-vocality was expressed in the collision and interaction of *types* – LaRue, Hunter, Furillo, Renko. In *NYPD Blue* the fragmentation of parts is much more *internal* to the characters, starting with Sipowicz himself. For Franz it was simpler to play him as a type – 'the core of his being is basically a good strong man' – but to be that, we need to know it from the inside, its depths and shadows in order to grasp the struggle of 'the little man standing up for what's right'.[50] In the pre-credit sequence of the pilot Sipowicz is outwitted by the Assistant District Attorney Sylvia Costas (Sharon Lawrence), who is defending the known gangster Alfonse Giardella (Robert Constanza). When Giardella goes free, they have a confrontation outside the courtroom. Costas says to Sipowicz, 'I would say *res ipsa loquitur* if I thought you'd know what it meant.' Sipowicz replies by grapping his penis through his trousers: 'Ipsa this you pissy little bitch!' For Franz, it was the line that captured the character and gave him drive: 'I'm gonna love saying it, the attitude, arguing with her, grabbing my crotch, everything about it was ugly and I loved every second of it.'[51]

According to George Toles, '[m]uch depends in film on our involvement with attributes of a performer that supplement the specific requirements of a character'.[52] But in film this collusion and its potential intensity is strongly bounded by the fact of a beginning and end that achieves a whole (however satisfactory or not) for the audience. In theory there is no less intensity possible in television performances: however, often we see the character played again and again over time, and the challenge is to ensure that neither character nor actor becomes a candle that runs down to the wick with over-usage. In network television at the time, shading and gradations of depth and layers were paced (which is not to say diluted) across 22-episode seasons, as in the case of *NYPD Blue*. The principle is one of accrual, accumulation and sedimentation of material that is not known very far in advance by the performers, the writers or the directors. In Milch's case, he would keep writing until the last minute, so that often actors would arrive on set in the morning without a script. Dustin Hoffman, who, at 74, had never played a character in episode television, nailed the issue in an interview in *The Financial Times* in 2012:

> In the theatre, after the third week of rehearsal, you might say, 'Eureka! I think I've found it.' In the third week of making a movie, if you say, 'Eureka!', the director looks at you and says, 'That's nice but you have to match the first three weeks.' You can't change the character because you're not shooting sequentially. With *Luck*, it's evolving, we're being led by what we did and we're discarding what doesn't work.[53]

Evolving takes with it the pressure of the past, both a constraint and a resource for writer and performer alike. As the audience we have an awareness that actors and the behaviour of their characters in the present are constantly providing further layers that in themselves draw on established patterns and habits (whose back story is either known or will be revealed to us). Such patterns neither dictate nor determine, but are shouldered, drawing on the congealed and supple aspects of shared memory and recall. In genres such as police- and hospital-based dramas, the sheer immediacy of the crises that these characters face helps to push this aspect into the background, where it continues, nevertheless, to shadow them. Equally (and in this we share something with the actors, particularly those who work to Milch's close deadlines), as an audience we have the future in mind as it begins to signal itself in the episodes we see. Hence this kind of television fiction structurally enacts the possibility of erasing or transforming the pain of the past into a resolution that, if it does not negate it, at least heals it to some extent. When asked by Pamela Douglas why he choose television as his medium, Milch responded by evoking Warren:

> Time. One of Robert Penn Warren's great poems about Audubon, the guy who painted the birds, goes something like, 'Tell me a story in this moment and century of mania. Tell me a story. Make it a story of great distances and starlight. The name of the story will be time. Tell me a story of great delight.' What we learn or fail to learn over time is what endows our experience with meaning, but to identify that as a 'theme' is to demystify the experience of life. TV makes available the large canvas: the opportunity to portray lives over time. For me, I have a pedestrian sensibility. I see things in small increments. I can render a moment without necessarily understanding its meaning. For that type of storyteller, the accumulation of moments is what ultimately shows the pattern of experience.[54]

NYPD Blue began a familiar format that revivified faith in episodic drama. It was a variation on both the ensemble episodic genre that was to constitute the revival of the hour-long drama in the 1990s (in shows such as *ER*, *Chicago Hope*, *Homicide: Life on the Street* and many others) and the buddy cop genre. Sipowicz was the less attractive, but wiser, sidekick to the main star, David Caruso, cast as John Kelly, a cop of Irish descent, clearly intended to embody sex appeal, courage and a fairly generic friction with police bureaucracy. Caruso's performance as an ethnic urban cop seems aloof from his surroundings in a way that Franz's does not, and in later episodes of the season Kelly was frequently shown moonlighting as a security guard for the rich, placing him in well-lit, luxurious interiors rather than the grubby confines of the squad room. Sipowicz in the pilot is a hard-drinking, violent, whoring figure, but pointedly good at his job. Milch writes in a cop character who resembles Sipowicz but misses crucial intelligence on the job; he is replaced by a recurring character, Mike Roberts, played superbly by Michael Harney, who again, has a moral weakness that makes him unfit for the force; the point is that whatever Sipowicz's moral failings, his heart is not one of them. While Sipowicz lacks the grand glamour of large-scale police corruption or villainy, his very mediocrity and ordinary failings make him an epic television character. One is reminded of the success, decades before, of Paddy Chayefsky's *Marty* (1953), with Rod Steiger's compelling depiction of the despair of ordinary everyday life.

The tone of the show, particularly the title sequence that follows Sipowicz's vulgar gesture to Costas, grates against the kind of figure that Caruso/Kelly seems to represent. It is a montage of fast cutting and movement accompanied by rapid drum beats. The visuals and music emphasise the perceptual disorientation as we are assaulted by disconnected slices of city life, and this is counterpointed by a mournful, elegiac orchestrated melody, based on an Irish folk tune, whose sadness suggests the end of things, an aspect emphasised by a shot of the demolition of an old building during its most poignant notes.[55] As a product it strikes the viewer as caught between the promise of titillation – sex, violence, bad language and crime – and something much more unsettling, as if a nineteenth-century reader had picked up a copy of *Moby Dick* expecting the same kind of thrills and exoticism that Melville offered in *Typee* or *Omoo*. The unsettledness of this world is initially communicated in the early seasons by a restless, constantly fidgeting camera, but this style was gradually abandoned as what in fact it is, a somewhat pointless stylistic underlining.

The pilot sets up a pattern that is essentially repeated throughout the twelve seasons of the show. Sipowicz's humiliation by Costas on the witness stand means that the gangster Giardella is free. Giardella's doughy bulk resembles that of Sipowicz; Milch describes him as someone whom Sipowicz regards as 'his own clownishly evil nightmare double' (the two actors played brothers in *Die Hard 2*).[56] Sipowicz retaliates by humiliating the gangster in his restaurant by pulling off his wig. Giardella's revenge is to ambush Sipowicz while he is in bed with his regular hooker, shooting him multiple times. Gradually, as this story is left behind and Sipowicz recovers, the episodes re-establish his competency as a cop, but the shooting establishes a diabolic pattern of the kind discussed in the Introduction – there is a sudden trauma, a crisis, and Sipowicz reverts to drinking, smoking, back to the 'filth of self', exemplified by his confession that he'd like to 'crawl inside a bottle and set up housekeeping'. There are rapid plot shifts in the first four episodes, but as Milch notes in one of his audio commentaries on the DVD for this season, a 'character like Sipowicz builds slowly'. The fact that he is really 'not a shitbird' becomes 'the viewer's private secret': we can see an aspect of Sipowicz that he does not know about himself (a tactic that Milch repeats in season one of *Deadwood* with Al Swearengen).

The dramatic architecture that allows this entry into his private world involves staging Sipowicz's private dramas in public spaces where we can see better his acts of concealment from himself, aspects that the performer, short of winking at the camera, can convey through gesture, pace of delivery and movement. In its first season Milch's project seems to get at an anthropological truth about the contemporary lives of cops, the costs and the doubleness they must undergo every day in order to 'do the right thing'.[57] To keep Sipowicz in the cycle whereby he is vulnerable to relapse, one also needed benign anchors, so that something more was at stake for him to lose or win. A story arc involving Dominic Bucci, a grieving father whose daughter had been abducted two years previously, allows Sipowicz to invest his spare time in trying to resolve the case. 'After the emphasis we'd given in the first three shows to Sipowicz's chaotic personal life, I always felt the doggedness Andy shows in pursuing his investigation in this case went a long way toward establishing his effectiveness and honourable nature as a cop'; this was the story Milch cited in *True Blue* as an example of the modulation of time that allows us to appreciate the 'qualities of character'.[58] At Bochco's suggestion, the daughter is eventually found alive.

Milch also became interested in particular in the relationship between Sylvia Costas and Sipowicz, which had begun the show with such sexist and unpromising hostility; by the end of season two they are married. With Sipowicz we share the experience (if we have been regular viewers) of the traumas and backsliding events of his past: it is available to us without being stated repeatedly and underlined stylistically, in the patterns and habits he exhibits in the present. And in a network show, built into the narrative form was the sense that time had passed – at least a week – between one episode and the next. We needed to believe that their lives continued during that time. For Sipowicz the ever-present threat was his return to alcoholism and despair. As Milch once told a director: 'despite my self centered conviction that I can ruin everything ... There is nothing so dark or so contradictory that in faith it can't be converted to joy. What I know is that what we think we're doing is very very rarely what we're actually doing.'[59] This evoking of the final lines of Warren's poem, 'I Am Dreaming of a White Christmas: The Natural History of a Vision', is of course a necessary slogan for Milch, or anyone, with a history so branded by trauma and self-blame that the sheer difficulty and expense of energy of attempting to transcend it can lead to relapse. It takes enormous energy to keep such things at bay (what Alcoholics Anonymous calls 'white knuckling it'). Embrace of the hand one has been dealt is also a relaxing into one's lot, sating the internal committee of critics, playing the hand out to the last loss. Milch told David Thorburn that Sipowicz was based much more on his father than himself, although he followed his father's bad habits on a far grander scale given the money he had available. Friendship with Bill Clark lent that identity the details, language and gestures that would anchor his central character to the realism that Milch equally wanted to abide by, and also added the impish, comic side to the character that we glimpse in *The Groundlings* and in Sal Benedetto's wisecracks. Sipowicz gives that side free rein, and it is a real joy, however grim the circumstances, to hear his comic lines – Milch is very underrated as a comic writer, partly because he juxtaposes the comic with the utterly ghastly in such an unexpected manner.

That sense of the gravitational pull of one's inner core as fundamentally, ineluctably toxic can be seen in a seemingly irrelevant digression in one of *NYPD Blue*'s first season episodes. After a decade of avoidance, Sipowicz is finally compelled by the pain of a toothache to see a dentist. As he is drilled (without anaesthetic since he is afraid of the needle – a wonderful reversal of Milch's relationship to heroin: 'something that gives you everything but that you must give everything to'), the dentist reminds Sipowicz that he is merely a 'mechanic', not a priest offering rebuke or confessional. But for Sipowicz the pain itself is a rebuke, its persistence a reminder of the range of neglect he has subjected himself to inside and out – he's not afraid of this minor criticism from the dentist, given the daily pincers and clawing of the Committee's judgements in his own head.

Suddenly, the dental assistant bursts into the scene – Dr Fleishman, the pedodontist who shares the medical suite next door, has climbed out of the window and is standing on the ledge threatening to jump twenty-eight floors to his death. When Sipowicz talks to him he is confronted with a concentrated version of his own self-loathing: Fleishman describes himself as a 'despicable asshole' who doesn't deserve to live and who has 'poisoned every personal relationship I ever had'. Rather than talk him down, Sipowicz tries to improvise some supportive noises, while admitting that his drilled tooth makes it hard to come up 'with a bunch of cheery thoughts'. But the tooth is a prop for this scene: Milch (who was in his late forties at the time) is using a standard generic trope (cop talks down suicide with common sense) to drill into something deeper:

> *Fleishman*: I know what I am. A 48-year-old one-man train wreck.
> *Sipowicz*: Don't you think people could change?
> *Fleishman*: I've tried to change a thousand times. That crap lasts a couple of months max. Eventually you go back to being the same disgusting asshole you always were. You get to a certain age, it's too late. You are who you are.

Sipowicz listens in silence as Fleishman turns to him: 'Officer, can you look me in the eye and honestly tell me I'm wrong?' The reverse shot of Sipowicz, brief, looking back at the sad man, then lowering his eyes reflectively asks a lot of us if we are willing to participate in his thinking: it *is* true, he *is* right as far as Sipowicz knows. Fleishman (flesh man or butcher in German) represents for Sipowicz those persistent internal voices that greet some of us first thing in the morning with such thinking, which they've been honing all night while we've been asleep. The immediate pain of his toothache, the product of years of neglectful dental habits, is juxtaposed with this longer term, seemingly ineluctable existential nagging: even cleaning them three times a day won't avoid the inevitable root canals and crowns. As a recovering alcoholic trying to get his life on some kind of even keel after the Giardella shooting, Sipowicz knows only too well the secret voice made public by Fleishman on the building ledge. The distant noise of the traffic below and their close-miked conversation encourages the viewer to take this as a very private moment in a very public world. They are talking above millions of human beings near the clouds. When Sipowicz answers only by lowering his eyes, Fleishman supplies the words: 'Of course not! Screw everybody!'

It is typical of Milch to button this terrifying sequence with some grim humour, as we get a reaction shot of Sipowicz blinking at the impact of Fleishman hitting the ground and delivering a quip with consonants mashed around his sore teeth and lips: 'There's the hostage squad now.' The Calvinist hooks that whisper that one is predetermined to ruin everything one touches, and then to hate and resent one's own self-hatred and resentment, to envy the holiday eyes of others and hate oneself more for that, is on full display here, leavened helpfully by that humour. The promises of change vaporise in the face of the continued, painful demands of the world, and the demands of the self on the self are so intense that one finally does not have the energy to 'white-knuckle' it through. These laws are the store of Sipowicz's experience of the world. But that's kind of funny too: that the long, hard-earned habits and self-training of tending to the heart, of loving, are at every instant vulnerable to relapse, temptation, backsliding. We end up like Fleishman anyway – 'a poor, bare, forked, animal'.

Later in the same episode Sipowicz is confronted by vestiges of the past when Lois the hooker, who set him up for the shooting, reaches out, wanting to 'make up' by having dinner (plus booze and sex) with him. 'That guy is wrong', Sipowicz says earlier in the episode to no one in particular; 'I think I'm done with the old times', he says to Lois. But the past is 'gum-shoeing closer behind' and is not done with him: long-form television is time-bound, too, and pitiless in its pursuit of ruin.[60] Thorburn's characterisation of Milch's repeated depiction of characters seeking redemption begins to acquire momentum over the course of the first four to five seasons of *NYPD Blue*. The show has characters and events that decontaminate or purge themselves periodically, before building towards a new crisis or failure. An emblem of this is Sipowicz's attachment to his pet fish: during their early courtship, Costas brings him over a new one and he is surprisingly distraught: 'You don't just introduce a sudden fish into the ecology like that!' This very legible analogy is reinforced by other characters in the squad complaining about their failure to learn from the past: Greg Medavoy's (Gordon Clapp) complaints about his journey into work along the Long Island Expressway (many cops, once they made detective, bought property on Long Island) follow the same pattern: 'I sucker myself in ... I have to learn the lesson over and over again. I wind up trapped.' Every episode has some sense that the past is coming back, recycling itself and looking to be purged or redeemed. Sometimes the drama allows that, and sometimes it does not.

In tension with the rebuke of the self against itself is the grace of human community and art. We may see this in the gradual formation of adult solidarity, especially that formed between those excluded from wider society – Jews, cops, criminals – who have found ways to operationalise their fundamental doubleness through a series of pacts that the rest of the world demanded of them. By *NYPD Blue* Milch had found a way to create sharply defined individuals, cut off from the rest of the world and yet compelled to act within it. Hence his continued interest in cops, and station-based or contained settings, threatened as always by the perils of the outside world. Like *The Pequod,* these places compel solidarity, but they sail alone, whether it be the fifteenth precinct squad of *NYPD Blue,* the town of *Deadwood,* the surfing community of Imperial Beach in *John From Cincinnati* or the denizens who infest the Santa Anita racetrack in *Luck.* That sharp defining around the edges of these groundlings cuts them off from others, yet they embody the possibility of moral flourishing in the most unexalted settings: where else would we notice them so vividly?

In the early episodes, *NYPD Blue* was in thrall to its own pitch: 'adult themes' meant the depiction of grim homicide and nudity (including the famous incident showing Caruso's bare backside in the shower). It sticks to the rather heroic narrative (matched by the first season of *ER* which premiered a year later) of hard work by decent people faced with very unpleasant experiences. The show exhibits its close proximity to accurate details, drawing on Clark's expertise (for example in the use of police codes, and numbers for official forms). Some episodes privilege one character over all the others, but even early on, Franz as Sipowicz dominates our attention.

In the seventh episode of the season, when a Polish father reports that his son is missing, Sipowicz remarks to a co-worker, 'I hate it when you know it' (meaning he knows the child is already dead). Franz in playing Sipowicz's moments of tenderness modulates his voice to a soft gravel, almost a whisper, juxtaposed ('spinning against') brilliantly with his medieval balding tonsure and planetoid midriff. By using the canvas of the entire city and its crimes Milch begins to approach Dostoevsky in terms of his peculiar handling of realism. John Jones, in his superb account of that novelist, calls the process 'his working his way backwards into the Nineteenth Century', and notes that Dostoevsky conceived of realism not in terms of documentation, but idealism or prophecy:

> Shrewd guessing at tendency is not the jewel in his casket. The interest of how things are resides in their figuration, discernible and expressible by the deeper realist of how things will be only in so far as that futurity is the truth and the end of how they are and always have been. His naturalism is apocalyptic.[61]

We begin to admire Sipowicz as an athlete of perception, who can read the world and make its acts legible for us. But because of Sipowicz's nature we find this reading deeply ominous at the same time. *NYPD Blue,* despite attempts to bolster its artistic merits via social relevance, is not a dissertation or meditation on the state of the nation.[62] The racist pantomime of Sipowicz is as much a device to trouble our relationship with that character, the spin that prevents him comfortably settling in our estimation.

When Milch introduced Andy Jr, Sipowicz's estranged son from his former marriage, he deepened the sackcloth aspect to his major character. Sipowicz manages to use his police connections to lessen a misdemeanour that Andy committed. Then he goes to his son to atone:

> Bad enough I was the kind of father I was. I'm not gonna sit here and piss and moan about it but I was glad enough to get the chance to maybe help you. And I'd like to be a better father or a friend or whatever the hell you need.

Franz handles the performance so that Sipowicz seems physically uncomfortable with his emerging virtues: he swivels his eyes as if recognising, suspiciously, some seam of good, hardly credible, somewhat embarrassing, a kind of love sheepishly welcome if unfamiliar. This anxious sense of the unpractised vocalisation of certain feelings is something that Franz excels at, and it is freighted with doubt. Is it real? Can I be seen? Is this weakness or strength? Right or wrong? Permanent or passing? All of those things.

By contrast, the character of John Kelly diminished in interest for Milch. While the shooting of Sipowicz provides Kelly with the moral impetus to exercise some police muscle, his own life is complicated by a series of women who provide the opportunity for the show to exhibit its 'adult' scenes. First, he has sex in the shower with soon to be ex-wife Laura (Sherry Stringfield, who made the wise decision to leave the show to join the cast of *ER*, where she excelled), as well as beginning a liaison with Janice Licalsi (Amy Brennerman, who likewise went on to do much better work). However, Licalsi is working for the mob boss Angelo Morino (Joe Santos), since her father – also a cop – is on the take. Hence by the end of the pilot episode we have a strong sense of a fractured, disintegrating world whose 'peacekeepers' are as infected with the same human frailties, temptations and misguided sense of honour as anyone else. Tellingly, when Kelly sits next to the wounded Sipowicz's hospital bed, he says, 'I don't know what's going on in your head.' Sipowicz's reply is to squeeze his partner's hand, another indication that the range of intimacy between cops will be a central focus of the show. Contrast this to the overbearing ambition of *The Wire*, which seeks to capture an entire societal breakdown through its institutional fragility and corruption; for Milch, unlike David Simon, such a breakdown has already occurred at the ontological level of the human social bond. Milch's dramas are looking to rebuild that bond in any way they can, with the most fragile and broken of materials. Notwithstanding the large egos reportedly common among Hollywood actors, one can understand Caruso's frustration that Franz's character was achieving depth and popularity, whereas his seemed an unlikely shell for further development.

This led, indirectly, to an event that was to change Milch's life significantly, at least on the surface. According to several accounts, including one in *True Blue*, during rehearsal or shooting for an episode, Caruso was unhappy with aspects of his scene and in front of the crew, including Milch, asked aloud, 'Who wrote this shit?'[63] Milch claims that he knew he was having a heart attack as he tried to explain the 'crosshatching' of ironies that the scene evoked, but he didn't ask Bill Clark to call an ambulance until he had finished explaining this to Caruso. Nearing his fifties, Milch's lifetime of bad habits had caught up with him – those 'constable clutches' of the past were now tightening his arteries and he had heart disease. He subsequently underwent a series of angioplasties; as Milch puts it, the event made clear what his priorities were:

> For me, the regimen of deadlines and responsibilities imposed by a television series has been a type of liberation. I had no great wistfulness about periods in my life that had been less encumbered but tended to end in unfamiliar cities and rooms.[64]

Bochco was busy setting up or running other shows, and there was no other lead writer, so Milch, despite regular visits to the hospital for treatment, continued to churn out the scripts. Clark helped, and increasingly his contribution was as much as a storyteller as a resource for plot stimulants. He had worked on hundreds of cases and was known as a breaker – the person to call if none of the other detectives could secure a confession from a suspect in the interrogation room (something taken directly into the plot of *True Detective*'s first season). The structure of *NYPD Blue* tends to remain the same in this sense: we begin with a gruesome homicide, suspects are arrested (although rarely do we hear the cops read them the Miranda warning informing them of their right to remain silent), then interrogated. The key point is that without a confession, the police have very little else that is reliable (witnesses, DNA, etc. are all too frangible in the courtroom), and the confession needs to be written out by the suspect *before they get within shouting distance of a lawyer*. This was the way the police worked, not the way they were usually depicted on television. Clark gave Milch this crucial insight, which was woven cunningly, largely through omission, throughout the show. This is also why quite a lot of *NYPD Blue* takes place not through the speedy, jerking camera style, but within traditional set-ups, shot/reverse-shot patterns in the dingy interrogation room, which becomes a stage for words, for lies, and for the excavation of lies. This is what Clark did in his job, and it would take hours and hours to wear a suspect down to a confession. Clark's point to Milch was the relief and friendship that the confessors had for him once they had given up the truth. Clark also told him about the calm he exhibited when standing in court when asked whether he had read the suspect his Miranda rights, while looking at him or her full in the eye and answering 'Yes'. They had an understanding about justice.

Clark is a contemporary of Milch and his own background was likewise an alloy of tragedy and the usual muddle of ordinary childhood. He grew up in Park Slope, Brooklyn, which by his teens – as with many of the neighbourhoods in and around Manhattan – was saturated with heroin. His brother, John, died of a heroin overdose: Clark chained himself to a radiator in his locked bedroom, knowing that he would kill the supplier – meaning that his parents would lose both sons, one to dope, one to prison – until he could trust himself not to take vengeance. Clark went on to join the army, doing tours in Europe and Vietnam. At one point he came across the body of a Vietcong soldier, dug a grave and buried the man. Like Milch burying the unfortunate chemist in Cuernavaca, one can see in the act a fundamental respect for the commensurability of human experience. 'Bill is a very violent man', Milch once told me over breakfast; 'but', he continued, 'you should see him with his birds, he is also the most gentle man.' Milch's Red Board complex of offices sings with the sound of Clark's various birds coming from his office; there is a homage to this in *John From Cincinnati* with ex-cop Bill Jacks's (Ed O'Neill) house full of caged birds. Most of the audio material that I was allowed to access during my research consists of Milch and Clark talking together about their proposed series *Last of the Ninth*, and much of the conversation underlines the brotherly friendship of the pair, right down to the aggressive, insulting intimacy that those of us who have brothers take, and know, as love.

NYPD Blue: Sipowicz and Costas

With Milch's health in question and Caruso hoping to launch a career in feature films rather than television, the show took a major turn in its second season. Kelly appearered for a couple of episodes and then was replaced by Bobby Simone (Jimmy Smits) as Sipowicz's new partner. It is during this and the next three seasons that *NYPD Blue* is at its best;

Milch finds a way to work within the genre that makes the characters prominent, so that plot elements are used to deepen and evolve them. To be sure this is one sided: the female characters, with one exception, tend to be somewhat neglected (and in one case totally erased). But Simone's Hispanic background (Smits grew up in Puerto Rico) helped ease Sipowicz's latent racism once the latter had established respect for his partner. Simone's back story was as a police driver – a kind of armed chauffeur – much to the disgust of Sipowicz, until he learns that this was in order that Simone could care for his wife who was dying of cancer. Simone also has a back story as a pigeon fancier, a kind of emblem of his higher spirit and lift in contrast to his more grounded and weighed-down partner. It is easy to see why Clark preferred Jimmy Smits's rendition of Simone to Caruso's Kelly. Kelly's version of privacy is extraordinarily hygienic as well as inscrutable; we see in him, to the degree that we can, a barrier to our fundamental understanding of any shared set of values. This is certainly not a factor with Sipowicz, and Simone's privacy has a happier public face.

Unlike Caruso's Kelly, Simone's ongoing series arcs had real substance and did not devolve into a stance that flattered the actor's vanity. But even for Simone, Sipowicz's repeated lapses, his backsliding, were a continual concern. The characters clearly had chemistry, such that their small lies to one another were emblems of intimacy by which each could acknowledge the other's need to cover himself in front of a friend. What Simone enables for Sipowicz is the possibility of imagining a future as a means of stabilising the chaos of the present, and to negate the fate that his internal critics regularly insist is his due. Such matters would more logically sit, it would seem, in a drama about, say, psychiatrists; but, as William Empson reminds us, 'Life involves maintaining oneself between contradictions that cannot be solved by analysis.'[65]

Midway through the second season of the show, in one of its most charming episodes, 'Travels with Andy', Sipowicz – by now as tough and familiar to the audience as a boiled potato – is pouring himself a coffee from the jug in the station rec room as he tells his colleague, Greg Medavoy (Gordon Clapp), that 'Sylvia made some Greek stuff for dinner last night. Usually gives me an upset stomach. I sailed right through it.' 'That's a good sign', replies his friend. Indeed it is. Clapp is a superb performer who, like many of the other regulars – after Sipowicz he was the longest-running character in the show – delivered exquisite incremental development as well as the usual alloy of confidence and doubt that we expect from Milch's characters. Sipowicz's ontological ecosystem is ultrasensitive to changes in his routine and habitat, and indications that his body is calibrating itself to his desire to please his future wife is no small thing. As we have seen, Sylvia Costas is Assistant District Attorney, a beautiful lawyer from a large Greek family who, on the face of it, seems an ill fit for Sipowicz's roly-poly cop with his expert knowledge of all things sleazy and deceitful. But when she breezes into the room shortly afterwards in order to fill her own cup, her conversation with Sipowicz is easy, open and convincing. She reports that she has spent the morning with her father making plans for an elaborate Greek wedding day. Sipowicz is moved by her (somewhat stereotypical) excitement, but suggests an alternative event, more of a private affair in Maryland:

> *Sipowicz*: It'll be nice and private, just the two of us.
> *Costas*: Like some sailor running off with a hooker?
> *Sipowicz*: No it doesn't have to be that.
> *Costas*: Andy I don't think you understand how much getting married means to me.
> *Sipowicz*: Listen, it means a lot to me too but do we have to make some production out of it where we both ... where flowers and...
> *Costas*: I don't think of it as an ordeal. And I *don't* want to take my vows in some marriage mill that smells like booze and cigarette smoke. I have to go.

As Costas speaks she dunks a teabag into her cup (which has a gold leaf imprint), rather than pour the regulation coffee. It is a gesture maintained calmly as she speaks more heatedly, so that in holding the cup with her palm underneath, like a chalice, then making delicate stirring motions with the spoon, the action reinforces the contrast between the refinement of the marriage ritual that she wants, and the 'get it done away from the eyes of the world' nature of Sipowicz's imagination. This is underlined by his holding a souvenir-grade mug of coffee with a Statue of Liberty imprint. On the word 'don't' Costas breaks eye contact with Sipowicz and they do not look at each other again until the end of the episode.

The sound of the world around them – the blurred clamour of the station, distant sirens – is recruited as a substrate of disorder to the beat of the lines. As Costas imagines how beautiful her orthodox wedding will be with its pomp and costume, a brief light is cast over her face, but this seems, from Sipowicz's point of view, only to confirm his suspicions of the showbiz display of the event; it briefly lifts Costas from the soundtrack of urban chaos and conveys a reverie of imagination, the possibility that even in the context of a grubby squad rec room, dreams of the future can lift us from the forces of shame and the need for privacy that Sipowicz embodies. He is worried that he will stand out as the ugly element in a beautiful ceremony. Sylvia looks like a star: Andy would rather be a black hole. As she storms out of the room, Sipowicz immediately feels a twinge of discomfort in his side – the Greek meal is reacting to the argument, his body spinning against the way it drives.

Sipowicz is the most resonant of the characters who display this self-loathing affliction at this stage of Milch's career, but part of his attraction, as Milch suggests, is the force of his 'soul reaching out'. Milch's characters maintain this self-division, not as binaries of good/evil, nurturing voice/critical voice, but rather as clusters of competing noise expressed in a range of ways. Sipowicz's enjoyment of the Greek food is rejected by the weathervane of his body as his external comfort is ruined by a reminder from his internal committee of the exposure that a wedding event on this scale would mean: how could you, a man like you, marry someone like that and have it celebrated as a grand spectacle?

As Walter Benjamin reminds us, in allegory anything can stand for anything else. Food signals both the sensual enjoyment of consumption and the necessity for digestion. Characters have an immediacy, but also leave lingering impressions on us, as this succession of immediacies becomes a history, a past to be processed. Fictional characters in long-form television require digestion, acquire intimacy with us through repetition. Yet fictionality is by definition unlike history, since it cannot be verified by external facts. Milch recounts Cleanth Brooks's advice to him on the distinction:

> Cleanth Brooks ... in trying to educate me a bit about the different kinds of truths, suggested that the truths of reportage or of history depend upon ... a correspondence to an externally verifiable reality. And the truths of storytelling are the truths of an internal emotional coherence.[66]

Brooks instructed Milch on the centrality of New Criticism's insistence on coherence, unity, as a salve for the shattered meaning of the modern world. Fiction depends on a pretend world populated by created entities – characters – whose compelling force depends to a large extent on their being like us. Plato's problem with mimesis is precisely that the power of characterisation runs the risk of infecting the actor or storyteller, and hence the reader or viewer. Some evolutionary narratologists see in this a long-standing human tendency to

> keep close track of the personality of others, because doing so helps to predict their behaviour and plan our own. Since personality remains relatively stable, it pays us in life to monitor it, especially if a person is complex enough not to be entirely predictable. Story offers us intense concentrations of character information.[67]

The problem with this reading, as with most formalist accounts of narrative and character, is that it is entirely ahistorical and misses the key aspect of twentieth-century art, which is its struggle to establish or ground meaning in any internal or external force.

However complex or deep character data are, it pays to look more closely at how characters such as Sipowicz withhold information from themselves and others, those whose 'data' are not legible packages communicated or relayed to audiences, but instead the result of evasions, contradictions or misdirection. Milch achieved, first with Sipowicz and later with many other characters, something far more than the stable entities that we take as 'characters' and that had been taken for granted over the past centuries.[68] More than this, the historical context in which he was writing saw an opening up of the private sphere to levels of public scrutiny and official interference that were unheard of before the 1980s: poor parenting, child abuse, toxic relationships, diet, exercise and other hitherto private activities gradually became targets of national policy across the West.[69] *NYPD Blue* had an enormous canvas on which to capitalise on this shift, by bringing every class, gender, race and age of suspect into its interview room.

The issue that is most prominent once we reach seasons two to four is the extent to which Benjamin's claim about allegory butts against Brooks's New Critical claims of unity. According to Charles Rosen, in an excellent account of Benjamin's work, '[allegory] rejects the false appearance of artistic unity, the fusion of meaning in the symbol, and presents itself as a fragment, a ruin'.[70] The various people and their crimes stand in for anything else, rather than meaning itself: the constant is the diligence and resilience of Simone and Sipowicz as interrogators.

At the Greek party where Sipowicz finally meets Sylvia's father, the writing conspires to put as much pressure as possible on his will to withstand his suspicion and mistrust of genuinely being welcomed into the family. The party is an over-thickened flush of communal togetherness and joy, a promising environment for healing Sipowicz's private doubts. As the Costas family raises a toast to Sylvia, Sipowicz – emboldened by this brief blast of collective familial goodwill – drinks too. This, for the first time, is not for himself but for her: 'There's no lightning bolts, the ground doesn't open up.' But the action, born out of gratitude and pleasure, signals to us that the devil has a hand here, too. Sipowicz, at heart, wants to show himself in 'all my degradation, my evil, my sheer loathesomeness'. Milch needed something in this sequence to humanise our abstract acknowledgement of a tired generic moment – the dance that we see, the spinning communal blessing of art, of unconflicted human sociality as it washes over them and anoints this formerly isolated fat man. When Costas discovers Sipowicz smoking after drinking more whisky, we see his dark-hearted joy exulting in self-hatred and then its projection across her and the group, like a black sun sweeping its rays across the planets that orbit it.[71] He insults her family, calling them 'moron shepherds' – the words seem to bite physically into Costas. After she leaves we have a shot of Sipowicz, alone in his apartment, except for the only remaining emblem of his commitment to regularly caring for other entities in the world: his fish tank. The tank represents the enclosed security of habit and routine, protected from the world, however filthy and disordered it becomes. After Costas refuses to see him, he calls Alcoholics Anonymous, but minor issues are inflated to become barriers to attendance ('Is it a non-smoking meeting?'). When he finally does attend, one of his former collars is there, speaking like an insane temperance preacher ('Booze will simplify your life – you will disappear!')

NYPD Blue's patterning tended to thicken strong story arcs around the main characters towards the end of the season. At the end of season two, Sipowicz has a bachelor party set up the way Benedetto or Buntz might have liked it, and we get to witness the resentment towards those like Sipowicz, who is trying to better himself, or at least deprive his demons of fuel, by avoiding pleasures such as alcohol that others take for granted. At the wedding ceremony, we have an explicitly ironic fairy tale ending: Costas's eyes alive and twinkling and a dissolve towards the twin towers of the World Trade Center and Manhattan at night: the city is healed in this act, a picture of unity and peace.

Part of the depth of the range of characters whom we only see briefly was down to Milch's research – in itself I suspect a means of putting off the writing until the very last moment, when he had to commit words to paper. Writing the final draft fixes the past, and only editing in post-production, which Milch ended up doing on nearly every episode, allowed him to adjust in what was the final 'rewrite'. According to casting director Junie Lowry-Johnson,

> David Milch has a wealth of background information on any character on any size part whatsoever ... the day players and the guest stars weren't used to having as much information as he could give ... that enriched our show greatly ... we were listening to every detail David Milch said, because he was creating that world, populating that world.[72]

Sipowicz does not stand out in that sense, as Buntz or Benedetto do, as a kind of anomaly in a world otherwise populated by thinner, flatter characters; but he is given more time and focus.

Everything we know about Sipowicz comes from his actions, talk and the way others respond to him. In the Greek party sequence nothing we have assumed about him is challenged or put in question: part of its pleasure is the way it draws on new material to confirm the aspect of Sipowicz that we recognise and acknowledge as fundamentally 'him'. The newness of the material – the various events associated with the wedding – is the part we delight in because it has discovered a fresh way to re-present to us Andy as Andy, and assert the continuity of an entity whom we have taken as an ordinary human. However, that familiar aspect of Sipowicz is by no means stable or fixed: to make that claim would be to miss the double way in which the same thing becomes different as it occupies, and moves through, historical time, the context that gives rise to it. A character in a long-running show accrues his or her own past as an identity that casts shadows forward as a framing of current and future behaviour. Such television characters are able to convey this doubleness, this embodiment of pastness that shadows ('gum-shoeing closer behind, with the constable-hand that clutches')[73] the present, which is, too, an everyday feature of any human life. But unlike most of us (the lucky ones), such characters are fated to return again and again in roles that are constrained by the requirements of storytelling plausibility and leavened by the desire for change and difference. Characters offer a continuity that inserts a fictional entity into the history and flux of the immediate present, but because that experience is patterned with the authority of intent, they too are features of an artwork. Sipowicz is perhaps one of the first, extended versions of this kind of character on television, and the modernist impulse at the heart of it is to internalise as part of his character that feature of repetition itself.

More than that, Milch treats such scenes *as characters* in conversation with other scenes. The notion of character, then, is extended across the entire plotting, ordering and patterning of each episode and season.[74] Which is to say, Milch's method, which for shorthand I am describing as 'modernist', is essentially *associational*: rather than relying on realist legibility or complexity, it instead brings into proximity human characters with their own *characterness*, their own patterns of repetition, history and potential futures. When station boss Lieutenant Fancy (James McDaniel) tells his adopted son Maceo (Alex Bess) that 'The future keeps telling us what the past was about. You make the past mean different things by the way you use the time that comes after', we can see Milch trying to operationalise Warren's view of past time as redeemable, a feat that Eliot attempts in *Four Quartets*. And since the show is regularly based around the interviewing of suspects, it stages precisely an interrogation about the past: its truth, its deception, the threat of a future either on death row or behind bars intensifying that sense of the future continually interpreting the past. Sometimes in confession there is forgiveness, and in yearning for forgiveness, the characters find confession.

But this realisation that the past is 'adjustable' – to put it in crudely instrumental terms – has to contend with the expense of energy required to tamp down the past's incessant chatter. We can't all share the quiet cottage settings that Warren and Eliot enjoyed for their poetic composition. Sipowicz's settled then upset stomach is a feature of his self-conflict that he shares with other major characters in Milch's work, most notably Al Swearengen (who develops life-threatening kidney stones) and Ace Bernstein. It is a tendency to contend with oneself in a ferocious, pitiless manner. It is not the Greek cooking that disagrees with Sipowicz but his own body's inclination to take any opportunity to turn against itself. In an interview with Charlie Rose in 1995, Milch expounds on the nature of Sipowicz's internal 'Committee' and its inflection in his voice:

> Closer to the bottom lines of Sipowicz's nature he's drawn much more on my father who was the same type of complicated personality in that he was enormously driven and in some ways very emotionally isolated and at the same time enormously generous. And at the depths of whatever behaviour he was engaged in you were always pulling for him, you could feel a soul reaching out and I think that might be at the heart of why people like Sipowicz ... Addicts sometimes talk about 'The Committee' – there are all these voices that are going on in your head saying, you're a bum or you're no good or you're this or you're that. And what you want, and a lot of times I think why people take drugs, is to just quiet The Committee down a little bit so your own voice can be heard. And I think what you see in Sipowicz is a man whose got a very active Committee, whose own voice when he's able to use it, is very kind and gentle. But he's got a lot of other people speaking through the same mike.[75]

This group of internal and seemingly eternal punitive energies generated by what Freudians might call the superego, the ones that constantly criticise, nitpick and discover blemishes and defects across one's entire range of thinking, physicality and behaviour, are what one episode title of *Deadwood* describes in a triple entendre (including sexual desire and the self-propulsive forces that need violence to close meaning) as 'A Constant Throb'. Like Sipowicz's toothache, there's no losing it, even when acknowledged, understood and therapeutically treated: it is a feature of one's self, not an alien force.

Sipowicz and Russell

The appeal of *NYPD Blue* lies its novelty as a revivification of a genre and a form within the industry, as well as its appetite for popular trends in crime and manifestations of authority. Fallibility and the pathologisation of modern privateness, a desire to turn the inside out and remove the stoic insistence on the integrity of boundaries between public and private, find their perfect stage in the police interview room, where the goal is to make the private public through writing out a confession on the yellow legal pad. But this is also what happens to Sipowicz and the other characters in the show. The close-knit, *Pequod*-like community that Milch has carefully established helps this, in which gestures and stomach upsets are noticed by those whose profession is precisely to notice details, especially of behaviour, as indexes of motive and interior intent. The inner narrating voices that one finds in Henry James and other novelists is not available in the same way to those writing for film or television, except awkwardly (although it can be done with skill as in *Alfie* [dir. Gilbert, 1965]). Milch provides access to interiority in a way that was inherited from his training at the Iowa Writers' Workshop, a model of writing in which access to interior meaning is offered via the vitality (or lack of it) in the detail of what characters say and do. As noted in Chapter 1, in Mark McGurl's account of the Iowa model he describes it as 'third person limited narration', the 'show not tell' school of creative writing teaching:

> Here a disembodied narrator is understood to hover above the focalizing character in a dimension whose impersonal separation from the space-time represented in the novel is built into its grammatical structure ... [It therefore stages] a *limitation* of knowledge – a substantial eclipse of the omniscience whose display, by logical implication, is always an option for the godlike author.[76]

This spectral effect of grammar, exemplified in the work of Flannery O'Connor, reinforces our sense of the limitations of the point of view of the characters. Like the mechanical observing camera, it appears neutral while also embodying selectivity so that we quickly learn to read patterns in its selection as providing or withholding moments of privileged access.[77] Hence what is *designed* is also effaced by what McGurl calls 'the disciplining of the egoistic authorial self with the whip of impersonal narrative form'.[78] Now, there are serious problems in translating ideas of narrative form from print to audio-visual forms. Cameras and microphones are instruments of selection long before we reach the editing process, and we cannot efface the *choice* of that selection. As V. F. Perkins is fond of reminding us, 'How is What': how the camera shows an object simultaneously reveals a viewpoint on it. And part of the selection comes in the performances themselves, the choices that actors make, that directors (and writers like Milch) guide in rehearsal and on set.

All these fundamentals return us to the claim of modernism that I made earlier. In a figure such as Sipowicz, and the satellite characters who surround him, *privacy*, especially the privacy of the self and its 'spinning against the way it drives', is made public; indeed, it is a central theme of the police procedural genre that a major part of the job is the detection and revelation of deception and concealment. The connection with the teaching model at Iowa is further deepened when we consider the ensemble workplace dramas that dominated US television during the 1990s, because these dramas consistently bind their protagonists and their performance at work to the scrutiny and evaluation of small groups. As McGurl points out, 'O'Connor was only an unusually extreme execution of the writing program aesthetic that understood the writer's process, on the Joycean model, as a disciplining of the individual authorial voice.'[79] This disciplining in the setting of a fictional police squad meant situating selective choices among others. In joining and writing for the television industry Milch was able to stay loyal to the techniques of authorial effacement, but was hostage to a technology that demanded emphasis. The solution was to dilute selection among a range of characters: but it was Sipowicz above all that held the gravitational pull of the series, and this in itself points to a great tear in Milch's obedience to authorial and egoistic effacement and its strong, almost overwhelming temptation to express itself.

Sipowicz's saving grace is not that he changes but that he is situated in a small, self-help group of cops: Simone in particular is a far more sensitive figure than Kelly, and constitutes part of a support network that is always being reached out to: 'in my office', 'talk to you a minute?' – the places and spaces of therapeutic intervention are never totally private (as in the rec room scene above), but their ad hoc nature raises the risk of revelation and hence their moment. *Understanding Fiction* includes the assertion that '[f]ormal considerations spring from deep personal urgencies':[80] whatever else that might mean, in *NYPD Blue* it involves respite from the forward momentum of plot strands in a more intimate space of reflection. This move corresponds somewhat with the description of Henry James's 'dialectics of personality', described in *American Literature: The Makers and the Making* as 'to do with the slow establishment of the self *as* a self, and then the effort to transcend the self in a nourishing communion with others'.[81] And yet, even with the forward-driving cases that they break each week, issues of deception and self-deception are foregrounded and socialised routinely. The stakes are high: as many of Sipowicz and Simone's clients are informed in the room, it's either the lethal injection or else they can be helped. Most of *NYPD Blue*'s vast range of crimes comes down to the interrogation room, with a variety of characters struggling to come to terms with their own attempts to lie either to the cops or to themselves. This is the lesson that the show repeats again and again: the detective work in the room involves watching how the suspects perform when faced with these mortal stakes, the impasses they introduce for themselves, and the melodramatic payoff when confession is made. Milch correctly judged that these interrogation scenes would not only display accurate police technique but had at their core a dramatic battle of wills for dominance in a setting stripped of distraction.

What is the dramatic and cultural achievement of this repeated form in the show? It is, at least in part, to instil in the viewer who wishes to make sense of events in the world the virtues of collaboration, of 'talking it out'. Bill Clark was routinely befriended by the often evil and dangerous suspects he drew confessions from, such was their relief at unburdening themselves. Unlike the restless camera that infected the show's titles even into its final season, the lesson of the interrogation room is to settle, be still and translate restlessness to reflection. It also tutors the audience to be patient: as Milch puts it in one of his commentaries on the series: 'By making the audience patient you help them to be good writers themselves. A lot of storytelling is just getting the story going in the viewer's mind. Then you get out of the way.' Simone and Sipowicz are in that sense avatars of writers *and* the audience. Milch, again talking about Simone, says: 'He's gaining access to her emotions, that's what a good detective does. That's also how a good writer works. You provide receptacles in the action for the viewer's original feelings and then you modify those feelings.'

Against this there is fancy. Not just Lieutenant Arthur Fancy, the black captain, named because Milch considered it 'fanciful' that almost every cop show had a black man in charge, as a way to deal with the diversity issue while casting an African-American actor in a role that typically offered less screen time than that of his white counterparts. I mean rather the fancy of hope in romance that we see in the developing relationship between Simone and Detective Diane Russell (Kim Delaney), Milch's first substantial female character, who is introduced in season two. Sipowicz, after his disastrous break-up with Costas after the wedding party, is now on the wagon, with a sponsor in Dan Breen (played by veteran actor Peter Boyle). But Breen is an ex-cop who has internalised the bureaucracy of Alcoholics Anonymous in a way that frustrates Sipowicz's desire to approach Costas. Breen too falls off the wagon and tells Sipowicz, 'It got bad I hid in the bottle'; Sipowicz replies, 'Regret for the past is a waste of spirit. That sound familiar?'[82] It is Russell who provides Sipowicz with a way to order his private life, and he draws on his experience in recovery as something he can teach her, cop-to-cop. He quickly intuits that she is an alcoholic and gets her into recovery. It is not clear whether Milch at the time had been regularly going to AA, although there are several talk show interviews in which he appears typically articulate, but also (for those who can see) drunk or high on something.[83] The theme of recovery and relapse haunts these seasons: in part it is because habit butts up against impulse.

When Sipowicz finally takes Costas out to dinner and describes his dedication to The Program (like the university-based writing programs, in fact a set of half-baked mystical rules that have the theological costume of religion without the burden of a particular institutional history or tradition to bow down to), she tells him she is 'Proud of your self-control'. Seconds later he blurts out, 'Why don't we get married?' His adolescent unreadiness and lack of control contrasts with the fierce and patient way he breaks down suspects into confession. However, their eventual making-up seems inevitable, and she finally agrees. This romance 'solved', Milch moves on to Russell and Simone. Costas gradually becomes invisible on screen after she becomes pregnant with their first child; in the meantime, Sipowicz is reconciled with his older son, Andy Jr, who now wants to join the police force after a stint in the military.

Sipowicz thus becomes a father twice – to the adult Andy Jr and in preparation for his new child. He tells the former: 'This is a good job for people like us. We don't have a lot of education but we can read and write. And we're honest. Don't ever embarrass this job.' The lesson the father gives is about attention to 'people, places, the things they do, the times they do them'. He recounts the moment he nearly killed a man who was working at a toy factory, whom he saw at night carrying a machine gun – a toy one. It was patience and control and the intensity of instinctual notice that saved the innocent man. But control over impulse is a responsibility of the writer too. When Costas gives birth to their son, there is a brief moment of crisis when she haemorrhages; Sipowicz and Andy Jr wait anxiously outside the delivery room, but we are treated to the ultimate spectacle of Sipowicz cradling his new son and telling him he loves him. But unlike the wedding that provided the final destination of the previous season, in the next episode we discover that Andy Jr has been shot dead in a bar. Milch kills off Andy Jr – and Sipowicz immediately falls off the wagon. The dark truth of this callous move is the fantasy that the compensation for such a tragedy is that we, as addicts, get a socially acceptable excuse to restore the comfort of our habit.[84]

It is a cruel betrayal of the intimacy established by the three characters before the birth. Sipowicz is thus sent back on the cycle again, but this time he reaches out to Simone: 'You gotta help me Bobby, I want these guys dead.' Of course, he blames himself as a bad father and teacher, for feeling too proud about his new son, his new family, his luck. We see how the death threatens to tear apart the fabric of the world; when Sipowicz visits Andy Jr's mother, his ex-wife, her grief is unbearable, and he barely wants to hold her, refusing intimacy rather than inviting her to express the vengeance he believes he deserves. Russell offers to protect him from his inevitable wish not just for revenge against the killers, but to cash out the enormity of the tragedy in the refuge wherein his deepest self believes it belongs. He rushes through the rain, the drops clinging to his face and coat as if he is melting. He reaches the bar and pulls out a pack of red Marlboros: 'Whiskey, line them up.' He disappears for days, and is thrown out of their home by Sylvia; in this abusive state Franz empties out the character into a mere type, emphasising the hollowness of the downfall. It is Fancy who pulls him out of his narcissism with an echo of Sipowicz's advice to his son: 'You're embarrassing the job.' In the meantime, Simone kills both of Andy Jr's killers in a confected act of self-defence. The show's gradual concrescence is achieved by our absorption of such moments: as Charles Affron puts it, '[e]motion filled moments are found in everyday events, each one a climax. Their accumulation is the fiction of a life not necessarily a plot we enjoy for its complications. Time itself is emotion-laden...'[85]

Simone has his own life beyond being the protector of a damaged soul like Sipowicz. But of course, it transpires that his life with Russell (they move into his apartment together somewhat quickly) is also one that requires dealing with damaged goods. As Milch puts it,

> In Simone's case, a cop like that may be shut down emotionally for years and years and years. Particularly if he lost the woman he loved. But if he sees a wounded bird he's gonna take care of her. Even if he's not functioning yet emotionally. His training teaches him to take care. So, now I had no articulate sense of that, but I kind of knew that whoever he was drawn to was gonna be a drunk. Again, I had no understanding at that time of why she was drinking ... although I came to find out what her emotional background was.[86]

Russell's drinking causes her work problems – she meets a rape victim in hospital who can tell she is drunk, she misses a firearm on a pat down, so the habit has mortal consequences for her colleagues too. Again, we hear a familiar Milchean observation in relation to this moment: 'This is the hand you got dealt. You don't admit that all kinds of strangers wind up in the game.' In the third episode of season four, Simone and Russell have dinner. Simone's monologue reflects back to the audience how we feel about these characters:

> You think our being happy is like some kind of trick you bring off – being so smart and pretty and all the lights going in bed? What do you think? If we get married, I'm gonna see behind the curtain. [Diane: 'Maybe.'] Well, seeing behind the curtain's when I fell in love. I like the lights, you know I like smart and pretty. But it was the way you were with your mother and your brother. It's the way you've been with me, you know, helping me get past myself. That's why I want to make a life with you.

The third season has large doses of the ideology of Alcoholics Anonymous, the secret society of truths that maintains that one is born that way, that rehabilitates sin, and the perpetual watchfulness over the self's desire to harm itself. The organisation is a remarkably fearful practicalisation of the tension between competing desires that is formalised not in the stiffening of will or resolve, but by a diminished sense of group support. Again, this model has similarities both to the Iowa model of group writing (and ritual humiliation in public), the television writers' room, and Milch's own proclivity to keep his work somehow in view of others. The danger, as with Sipowicz, is that recovery does not remove the danger that made the character compelling in the first place, and the AA model provides this by branding its members Alcoholics for Life, in 'permanent recovery', as if it were a genetic mutation.

Nevertheless, their relationship flourishes, but it does so under the shadow of the show's dark house style. The sacrament of the ordinary events of the world is shaded by the show's need for the detectives to encounter ever more extreme and vicious crimes. It is as if Moby Dick was just one of an increasingly twisted pod of evil whales coming after *The Pequod*. Towards the end of episode two in season three, Simone and Russell enjoy sex in their apartment shortly after a conversation about a sadistic sex killer. Near their bed a large clock face has been prominently placed, as if to remind us of the limits within which such romantic involvement takes place – it is a matter of time before they will both have to face the next egregious atrocity.

Diane Russell is Milch's most complex female figure (after the show's experiments with a series of lesbian cops) who absorbs into herself the family disruption that Sipowicz tries to hold at bay. When Russell's mother shoots her husband, Russell attacks herself for missing the clues of beer bottles under the bed. (Her mother: 'He said he was gonna beat my half-brain out of my head.') Sipowicz walks outside with her, but like the scene in *Billy Budd*, we are not allowed to hear their conversation. By the next episode it seems that normality has returned, with Simone and Russell dressing together for work in the morning; and it ends with them in bed after showering but, for once, not having sex. 'I'm trying so hard to believe people don't have to be trapped by who they are or how they've lived. You don't think I'm trapped do you?', asks Russell.

The recognition of patterns of coupling in the station family is acknowledged by perhaps the best shot in the entire series, a tableau that offers us an opportunity to grade reactions. Detective Martínez (Nicholas Turturro) and Detective Adrienne Lesniak (Justine Miceli) finally couple off and as they walk down the stairs towards the exit we get a group shot of Simone, Russell, Sipowicz and Medavoy looking down at the newly formed couple. Their looks calibrate our knowledge of their experience of the turbulent climate of relationships within the Job. They say nothing, but the different wisdom of each seems deepened by their silence: Simone is patient, observant, bright and cool, slipping a stick of gum in his mouth; Sipowicz has seen it all before, but is curious that life repeats; Medavoy is meditative, tapping his hand on the balustrade, as if envious; Russell sticks her tongue in her cheek and looks to Simone – what is in store? (In fact, we never find out as Lesniak does not appear in the show again; she simply vanishes from the next season, as if one more repetition was too much for even this show to bear.)

Russell's character takes a turn when the stability of the crew at the fifteenth precinct is contrasted with her actual family: her father and mother at the limits of a disintegrating marriage, largely because of his drinking as a way of avoiding his wife's irritation towards him. This allows us to deepen our understanding of the source of Russell's unsettledness and need for alcohol. But she also repeats the pattern established by Sipowicz in earlier seasons whereby personal trauma is folded into a question of will. Simone discovers Russell drinking beer in a bar in the next episode, and this in turn creates conflict with Russell's AA sponsor, Sipowicz. As the latter morosely tells Simone, 'There's no helping anybody.' Like his racism and alcoholism, such traits are resources available to the writer to be brought into prominence, a kind of economy of flaws always trading beneath the surface.

When we see Russell visit her psychiatrist (Lindsay Crouse), she mirrors Sipowicz's self-loathing: 'Maybe I don't want to marry and have kids, maybe I'm not good enough for that kind of life'; shortly afterwards Simone and Russell break up. But it was at this point in the writing that Milch, in figuring out the reason behind Russell's drinking, introduced the story that her father had abused her when she was a child. This is the storyline revealed in episode twelve of the fourth season, when Russell goes missing and eventually turns up in Simone's apartment. There she confesses to Simone that her father molested her:

> I had to keep a secret. Daddy's pretty pet. I don't wanna be this way, I can't stand if I'm gonna be like this ... I think something happened ... I didn't want to yell so I must have flirted. I was only twelve. I just woke up and he was finished.

Unlike Milch, there is no sense that Russell has forgotten these events. Working undercover to get close to a dangerous gangster has put her next to both booze and the role of being a whore to a powerful man. As she tells Sipowicz:

> *Russell*: If I could drink then I'd be with Bobby. The job knew what I was ... I wanna drink! ... when I could drink I could work good and not feel like such a whore.
> *Sipowicz*: Don't talk like that.
> *Russell*: You feel how you feel Andy. Sending me back undercover, shaking it up for Liery [the gangster they are setting up] ... it's like the job knew what I was. Bobby, the squad, I was kidding myself with all that.
> *Sipowicz*: You know what you're sayin's not right.
> *Russell*: I wanna drink. [She covers her face with her hand.]
> *Sipowicz*: You add hiding to everything else.
> *Russell*: Hiding's got a lot of places.

Russell's comment that the 'job knew' mirrors Milch's frequent remark about Conrad's *Heart of Darkness*: sooner or later the jungle will find out what you're doing there. After her confession, the following episode begins with Simone and Russell at their morning ritual of getting ready together to go to work. The week between episodes – on network broadcast television – has given us the time to absorb the urgency and impact of Russell's trauma.

The season then makes its boldest move, in a sequence inspired by Milch's knowledge of the writer Hubert Selby's life. Selby, who wrote *Last Exit to Brooklyn*, was beaten and abused by his father as a child (according to Milch he attempted to boil Selby alive on occasion). He suffered from tuberculosis and was hospitalised for a considerable period of time; he was also an alcoholic like his father, and once married he beat his wife, who eventually left him with their only child for fear she would be murdered. After he managed to get sober his father would visit him in dreams. Eventually, he called his father by phone; they had not been in contact for years and it turned out his father was dying. Why, Selby asked his AA sponsor, did his father keep returning to him in dreams? Milch argues that he needed to be the son who showed his father the cruelty a human being is capable of; in his dream his father would say, 'I'm sober now, but I can't stay sober unless you do.' It was Selby's belief that human motivation fell into only two camps: fear or faith. Given the centrality of the father–son dynamic, this parable had enormous resonance for Milch. In the episode following Russell's confession we have an astonishing opening sequence in which father and son meet in a dream.

Sipowicz walks into a busy diner somewhere in the city, bathed in early morning light. He sidles up to the counter and as he does so he notices Andy Jr sitting at the counter drinking coffee. Since the diner is full he asks the person sitting next to Andy (played by Jim Beaver, later to play Ellsworth in *Deadwood*) to swap seats. They talk. 'I'm dead', says Andy Jr, 'but I'm doing alright.' Typically oversensitive to criticism, Sipowicz is offended by Andy Jr's suggestion that they didn't see much of each other when alive. But Andy Jr clarifies: he just meant he wanted to see more of Theo (Sylvia and Andy's new child) and the whole family. Sipowicz is relieved: 'The little guy, he's a real pisser, and in forty ways he reminds me of you. I never say that to Sylvia cause she would be upset.' Then a beat: 'Did I just ruin something now with my nature?' Then Andy Jr has to leave the diner; Sipowicz turns to the man played by Jim Beaver: 'My son.' 'A good looking boy.' Sipowicz goes on: 'I did something here, I pulled him.' Man: 'That it for him here, or is he coming back?' Sipowicz is suddenly distraught and we hear the sound of a phone ringing; 'I can't talk no more', he says and wakes up from the dream in order to answer the phone.

Apart from Jane Cannary's recounting of her dream in the third season of *Deadwood* (which is a masterpiece of writing), and the strange events that are *dreamlike* but never really dreams in *John From Cincinnati*, this is the only time in Milch's work when we have a dream sequence at all, the only time he has figured the unconscious in dramatic space. Somewhere between the remembrance of his own abuse and its connection to the racetrack and his father, Milch felt the need to insert this strange moment.

It is a moment that is directly religious, explicitly Christian in its values and motivation. It is probably the turning point in Milch's career, at least as it appears on screen, between a relatively secular before and a strongly devotional after – between fear and faith. Later in the episode, Sipowicz walks into a bar – it is one of those bars where time is uncertain (it could be middle of the day, early morning, or late at night, the ambience is the same – an alcoholics' bar). Once again, he sees the man (Jim Beaver) who enigmatically tells him, 'Shoulda talked across me' (a reference to when they swapped seats in the diner earlier), and we see Andy Jr sitting at a table. When Sipowicz says he has Sylvia and Theo around to say hello, Andy Jr says, 'Think him seeing me murdered is going to make a happy memory?' Sipowicz then realises that this is the bar Andy was killed in; he notices two men at a nearby table, one lit by a spotlight: the murderers. After hitting them both he turns back and Andy lies still, blood pouring from his head, murdered:

> *Sipowicz*: What did I do, what did I do? [walks over to the man played by Jim Beaver] What's your problem?
> *Man*: I gave you my seat at the diner.
> *Sipowicz*: We're going to be lifetime companions?
> *Andy Jr.* [off screen, voice over]: That's Jesus Christ, Dad. Congratulations pissing off Jesus Christ.
> *Sipowicz*: That's your boss, he's travelling with you?
> *Christ*: Dead as when he started.
> *Sipowicz*: What I do?
> *Christ*: What did I tell you?
> *Sipowicz*: I don't recall.
> *Christ*: Talk through me. Talk through me.
> *Sipowicz*: Please give me another chance.
> *Christ*: What did you just have?
> *Sipowicz*: I loved him as bad as I am.

That final line could have been said by either Milch or his father, just as much as it sits well with Sipowicz and most of Milch's other characters. They had feelings at least: compare this to the fate of John Marcher in Henry James's masterpiece 'The Beast in the Jungle', whose final discovery is that he had missed his own life, missed the very feelings that were available to anyone.

By season five, Milch was turning the screw on the child abuse storylines with probably the most disturbing episodes of the entire show. Entitled 'Lost Israel', the story is split into two consecutive episodes that effectively recount Milch's own story of being abused at camp. A child is found murdered and his father blames a mute, homeless man named Israel; however, Israel hangs himself and it transpires that he was framed by the child's father, who was in fact sexually abusing his son. During his confession, the father, Steve Egan (Brian Markinson), admits he was abused at camp by 'Uncle Gil'. He continues:

> *Egan*: You live with what you live with, I mean those were the cards I was dealt ... I am not so presumptuous or egotistical to pretend I can communicate with God. What I do know is what's necessary for life not to become a grotesque insanity and to protect a child you love. I know the burden of what has to be done. Because previously you can't forgive yourself, and you've beaten that in him, you can't forgive your own erection lying next to your councilor and you know you must be foul and so you beat yourself and your boy. I don't presume to communicate with God. But can you believe in any God who didn't want his child protected when he sees him crying at night and wetting himself? And some monster making him lie and hide and be so sad and afraid – how wouldn't God want him taken away? Kill me please, please. Shoot me in the head.
>
> *Simone*: I can't.
>
> *Egan*: Help me confess. Hurry get the pencil and paper.

After the confession scene Simone admits in a kind of rage to the squad room how much he despises Egan's rationalising of his evil – that God wanted him to kill his son so that he would stop abusing him: 'There is no forgiveness for that.' Sipowicz manages to add something comic, again in a ghastly way: 'He asked you to shoot him? He was asking the wrong guy.' What is even more striking about the scene is that Egan's wife, who comes into the squad room moments later, is understandably guilt-ridden and distraught ('I must have collaborated!') Sipowicz comforts her with some conventional police wisdom: 'Sometimes people who do something horrible know how bad it is and they hide it very good.' But then he picks up a Bible and begins to read from Psalm 119 (specifically verse 88): 'Quicken me after thy loving kindness; so that I shall keep the testimony of thy mouth.' As Milch says on the commentary to the episode in which Russell reveals that she was abused:

> We did a really good [story] – I guess it was the fifth season – a father actually murdered his son, because his son was about to tell, and he framed this deaf-mute – oh, it was horrible, and that was when I realised I'd been sexually abused, you know, a long time ago. I had just made myself forget about it ... We all live with such levels of denial. We don't wanna get well, we get comfortable with our illness.

By now Milch's conversion to a religious mode of understanding his characters was on display for all to see, and he had also reached a point, by December 1997, of remembering his own history and its convoluted connection to his father and the racetrack. Even before this point in the show, the vast majority of stories were about inter-family violence, alongside the usual street and drug-related killings. Events following this take on a regular pattern of tragedy and redemption: Russell becomes pregnant but loses her baby; Sipowicz discovers that he has prostate cancer but is given Viagra after his surgery which allows him to enjoy a second honeymoon with Sylvia; and in the final episode Simone and Russell decide to marry.

Behind the scenes the show was unravelling, despite its continuing popularity. For Franz, Milch's dialogue was becoming more difficult; its convoluted locutions began to get in the way of performance:

> It was a challenge that became more and more insurmountable as we went on ... usually when you speak you have an A-B-C connecting dots, one word will remind you of the next ... and the next ... when he would write in complete chaos and there was no connecting link sometimes ... and you would just have to phonetically memorise this thing, it was a challenge ... to decipher it ... We didn't always have scripts; we'd show up in the morning we'd have nothing ... David would show up, he'd sit on the floor; he would have somebody by him who would write down his thoughts. It was on the spot. We would do episodes like that ... Everybody backed off David. David would show up on the set, you'd wait for him, even though there was a director to see what he was going to write or how to direct it. He would sort of direct and the directors would work and direct with him ... and then David would leave and go edit the day before's work ... then he'd go write ... then he'd show up later on to see how you were doing the scene ... you could not ask more from a human being for hands-on involvement that we got from David Milch. Everything he did was about that show, that was his life.[87]

However, Jimmy Smits could no longer cope with Milch's process and negotiated to leave in the sixth season. His character suffers from – what else? – a heart condition that turns out to need a transplant, which ultimately fails. The episode, 'Hearts and Souls', won Milch another Humanitas prize, but for me it is so sodden with unearned sentimentality, given that the reasons for Smits's departure were well known, that it has little value compared to the achievement of the previous seasons. The rest of *NYPD Blue* continued on a treadmill, but Milch never again found the spark that made seasons two to five so electrifying.

In one sense, Milch had run out of character. This doubleness, unruliness, the edges not meeting in unity is an important recurrent theme in Milch's handling of character. Few other artists have so consistently and with such devastating attention to the webs and currents of manifold human deception (especially self-deception) been able to track so precisely the circumlocutions of human worthlessness, misdirected desire and the destructive patterns and habits that drive and confine people. This is his version of 'realism', its aim being to hear in the grubby, repellent behaviour of degenerates what Stanley Kunitz calls 'the deep rhythms that connect us with the stars and tides'.[88] In watching his characters we are faced with human beings in a dark search for what might transcend their habit of self-loathing as an autochthonous growth. But after season five it was hard to find much that could be any darker than it already was. This is why the social and historical, while providing the vitality of setting, tend to take second place in his work. As Jason Vest puts it:

> *NYPD Blue*'s isolated moments of social and institutional criticism offer excellent narrative texture to its ongoing story lines, but such moments are not frequent enough to pronounce the series a triumph of social realism. *NYPD Blue*'s fascination with Sipowicz, its willingness to explore the hostile aspects of his personality, and Franz's superlative acting instead transform the program into a triumph of deep, sophisticated, and detailed character development.[89]

A lot of academic work on *NYPD Blue* (and shows like it) takes at face value their sensitivity in the representation and exploration of 'social issues' such as racism and masculinity. When Sipowicz masters the Indian name Asha Mukhopadhyay (Janice P. Lal), an entire history is gathered up in what on the surface is his immediate 'racist' attitude. When a homicide victim is found dead in a BMW, Sipowicz is immediately drawn to half-baked racist notions as to the cause. Simone continually points out to him that Sipowicz's identity is as an immigrant, and the audience is encouraged to experience rather than share his limitations. It is important that the African-American Fancy and the French-Portuguese Simone are shown reacting to Sipowicz's casual racist musings – they model the response at the heart of the show's aspiration to reach a certain pitch of liberalism. Sipowicz's cultural provincialism is not a fixed but a fluid thing, born more of habit and inexperience than sheer malice or hatred. We see him change through a series of incremental adjustments prompted by personal experience rather than the instructions of 'sensitivity training' or regular vivid confrontations, although there are quite a few of those. Bochco heralds these as the achievement of the show – I believe this utterly underestimates and trivialises its artistic achievement, while managing to patronise an audience that made him a pretty good living.

That said, in the first season Sipowicz's racism is made into an issue; in episode ten Fancy takes him out to a restaurant and confronts him about it. But there was further controversy off-screen. In 1994 Milch gave a seminar for the Paulist Fathers, a New York originated Catholic group, shaped in part to interpret American history and culture through the writings of St Paul. The seminar was for up-and-coming writers, since the group funded the Humanitas prize for film and television writing that 'explores the human condition in a nuanced, meaningful way which, ultimately, inspires compassion, hope and understanding in the human family'. According to Milch, at one point he

> proposed that one reason so many television dramas portray black characters in positions of authority might be that these shows wanted to have the credentials of liberalism without having to portray in scope or depth minority characters with whom their writers were less comfortable or had less familiarity or whose fuller treatment they might think the audience might resist.[90]

This became an argument about whether Milch enjoyed writing a racist character. Milch went on to claim that it was difficult for black writers to write commercially successful work since 'When they wrote out of the complexities of their own experience in full scope and detail, the result might be powerful and compelling as art but not commercially successful.'[91] Milch was subsequently accused by the press of admitting he was a racist in a seminar, and although he was defended by Bochco, the head of the ABC network, Ted Harbert, attacked Milch on the phone after he had been called by Jesse Jackson to explain the event.[92] Hiring David Mills, one of the show's best staff writers, was one response, but the fact was that Sipowicz, the white underling, was hardly the show's most racist character. In the eleventh episode of the season, Borough Commander Haverill (James Handy) pressures Fancy to leave and it is Sipowicz who stands up for him. This suite of episodes in season one gradually brings Fancy much more into the foreground, including his home life and his desire to adopt the son he is fostering. Whatever the representation, I doubt we will get very far with making a judgement about Milch or his work based upon its putative racism.

Milch's 'inner relationship with history' is precisely hewed to this therapeutic sense of personal adjustment. The coercive nature of the reification of a therapeutic ethos in public and private institutions *demands* a defined set of emotional and interpersonal dynamics; this is an ethos that effectively prescribes healthy emotions. Such rules cannot exist in art, and Milch's characters would fail all their courses. Since the tracking of the currents and flows, the negotiations, confrontations, moods, the fluctuations in intensity of companionship and love, the whole dense web of conflict and community between human beings is the stuff of drama, any attempt to impose codes of conduct on such interpersonal matters is bound to create conflict. Sipowicz's kicking back against such codes is not a result of racism: it is because he is a human being with a private life and a heart that will not and should not be violated by a system looking to avoid lawsuits. Sipowicz is then in a sense the 'last man': Simone or Fancy do not resist in the same ways (they have no need to); thus I take it that the show pitches Sipowicz as a historical lens through which such matters can be explored. The organic connection between Sipowicz's difficulty in adjusting to the increasing conformity of the modern world and its attempts to use bureaucratic and workplace discipline to cloak real divisions and conflicts involves hypocrisies that a man such as Sipowicz can sense from three blocks away.

Sipowicz was understood by critics and academics as a fairly typical anti-hero, and praised by many in academia as an emblem of the crisis of masculinity, a notion that by the mid-1990s had acquired a pathological character in the West. A lot of academic work on television seems overly occupied not by shows or their characters per se, but rather the way that they embody or articulate aspects of the social world that such scholars deem egregious or laudable. The media quickly took up this tendency as well, so that films or television programmes are frequently assessed via their putative attitudes to X, Y or Z issue of the moment. It is taken for granted that masculinity is a pathology, and such criticism also flattens out the accumulation and momentum of a show's development, distilling formal patterns of narrative organisation as if they were the true 'formula', and failing to realise that such patterns and methods are merely the hangers – the scaffolding for the diverse and developing content of a show, which in Milch's case is always centred on character rather than plot or the fate of putative masculine or feminine attributes. That such matters are aspects of the design of the show, part of its creative intentionality, is hardly considered as an issue.

Conclusion: the weight of the past in the present

The pressure of the past is rarely revealed in a flashback (although as we have seen, it is in two of Sipowicz's dreams about his son): the show relentlessly progresses in real time, incorporating the distance of the network week, though occasionally eschewing that. The key to the show in its forward momentum is its attempt to make sense of the mystery of reasons for past actions that have to be made public in order to be intelligible to oneself and to others. The gruesome murders that tend to begin each episode are situated among scenes of ordinary life in the city. The sense of and wisdom about the nature of their own impulsive behaviour that the cops share is equally a product of their own observation of its mortal consequences on the street. Sipowicz shares with later characters such as Al Swearengen and Ace Bernstein the gift (which is also a curse) of *noticing*: his swivel-eyes pick out from the world details that make its deeper deceits legible at once. The world is cracked around Sipowicz, but his dogged sense of justice ultimately acts as a bulwark against the temptation of self-annihilation. When Costas tells him she was raped, they sit separately facing the camera, Sipowicz's face fixed in a look of blasted trauma. The weight of Sipowicz's love, his forgiveness (for what? for his own silent, perhaps prejudicial reaction – can we blame him for this?) is all the more powerful in this scene because he is not given to easy acceptance or rapid forgiveness. His sense of ageing, and its humiliations, initially conveyed by his need to wear spectacles and the prostate exam he undergoes, is expressed through the difficulty of admitting what are ordinary but persistent tacks pricked into the mind on a daily basis and, in his case, expressed physically: 'I have a pain for every bad thought I ever had'; 'What am I going to tell you about Sylvia? I'm peeing in two directions, I'm falling apart in all systems.' Television fiction, at its best at this time, gave the lie to the idea that 'talking out one's pain' was a healing technique. For some, perhaps. For others, it is worse than the condition that gives rise to it.

Another issue is the withholding of one's natural impulse to punish evil. When one of Sipowicz's witnesses, a French woman, is kidnapped and killed, 'all burned up, her teeth were all snapped out and her fingertips were cut off', we get a sense of the depth of evil that cops such as Sipowicz have to absorb regularly. As he tells the perpetrator, 'I'm gonna get a migraine tonight 'cos I didn't beat you.' His holding back might frustrate the audience but it bring us to an awareness of our own thirst for violence in order to close meaning. As much is hidden as is shown to us in the show. When Sipowicz tells Simone, off-handedly, that 'I gotta go take a piss', we cut to the latter looking at Russell. But this is a misdirect: we later discover that Sipowicz has been using toilet breaks in order to weep. He finally talks to the priest who is to marry him to Costas; the cleric says, 'You see things that are hard to deal with, have you lost your faith?' 'Yes.' 'Don't give up on God, he may not be through with you yet.' The show ultimately asks us to think of heroic virtues, 'loyalty, courage, tenacity and endurance', as continuous with ordinary life with its fears, anxieties and cowardice. This is magnified in the show by the repeated little moments of friendship, loyalty and camaraderie that put the frequent slights and resentments in the light they deserve. In *NYPD Blue* this means the situating of heroism, bravery and stoicism in the ordinary grubby world of the station house. And here we also get the vitality of the show's absorption of its time and place signalled afresh in each episode in the contextualising shots of the exterior cityscape, resolutely ordinary and in motion. The characters thus embody and express not only their history and the history of our involvement with them, but also a time, the present, that recedes as the show moves forward into its next moment of transmission.

One further issue that unravelled Milch was the decision to create a second cop show, this time focusing on the lives of uniformed police: this was *Brooklyn South*, which ran for just one season on CBS between 1997 and 1998; it was intended to be about the community of uniformed cops and their solidarity, as well as showing more of their home lives and the tensions there. The pilot begins with one of the most extended shoot-outs in television history, with dozens of police shot by a sniper. They started making it in the fifth year of doing *NYPD Blue*, and it just became too much: according to Bochco it was 'hubris' to think they could do two shows. Forty-four scripts a year was the pace, with Milch on the set the whole time as usual, with 'people trying to do their jobs – there's no scripts'.[93] Bochco effectively fired Milch from *Brooklyn South* so that he could at least keep up with *NYPD Blue*. But by this point, after the discovery of his memories of abuse, his turn to Christianity (in whatever version that he adopted) and his decision to become sober, Milch's investment in the show that he wrote for longest was coming to an end. Bochco described him as 'burnt out': Milch's view was that 'I lived a shadow life. Somehow I was able to find more constructive accommodations for all these impulses. There was my work. There aren't too many people that I write about that I can't imagine being.'[94]

One thing that Milch had not been, despite his immense work on *NYPD Blue*, was either sober for an extended period, or the sole boss of a show. That was to change, and so was his fiction over the next decade.

Notes

1 Milch lectures 2001, second lecture. In a less clear series of statements later in the series he says, 'I can testify to you that in the absence of some sense of humility in myself as a storyteller, which manifests itself as a rigorous commitment to identifying the signifying reality of my characters, presenting them as identifiable [in] an experiential world but also somehow enhanced, if I don't commit to that – and believe – although I don't have to believe it consciously – but feel in that process I am answering the deepest need of my spirit, I'm screwed. I don't know

what to write ... When I submit myself to the reality of my characters' respect for their situation, a desire to put them in an environment most congenial to their discovery of their deepest nature, I'm okay. And that sort of mantra that I've just given you is the final expression of the exercises we'll be completing this week.'

2 Hannah Arendt, 'What is Authority?', in *Between Past and Future* (New York: Penguin, 2006).

3 Gary Edgerton, *The Columbia History of American Television* (New York: Columbia University Press, 2009), p. 308.

4 Edgerton, *Columbia History*, p. 308.

5 John Thornton Caldwell, *Televisuality* (New Brunswick, NJ: Rutgers University Press, 1995), p. 63.

6 Caldwell, *Televisuality*, pp. 64–5.

7 Steven Bochco, Archive of American Television interview, www.youtube.com/redirect?v=G7vvWJNJEYs&event=video_description&q=http%3A%2F%2Fwww.emmytvlegends.org%2Finterviews%2Fpeople%2Fsteven-bochco&redir_token=VL5iXHOwPf1KmRvVCfygPAp70Yx8MTUyNDUxODc5OEAxNTIoND-MyMzk4 (accessed 23 April 2018).

8 David Bianculli, *The Platinum Age of Television* (New York: Doubleday, 2016), p. 427.

9 Steven Bochco, *Truth Is a Total Defense* (self-published, 2016), p. 86.

10 Bochco, *Truth Is a Total Defense*, pp. 86–7.

11 Bochco, *Truth Is a Total Defense*, p. 88.

12 Bochco, *Truth Is a Total Defense*, p. 88.

13 Bochco, *Truth Is a Total Defense*, ch. 13.

14 Steven Bochco, Archive of American Television interview, www.youtube.com/redirect?v=G7vvWJNJEYs&event=video_description&q=http%3A%2F%2Fwww.emmytvlegends.org%2Finterviews%2Fpeople%2Fsteven-bochco&redir_token=VL5iXHOwPf1KmRvVCfygPAp70Yx8MTUyNDUxODc5OEAxNTIoND-MyMzk4 (accessed 23 April 2018).

15 Ezra Pound, 'T. S. Eliot', in *Literary Essays* (New York: New Directions, 1968), p. 420.

16 According to a lunch conversation, Milch had experience at some unspecified point in the 1960s or 1970s of working very briefly in the television industry on a variety show. That job ended when he was asked for advice about whether a black performer could walk down some glittery stairs towards the audience alongside a white woman: his response was that it would be fine, as long as the man's penis was draped over her shoulder. Over breakfast in 2011 he told me of several examples when the Hollywood industry, so eager to demonstrate its liberal sensitivity, had exhibited racist ignorance in his presence.

17 See Charles Barr, '*Straw Dogs, A Clockwork Orange* and the Critics', *Screen* 13.2 (1972), for a compelling account of *Straw Dogs*' moral complexity.

18 Harry Frankfurt, *Necessity, Volition, and Love* (Cambridge: Cambridge University Press, 1999).

19 Clive James once predicted in his *Observer* column that because 'American production centres, having fed their shows to the networks, might go on picking up secondary earnings by flooding the world with stuff priced low because it had already made a profit in the home market, the droll sarcasm of the desk sergeant Phil Esterhaus ... in *Hill Street Blues* would be about as clever as their effort would ever get.' Reprinted in *Play All: A Bingewatcher's Notebook* (New Haven, CT: Yale University Press, 2016), p. 1. In that book James recants in the face of more recent US drama.

20 See Robert Pippin, *After the Beautiful: Hegel and the Philosophy of Pictorial*

Modernism (Chicago: University of Chicago Press, 2015); Michael Fried, *Why Photography Matters as Art as Never Before* (New Haven, CT: Yale University Press, 2008); and Walter Benn Michaels, *The Shape of the Signifier* (Princeton, NJ: Princeton University Press, 2006).

21 V. F. Perkins, *Film as Film: Understanding and Judging Movies* (London: Penguin, 1972), p. 158.

22 Blake Bailey, *A Tragic Honesty: The Life and Work of Richard Yates* (New York, Picador, 2003), p. 560.

23 See, for example, Leslie Fiedler, *What Was Literature? Class Culture and Mass Society* (New York: Simon and Schuster, 1982), which praises *Starsky and Hutch* and *Kojak* as well as *Hill Street Blues*.

24 Mark McGurl, *The Program Era: Postwar Fiction and the Rise of Creative Writing* (Cambridge, MA: Harvard University Press, 2009), pp. 153–5.

25 Stephen King, also an alcoholic and drug addict during his early career, recounts being asked by a doctor how much he drank: 'All of it.' Like many who use alcohol to medicate and subdue the powerful committee of critical internal voices, Milch suffered from 'last man standing' syndrome, whereby in the early hours of the morning he often found himself drinking alone amid passed-out revellers, still not able to quiet the incessant attacks or find solace in sleep.

26 A personal account of this can be found in chapters 14 and 15 of Bochco, *Truth Is a Total Defense*.

27 While preparing for this book I watched all seasons of both series, and *NYPD Blue*, in particular its second to fifth seasons, had a hypnotic, slightly deranged quality – in many ways because of the extraordinary performances of Smits, Delaney and Franz. The intensity is remarkable when time is compressed at that level and the apocalyptic sensibility is greatly amplified.

28 Stanley Cavell, *The World Viewed: Enlarged Edition* (Cambridge, MA: Harvard University Press, 1979), p. 32.

29 See interview with Dennis Franz, www.emmytvlegends.org/interviews/people/dennis-franz (accessed 16 December 2016).

30 There is actually an edited collection of essays entitled *What Would Sipowicz Do? Race, Rights and Redemption in NYPD Blue* (Dallas: BenBella Books, 2004). It offers little more than one would get by actually watching the show itself.

31 See, for example, the photograph in *True Blue* with Milch and Bill Clark (between pages 124 and 125) with the caption: 'David and Bill before David lost fifty pounds'; David Milch and Bill Clark, *True Blue: The Real Stories Behind NYPD Blue*, rev. edn (New York: Avon Books, 1997).

32 Delmore Schwartz, 'The Heavy Bear Who Goes with Me' (1938), in Cleanth Brooks, R. W. B. Lewis and Robert Penn Warren, *American Literature: The Makers and the Making, Book D, 1914 to the Present* (New York: St. Martin's Press, 1974), p. 2944.

33 Cavell, *The World Viewed*, p. 56.

34 Compare this with Mark's speech in the 'I hate all the openings, all the wholes' monologue in *The Groundlings*.

35 Brooks, Lewis and Warren, *American Literature: Book D*, p. 2480.

36 Brooks, Lewis and Warren, *American Literature: Book D*, p. 2454.

37 George Toles, 'Writing about Performance: The Film Critic as Actor', in Alex Clayton and Andrew Klevan (eds), *The Language and Style of Film Criticism* (London: Routledge, 2011), p. 95.

38 Joseph Conrad, *Heart of Darkness* (London: Penguin, 1978 [1899]), p. 8.

39 Toles, 'Writing about Performance', p. 95.

40 It underlines LaRue's cruelty in his satisfaction at the gore he must see; its

equivalent is Dennis Price's look after the final murder in Robert Hamer's *Kind Hearts and Coronets* (1949).

41 David Milch interviewed by David Thorburn at MIT, 2006, www.youtube.com/watch?v=MDTVIP8bvE8 (accessed 23 April 2018).

42 See interview with Franz, www.emmytvlegends.org/interviews/people/dennis-franz (accessed 16 December 2016).

43 Horace Newcomb and Robert S. Alley, *The Producer's Medium: Conversations with Creators of American TV* (Oxford: Oxford University Press, 1983).

44 Bochco, *Truth Is a Total Defense*, p. 116.

45 Bochco, *Truth Is a Total Defense*, p. 153.

46 Bochco, *Truth Is a Total Defense*, p. 154.

47 Interview with David Milch and Bill Clark on Charlie Rose (1995), www.youtube.com/watch?v=oYP1gSYZC3g (accessed 19 December 2016).

48 Clark has joked about the rather touching homosociality that *True Blue* exudes, quipping to an intern that 'that pic of us on the back cover looks like we're just off to a gay bar'.

49 Interview with David Milch and Bill Clark on Charlie Rose (1995), www.youtube.com/watch?v=oYP1gSYZC3g (accessed 19 December 2016).

50 Interview with David Milch and Bill Clark on Charlie Rose (1995), www.youtube.com/watch?v=oYP1gSYZC3g (accessed 19 December 2016).

51 Dennis Franz interview, Archive of American Television, www.emmytvlegends.org/interviews/people/dennis-franz (accessed 23 April 2018).

52 George Toles, 'Trying to Remember Clementine', in Christopher Grau (ed.), *Eternal Sunshine of the Spotless Mind* (London: Routledge, 2009), p. 139.

53 *The Financial Times*, 12 February 2012. Reposted at *Slate* online, www.slate.com/articles/life/ft/2012/02/luck_s_dustin_hoffman_discusses_his_transition_to_tv.html (accessed 19 December 2016).

54 Pamela Douglas, *Writing the TV Drama Series* (Los Angeles: Michael Wiese Productions, 2007), p. 29.

55 Jonathan Bignell has written an excellent account of this pilot and other aspects of the show: 'The Police Series', in John Gibbs and Douglas Pye (eds), *Close-Up 03* (London: Wallflower Press, 2009).

56 Clark and Milch, *True Blue*, p. 59.

57 See interview with David Milch and Bill Clark on Charlie Rose (1995), www.youtube.com/watch?v=oYP1gSYZC3g (accessed 19 December 2016). It strongly resembles the first season of *ER* in this respect: a conscious building of respect for the emergency services.

58 Clark and Milch, *True Blue*, p. 45.

59 Interview, 27 March 2008.

60 See the discussion of ruins that concludes Jason Jacobs, 'Issues of Judgment and Value in Television Studies', *International Journal of Cultural Studies* 4.4 (2001).

61 John Jones, *Dostoevsky* (Oxford: Clarendon Press, 1983), pp. 200–1.

62 In my book *Body Trauma TV: The New Hospital Dramas* (London: BFI, 2003) I describe the way in which the medical drama genre morphs according to its predictive capacity to anticipate trends emergent in society; *NYPD Blue* does something like this, but it is at its weakest when preaching American liberal values at its audience. This frustrates some critics who want to admire Milch's creative genius but are suspicious of his politics and religious talk.

63 See Clark and Milch, *True Blue*, pp. 87–92 for a full account, including medical details of the heart attack.

64 Clark and Milch, *True Blue*, p. 94. Milch has his revenge of sorts by showing, in season two, Kelly's primary reading material as Arthur Hailey. Later both

Caruso and Milch found themselves together again at their respective daughters' graduation at Yale.

65 Quoted in Andrew Klevan, 'Notes on Teaching Film Style', in John Gibbs and Douglas Pye (eds), *Style and Meaning: Studies in the Detailed Analysis of Film* (Manchester: Manchester University Press, 2005), p. 215.

66 David Milch interviewed by David Thorburn at MIT, 2006, www.youtube.com/watch?v=MDTVIP8bvE8 (accessed 23 April 2018).

67 Brian Boyd, *On the Origin of Stories* (Cambridge, MA: Belknap Press of Harvard University Press, 2009), p. 222.

68 For example, for Amie L. Thomasson, fictional characters are 'abstract creations relevantly similar to stories, marriages, innings and laws'; *British Journal of Aesthetics* 43.2 (2003).

69 Christopher Lasch was particularly prophetic in anticipating this in his writing; see in particular *The Minimal Self* (New York: W. W. Norton, 1984), and *Haven in a Heartless World: The Family Besieged* (New York: W. W. Norton, 1977).

70 Charles Rosen, *Romantic Poets, Critics, and Other Madmen* (Cambridge, MA: Harvard University Press, 1998), p. 155.

71 See Julia Kristeva, *Black Sun* (New York: Columbia University Press, 1989), for a good account of this kind of self-loathing.

72 *NYPD Blue* 2002, 'Cast Blotter', featurette Season 1 DVD.

73 Robert Penn Warren, 'Homage to Theodore Dreiser', in John Burt (ed.), *The Collected Poems of Robert Penn Warren* (Baton Rouge, LA: Louisiana State University Press, 1998), p. 295.

74 Thorburn interview with Milch, 2006.

75 Charlie Rose interview, https://www.youtube.com/watch?v=0YP1gSYZC3g (accessed 21 December 2016).

76 McGurl, *Program Era*, p. 142.

77 Point of view in movies and television is a vastly more complex issue, of course: for the best starting point, see George Wilson's *Narration in Light*, which is, alongside Perkins's *Film as Film* and Cavell's *The World Viewed*, one of the three essential works in film scholarship. George Wilson, *Narration in Light: Studies in Cinematic Point of View* (Baltimore, MD: Johns Hopkins University Press, 1986).

78 McGurl, *Program Era*, p. 143.

79 McGurl, *Program Era*, p. 144.

80 Cleanth Brooks and Robert Penn Warren (eds), *Understanding Fiction*, 3rd edn (New York: Pearson, 1979), p. x.

81 Cleanth Brooks, R. W. B. Lewis and Robert Penn Warren, *American Literature: The Makers and the Making, Book C, 1861 to 1914* (New York: St. Martin's Press, 1973), p. 1371.

82 It sounds familiar because it is a reference to Shakespeare's Sonnet 129.

83 Blake Bailey describes Milch as 'the most spontaneously articulate human being I have ever encountered'; *A Tragic Honesty*, p. x. A lot of the time, in the early stages of becoming drunk, one can be extremely articulate: Martin Amis gives a good account of his father's view on this in *Experience* (New York: Talk Miramax Books, 2001). See also Milch's account of how he would prepare to appear on talk shows in *Dinner for Five*, season 1, episode 4, www.youtube.com/watch?v=OFEHp9aNeqk (accessed 31 December 2016).

84 As with the killing of William Bullock in *Deadwood*, this is one of the most callous writing moves Milch has given us, comparable to Raymond Carver's ending to his excellent short story, 'A Small, Good Thing'.

85 Charles Affron, *Cinema and Sentiment* (Chicago: University of Chicago Press, 1982), p. 162.

86 *NYPD Blue*, Season 2 DVD, Special Features interview.
87 Dennis Franz interview, Archive of American Television, www.emmytvlegends.org/interviews/people/dennis-franz (accessed 23 April 2018).
88 Stanley Kunitz, 'Reflections', introduction to *The Collected Poems* (New York: W. W. Norton, 2000), n.p. The full sentence is: 'Poems would be easy if our heads weren't so full of the day's clatter. The task is to get through to the other side, where we can hear the deep rhythms that connect us with the stars and the tides.'
89 Jason P. Vest, *The Wire, Deadwood, Homicide, and NYPD Blue: Violence Is Power* (Santa Barbara, CA: Praeger, 2011), p. 71.
90 Clark and Milch, *True Blue*, pp. 169–70.
91 Clark and Milch, *True Blue*, p. 172.
92 Milch 'made it right' with Jackson, in ways that will be understood in both Hollywood and political circles.
93 Interview with Steve Bochco, https://interviews.televisionacademy.com/interviews/steven-bochco?clip=84122#interview-clips (accessed 30 May 2019).
94 Bernard Weinraub, 'The Demons That Have Driven *NYPD Blue*', *The New York Times*, 18 June 2000, www.nytimes.com/2000/06/18/arts/television-radio-the-demons-that-have-driven-nypd-blue.html (accessed 31 December 2016).

Vision 3

> I'm not a good witness about that stuff, about my own creative biography. The big thing for me was I was loaded when I was doing *NYPD Blue*, and I got sober. And I think that accounts for a lot of the changes.
>
> David Milch[1]

It is unlikely that David Milch's name would have become as prominent as it did in the 2000s on the strength of *NYPD Blue* alone. John Wells, a magnificent writer and producer who created *ER*, certainly did not enjoy the same critical approbation that *auteur*-like figures attract, and Denis Dutton's astute observation that human beings are particularly attracted to displays of high *individual* skill may go some way to explaining this. However, you need to have the opportunity not just to display that skill but for it to be acknowledged and recognised.[2] *Deadwood* (2003–06) did just that for Milch. How this happened is not a straightforward story, and those who have written about it largely misunderstand the show's origins.[3]

The fact is that some time – probably between 1998 and 1999 – before leaving *NYPD Blue* in 2000 Milch became totally sober, abandoning alcohol, heroin and gambling, and adopting in their place the role of teacher, leader and boss by setting up his own production company, Red Board Productions.[4] As co-creator of *NYPD Blue* his profit participation was 25 per cent, and his new contract with Paramount to create TV series and develop movie features was reportedly generous.[5] In his mid-fifties, Milch could look forward to forging his own ideas, away from the enthusiasms and demands of Bochco and the limitations of network television. The shift by HBO into signature *auteur* television, spurred on by *The Sopranos* (HBO/David Chase, 1999–2006) and *The Wire* (HBO/David Simon, 2002–08) meant they were open to listen to signature pitches, and Milch cut a deal with them and Paramount that would in fact get caught up in the cancellation of the key show that made his name as a television *auteur*: *Deadwood*.

As I made clear in this book's Introduction, I do not believe in the *auteur* theory (which is not one theory anyway) any more than Milch does: the conditions of commercial film and television making do not allow that kind (and there are many kinds) of criticism to hold much substance. However, the life of *this* writer is ineluctably bound up with the work he has produced. *Deadwood* made his name and has become synonymous with that period of television which produced 'high-quality' output, work of 'literary' merit (as if that were a guarantee of value). In this chapter I want to examine Milch's working practice, which is more or less his talking about his work as much as his doing it, and place that show and *John From Cincinnati* in the context of collective imaginative fiction making.

Milch has two primary aspects to his creative persona: there is the voice that writes and there is the voice that communicates to everyone else the meaning of the voice that writes.[6] Both are absolutely fundamental to any writer for screen, but for Milch they also form part of the doubled substrate, his creative self, driving against the way it spins. Any writer has a different voice when they write, and that voice is not the one we have when we get up, take a piss, drive to work. From his time at Yale, as a student, as a research assistant and a teacher, throughout his time working on *Hill Street Blues* and *NYPD Blue* and, critically, after becoming sober, Milch became familiar with that writing voice, the one he morphs into when he writes. And then there is the other voice, the salesman for his writer's voice, the one familiar to those who have interviewed him, attended talks and lectures by him, worked with him. That is the voice that makes palatable, sociable, the other one. Like a companion, it is the voice that helps his writing voice find its place in the world. What is unusual about Milch is that both voices exist in very close proximity and he is able to pivot between them fluently on a sixpence.

His first production for Paramount was a network series aired on CBS called *Big Apple* (2001). Big Apple is the nickname for New York, but its other meaning is clearly Christian: the Abrahamic creation myth in which eating the fruit of knowledge, after Satan's encouragement, causes the Fall of Man. The title itself is something that Bochco would never have endorsed, and the intimation of apocalypse (as Sontag reminds us, not 'apocalypse now' but 'from now on')[7] in this show, *Deadwood*, *John From Cincinnati* and *Luck* creates a group that tackle in various ways the possible future for mankind. Milch's 'theme' continues Thorburn's correct identification of a cycle of despair and moment of purification among its characters but is set to an eternal, historical beat. As Milch once quipped to Jimmy Breslin during an interview, we do things for many, often mixed and contradictory reasons. It is hard to pin down one thing, or cluster of things, that set Milch on a more visionary path, except to say that it happened around 1997 and continued at least until the production of *Luck* began in 2010.

One piece of evidence for his desire to return to a kind of evangelical teaching of writing 'as an act of faith' occurred while he was still working on *NYPD Blue* in 1997: he hired a space in Los Angeles, which effectively became a lecture theatre as Milch played clips from the season just past and talked about the writing process. These were filmed and provide the spectacle of a charismatic teacher offering a dense pedagogical act of exegesis that holds in front of us the multilayered associations of meaning in play, ever attentive to the moment-by-moment responses, allegiances and moods of its audience. He talks in a deep voice that seems to dominate the sparse room and the white rectangle of the screen behind him with a kind of good-mannered menace, as he tracks us through the scenes with the voices, forms and moods of the characters he has created.[8] Milch had won an Emmy twice in a row for the 1996–97 and 1997–98 seasons of *NYPD Blue* for Best Writing in Drama, so these weekly sessions offered a genuine sense of reaching out and giving back wisdom to the screenwriting community.

However, we also get a sense from this lecture series of Milch's approach not merely to teaching but directing as well. By 'directing' I mean talking to, guiding, coaching and handling the performers, a critical aspect of the directing job that is often neglected since it is less evident and rarely recorded, except in fragments of screen tests or biographies distant from the event. Milch was an unstoppable force in his access to and conversation with actors, unfolding and unpacking the lines they were given with background, back story and no doubt a number of literary allusions and parables.[9] The final seasons of *NYPD Blue* also emphasised the transfer of wisdom, by pairing Sipowicz with Danny Sorenson (Ricky Schroder), the latter from a very troubled background; Sipowicz sees something of Andy Jr in Sorenson and makes attempts to school him (we need to realise that by this point Sylvia Costas has been shot dead, with Sipowicz this time not seeking comfort in the bottle). Both *NYPD Blue* and other long-running, long-form dramas such as *ER* were reaching the point where the amount of disaster and emotional catastrophe piled on to their central characters was so intense and frequent that it pulled too hard against the highly wrought aspiration to naturalistic workplace realism that the shows had tried to establish in the first place.

Big Apple

Big Apple is important as it was Milch's first solo flight using his new production company, Red Board Productions, without the comfort of his insertion into a well-established show, or of co-creation with the weight, reputation and ability to parlay with network executives that Bochco offered in bringing Milch on board *NYPD Blue*. Bill Clark remained an important source of intelligence for a show that was one of the earliest to see information, or as we know it post-2010 'big data', as a critical aspect of new police technology, and one that was to transform the typically strained interpersonal relations between different law enforcement entities, in particular the FBI and the NYPD. As with *NYPD Blue*, the cops are distilled to a pair: one older and wiser, Detective Mike Mooney, played by Ed O'Neill (a contemporary and drinking friend of Milch), who was best known at that time for his role as Al Bundy in the sitcom *Married ... with Children*; and the younger, handsomer figure of Detective Vincent Trout (Jeffrey Pierce). In the pilot, aired in March 2001, we see the pair on a case involving the bloody murder of a woman, probably an escort, in a luxury Manhattan penthouse. It transpires that this killing is connected to a long-term, ongoing FBI investigation into both local New York organised crime (emblematised by Terry Maddock, played with impeccable nuance by Michael Madsen) and incoming waves of Eastern European and Russian organised crime (a theme that seemed to shadow over a decade's worth of crime fiction, including Cronenberg's *Eastern Promises* [2007], Guy Ritchie's *RocknRolla* [2008] and *True Detective* [second season, 2015]).[10] Maddock, however, is an FBI informant, reporting to Agent Jimmy Flynn, played by Titus Welliver. Flynn himself is not trusted by his own boss, Bureau Chief Will Preecher (David Strathairn), who brings in newcomer Agent Sarah Day (Kim Dickens) to 'audit' the unit's use of surveillance assets – the audio bugs and mini-cameras located across almost every inch of New York City, all linked to FBI laptops. Preecher, realising that the killing of the woman is connected to the wider investigation, decides to 'deputise' Mooney and Trout so that the investigations do not compromise one another.

That, in summary, is the pilot set-up, and there is not much to be said for developments in the episodes that follow, except that – in a mode we have come to expect from almost every US network drama since (including most video games that have narrative components) – the real kingpin criminal is none other than a rich politician with connections to powerful financial interests. The rapidity with which capitalism began to loathe itself in popular fiction after 1989 is the topic of another thesis of course, but Milch was to repeat this move at the end of *Deadwood* with the arrival of the sheer power of mining magnate George Hearst and his shareholders. Again, plot is not typically Milch's finest achievement unless it is in service to deepening and revealing character.

There is little to choose between this account of the pilot and an episode of *NYPD Blue*, except of course what is missing – long-established and loved characters such as Sipowicz, Simone and Russell. The show was aired by CBS in direct competition with NBC's *ER*, which was beginning to turn the corner from the excellence of its early seasons to more extreme and narcissistic plot gimmicks. Nevertheless, it had a strong cast: Strathairn, Dickens and Welliver are superb character actors, but each was a decade away from leading their own show. Madsen and O'Neill, both large and menacing men, work better either on the big screen or in comic roles where their threatening, slightly lumbering size can be fully realised for comic or violent ends.[11]

These minor quibbles aside, *Big Apple*'s pilot had considerable ambition: it begins with an aerial view from a helicopter approaching Manhattan that carries Preecher and Day. We see them flying over forests and meadows until, according to the script: 'NEW YORK CITY. Dominating the horizon, sparkling in the morning sun like a mile-high pile of diamonds.' Preecher comments, 'That was all forest once, too.' There is a sense of *The Great Gatsby*'s lyrical ending in this sequence, at least as it is written, that what has been built may fall and what was lost may come again. This is reiterated when, for no reason of plot, the helicopter experiences an emergency failure and drops out of the sky like a stone into the city:

> the WORLD TRADE CENTER TOWERS thrusting volcanically into view off port, its WINDOWS WHIZZING UPWARDS like some sickening slot machine [...] the world going SILENT but for an ethereal WIND as, dropping now like a rock – GLASS STEEL GRANITE FLASHING past...

In plot terms the sequence is meant to tell us that Sarah Day can keep her head in the face of imminent death, but of course it also points forward to the immanent sense of catastrophe – shortly to be realised – that American culture had been turning over and over in its cultural production – films, novels and, latterly, television – since the turn of the century.[12]

Milch effectively uses the technology of the FBI to monitor and surveil all things as a riposte to Kant's claim that there is no God's-eye view from a human perspective, and therefore that we cannot 'know things in themselves'. In the script he describes the interior of the FBI's offices as a kind of hellish laboratory of watching trivia (perhaps a reflection of his view of media audiences). The script puts it this way:

> INT. BUREAU MONITORING HALL – DAY. A sprawling 4,000-square-foot room, as ON THE CUT, the CAMERA PANS 200 identical cubicles occupied by Bureau tech-support staff, struggling to inventory the sea of data flooding in on audio and video monitors from court-appointed bugs and cameras positioned throughout the city ... interior and exterior glimpses of: A JACKSON HEIGHTS COLOMBIAN BODEGA, A BAYRIDGE USED CAR LOT, A GARMENT-DISTRICT OFFICE-SUITE, AN AIRPORT DEPARTURE GATE then – A video monitor showing THE NORTHEAST UNITED STATES from 200 miles up: you can actually see the curvature of the earth –

As an operator adjusts the coordinates on one monitor we go from the cosmic shape of the planet to the size of newsprint:

> THE CAMERA FEED ON THE VIDEO MONITOR starts ZOOMING DOWN toward earth, slowly at first – New York State, the HUDSON VALLEY, the BOROUGHS, MANHATTAN – then FASTER AND FASTER – DOWNTOWN, BROOME STREET, the FEDERAL PLAZA, a MAN at a bus-bench, the NEWSPAPER in his hands, and finally, a FREEZE-FRAME EXTREME CLOSE-UP of the sports-page HEADLINE "BILLS STAMPEDE JETS 21–7"

Olsen, the soon-to-retire veteran black FBI agent who is taking Day on a tour through the technology-laden office space, quips, '"The sky's the limit" ... as they say.' Just before this moment, as Preecher prepares to walk Day around the 'tech sector', Flynn says, 'That's like the guided tour from Einstein', to which Olsen replies, 'Or Virgil'. 'I just felt a reference go zooming over my head', responds Flynn, but of course he gets it: this is the hellish world in which everything can be *seen*, what it might really look like if we had a God's-eye view. Milch in interviews has mentioned several times his difficulty with technology, for example, using mobile phones (which he does not answer, despite owning them) or computers. Thematically, technology is not something his work handles well – it is a blind spot in his artistic metabolism such as we sometimes see in great artists (Hitchcock, for example, found it hard to handle courtroom scenes – see *I Confess*, *Rebecca* and the particularly excruciating inquest sequence in *Vertigo*).

The friction between the FBI and the NYPD is handled well (Mooney: 'You know what FBI stands for? – '"Famous But Incompetent"'), although it is conventional. There is not a shred here of Milch's famous handling of language in complex, hard-to-deliver locutions. In a stand-off argument with Flynn, Mooney makes the kind of claim we would expect to hear from Sipowicz:

> But I *don't* work for the government Flynn. I work for the *victim*. People without a voice because they're dead like that girl, or being framed like that poor Russian fuck, so if you're wondering if I'm fighting this clearance the answer is Hell Yeah, Baby, bring it on!

As is usual with Milch's work, the pilot script underwent many revisions before it was viable as a plan for production. Milch would 'write' scene fragments and sentence-length outlines of the final act, then work them over and over before they were shot. Because FBI agent Flynn knows what Maddock is doing as a result of secret, unauthorised surveillance, whatever Maddock says to him in person Flynn uses to calibrate the reliability of their relationship. Day's audit eventually reveals that the camera is not sanctioned by a warrant: in fact, in a gesture of truce, Flynn admits as much as he hands over his inventory to her. There are outlines to episodes, despite Milch's later claim (in his four-day session of public talks during the writers' strike in December 2007) that he does not do them – and their brevity and lack of texture suggest that he switched to daily monologues in the writers' room in order to set the tone for scenes, rather than rely on what is a fairly sterile format of an A4 page of scenes and beats split into three acts.

However, something else far more significant is added here that is new to Milch's dramatic inventory. Mooney's sister Lois (Brooke Smith) has motor neurone disease (specifically, ALS or Lou Gehrig's disease) and is near death. That Mooney was 'given' this additional emotional burden to deepen his character struck me at first as one of the clumsiest moves in all of Milch's writing. However, in an otherwise conventional show, it stands out as probably the best thing he had written up to this point. O'Neill and Smith are very good in their scenes together, particularly the moment in episode three when Mooney and Lois discuss the significance of having a feeding tube and of not having one. O'Neill has never put in a better performance on screen than at that moment, when he realises that Lois is saying she wants to die. His reaction is 'not to react' – he says nothing but uses his face to absorb the information, mask his response, and in using the mask, show his response. This deception has a reason, and in deception we can see the reason. He doesn't want his sister to see him fall apart in front of her, because of her own choice, one that must come from deep courage. To do so would be to make a terribly hard decision far more difficult to bear. The problem with having this aspect of Mooney's life shown to us in order to provide a reason for his isolation from the other cops is that it throws into relief the relative absence of any private lives among the rest of the characters. This was an omission that Milch was careful to avoid, once he had the luxury of doing so, in his next project.

Eventually the plot evolves so that Terry Maddock is put into a position where he has to wear a wire as an alternative to testifying against his gang member friend. Then the series was cancelled after episode eight of its scheduled thirteen in April 2001. Milch's ambitious first solo attempt was a failure, though not in terms of the themes he was feeling his way into. Two of these stand out strongly, and while they were arguably latent (though sometimes explicit) in the *Hill Street/NYPD Blue* period of his career, here they find a path outwards, almost in a return to the strange liturgical references that we hear in *The Groundlings*. These themes are leadership as a form of teaching (and vice versa) and the origins and holiness of communication. Milch clearly wants to teach us something about the ways in which we talk to one another, and he does this by allowing his characters their own means of revealing themselves and their deepest natures through language. This is something that has been almost totally ignored in writing about Milch during the successful part of his career during and after *Deadwood* in the 2000s – the centrality of religion and his religious belief to his drama.

Amy Hungerford, in her book *Postmodern Belief: American Literature and Religion since 1960*, tracks the ways in which major post-war US literary figures attempted to incorporate and insist on the existence of 'something deeper', a religious force that had no institutional or historical affiliation as such, but rather formed or was manifest in the metabolism, substrate, status or authority of the language they use itself. Among these are J. D. Salinger, Allen Ginsberg, Don DeLillo, Cormac McCarthy, Toni Morrison and Marilynne Robinson, who all attempt to locate some anchoring source or force around which meaning or meaninglessness can orbit in literature. For Philip Roth, the most secular of post-war novelists working at this artistic altitude, the force is clearly desire and the mummification and vivification of selves (narrational or authorial or both) that are generated in its practice and denial. For all of those artists, language, especially spoken language, is central to this search for authority, since it connects, as a signifying practice, contemporary civilisation to the earliest forms of human expressiveness. We can see here the impact of some of the radical shifts in early twentieth-century anthropology and archaeology on post-war writing, particularly in the face of apocalypse: McCarthy's *Blood Meridian*, for example, includes in one of its epigraphs a newspaper report of a '300,000-year-old fossil skull [that] ... shows evidence of having been scalped'.[13] For writers working in a nation whose ascendancy post-war had not delivered on the promissory note of modernism (in fact, alienation, anomie and narcissism were increasing in intensity, a topic that Christopher Lasch devoted much of his work to exploring), finding some external and eternal anchoring point was essential if meaning itself was not to vanish (or if it was, for this to have meaning in itself). This is why the sound of language, the noise of voice takes on enormous significance.

Hungerford uses the example of Jimmy Breslin, one of Milch's close friends and a Pulitzer prize-winning journalist, who remarked about his Catholic schooling:

> There are two things that you can learn only by rote ... grammar and religion ... you came out of school with the structure of an English sentence and the mystical structure, the manner in which a religion is held together ... Faith in the sentence and faith in God.[14]

Hungerford goes on to link this to the sound of the Catholic liturgy which, since most Catholics did not understand Latin, implied that

> [t]he "secret language" of the Latin Mass ... represents an interior secret, a secret held and protected by a group that does not know the secret but nevertheless believes in it. Like grammar and the "mystical structure" of the religion, Latin is something memorised, in which one has faith.[15]

Each of the writers she considers turns to religion in a different way: some 'place their most potent evocations of literature's religious or supernatural power at the endings of major novels', while others 'find a belief in the religious powers of language, not surprisingly, at moments of sustained high style – as for McCarthy in his breakthrough literary masterpiece *Blood Meridian* or ... in his defining novel *The Road*'. She goes on:

> Each in their own way at the top of their respective fields, these writers aim to 'reenchant' the literary world, urging it away from rationality and realism even when working in realist modes, insisting on a species of meaning that is not reducible to historical context and cannot be fully perceived even by the most sublimely literate reader.[16]

Most importantly for Milch's case, Hungerford makes a distinction between two kinds of response to postmodernism, one of which, in her words, 'questioned the literary artifact as such, the power of the author, the metaphysical capacities of literature, the grand narrative and the possibilities of meaning' (as represented, say, by Beckett), while the work of DeLillo, Morrison, Pynchon and McCarthy, on the other hand, hewed much more to the 'world-encompassing tradition of the novel that Joyce represents'.[17] For these latter writers, 'the turn to religious authority as a renewable resource for literature can be seen as an attempt to restore to literature the traditional cultural authority that deconstruction and multiculturalist critique called into question in the latter half of the twentieth century'.[18] What, if anything, has this to do with Milch?

Part of the answer may lie in a theme taken up by Stanley Cavell's only extended essay on television, 'The Fact of Television'. Towards the end of that essay, when Cavell is clearly searching for some meaning with which to characterise a medium that he has had considerable difficulty handling up to that point, he references Norman Mailer's briefly influential essay, 'The White Negro'; this is the full context:

> But the role of television in explanations of catastrophe was in preparation before the war in Vietnam. Consider that the conquering of television began just after World War II, which means, for the purposes of the hypothesis I wish to offer here, after the discovery of concentration camps and of the atomic bomb; of, I take it, the discovery of the literal possibility that human life will destroy itself; that is to say, that it is *willing* to destroy itself. (This, too, had been in sufficient preparation; it was realistically described by Nietzsche. In my taking this as a lesson of the Second World War, the lesson there seems no way for us to learn realistically, I detect the lingering effect, for all its excesses, of a once well-known essay of Norman Mailer's, 'The White Negro.') And the conquering continued with the decline of our cities and the increasing fear of walking out at night, producing the present world of shut-ins. Not to postpone it any longer, my hypothesis is that the fear of television – the fear large or pervasive enough to account for the fear of television – is the fear that what it monitors is the growing uninhabitability of the world, the irreversible pollution of the earth, a fear displaced from the world onto its monitor (as we convert the fear of what we see, and wish to see, into a fear of being seen). The loss of this inhabitability would mean, in Heidegger's view, the loss of our humanity, whether or not we remain alive. Of course, children may not have contracted the fear; and the child in us is capable of repressing the fear, ambivalently. My hypothesis is meant to respond to the mind's demand of itself to take up the slack of mismatch between the fact of television and the fact of our indifference to its significance – as though this slack were itself the expression of the fact that a commodity has conquered, an appliance that is a monitor, and yet that what it monitors, apart from events that preceded its own (cultural coverage, sports, movies), are so often settings of the shut-in, a reference line of normality or banality so insistent as to suggest that *what* is shut out, that suspicion whose entry we must at all costs guard against, must be as monstrous as, let me say, the death of the normal, of the familiar as such.[19]

Milch's turn to television, in Cavell's terms, was a turn towards a medium where the ordinary, the everyday, the familiar 'as such' was undergoing, from *Hill Street Blues* onwards, a self-examination that could be characterised as modernist. Milch, following Warren (following Eliot), sees *time* as essential to the medium and it is certainly the case that US television's turn to the *historical costume drama* (in shows such as *Deadwood, Mad Men, Quarry* to name some vivid examples) exhibits this fascination with seeing the present through the lens of the past, where both seem uncannily similar, with mere details of difference – racism, sexism, misogyny, the time before the medicalisation and pathologisation of 'the normal, the familiar as such'. For Milch, sobriety – and this meant a radical shift in personality – allowed him to calibrate the difference between being another successful television writer with a named parking space at the offices at Santa Monica, and an artist who would have a place in the putative book 'E' of *American Literature: The Makers and the Making, 1945–Present.*

Hence, Milch's first solo work connected directly to the tradition that Hungerford identifies in post-war US literature, even though it is set in 'the present'. Its relevance lies in the way the meaninglessness of the urban setting has a religious spin even when the numinous is brought out only 'as a glow brings out the haze' in the gradual building of human social bonds against a backdrop openly hostile to trust. *Big Apple*'s poster, with its depiction of Adam and Eve in front of an iconic image of the Manhattan skyline, certainly points to a shift towards more explicit religious signposting in Milch's work. But with that show cancelled, what Milch worked on in the interim between then and the attacks of 9/11 is largely unknown. He taught for a time in the UK at the College of Music and Drama in Cardiff, Wales in August 2001.[20] This indicated his continuing interest in teaching, although all that was billed was a 'masterclass' rather than a series of events, lectures or tutorials.

Talking after 9/11

Shortly after returning from the UK and exactly a week to the day after the attacks on the Twin Towers, the Pentagon and Flight 93, Milch began a five-week evening class for writers. It was during this time that all of Milch's subsequent quotes, references, exercises and modes of public locution, including his notorious candour about his past as an addict, were established for the first time. The transcripts of the classes indicate the mode now familiar to those who have witnessed Milch interviewed, lecturing or participating in panels. It is useful to put this and Milch's working process in the historical context of the writer trained in post-war North American creative writing programmes.

As Mark McGurl details in his book *The Program Era*, the mantra of 'show not tell' – the hiding of authorial or narratorial presence and comment – was radically overturned, particularly with the publication of Roth's *Portnoy's Complaint*. Explicitly based on the stand-up rhythms and style of Jewish comedian Lennie Bruce, the narration in that novel is all about showing until the very final punchline moment when we discover that we have been reading a 'telling'. For McGurl:

> Roth announces a new turn in the dialectic of program era fiction as dramatically as we could wish. This, in narratological terms at least, is the true import of Portnoy [as] he is a symptom of a profoundly (let us dust off the term) phonocentric literary historical moment, when the New Critical ideal of narrative impersonality was rotated into a minor position in relation to a dominant ideal of vocal presence but persisted in the assumption that this presence should not speak directly to the reader but should be staged. The 'staginess' of voice is therefore the trace of institutional space of its emergence, and of the artifice – indeed of the technology – that enables a textual performance of vocal authenticity.[21]

This was congruent with the emergence of a valorisation of orality and oral traditions of storytelling over print culture, most clearly emblematised by Marshall McLuhan and Walter J. Ong; while at the same time Wayne C. Booth's *Rhetoric of Fiction* (1961) had proclaimed the inadequacy of the telling–showing distinction, replacing it with the 'more comprehensive concept of "voice"'.[22]

McGurl continues:

> Booth's arguments for the artistic respectability of novelistic 'telling' and the inevitability of authorial self-implication were thus part of a widespread return to the idea that a human being might remain present, in some way, in the dead print the reader holds in her hands ... it also made an aesthetic appeal. In this context, a reflexive narrative staging or quotation of the act of storytelling, even as it might in fact mask the identity of the actual author, or induce readers to confuse him with his narrator, was one way of folding some of the higher dimensional vivacity of oral performance back into the very medium thought to have killed off oral traditions.[23]

As Frank Furedi points out, this coincided with a '1960s mood of estrangement from modernity [that] went so far as to encourage a romantic reversion to the ancient Socratic glorification of orality'.[24] But for Furedi this was no mere hesitation in the face of the rise of other forms of communication such as radio, television and the computer:

> Disenchantment with the value of reading was an indirect expression of a wider climate of disillusionment with many of the fundamental values that Western civilization claimed to uphold. The ideals of progress, the assertion that modernization represented a superior alternative to the pre-modern traditional world, and the contention that the literate culture of the West represented a qualitative advance over the pre-literate communities of the past, were all called into question by critics of modern industrial society ... Others went a step further and imagined that pre-literate oral cultures possessed important virtues that literate societies had lost.[25]

It was, of course, Marshall McLuhan's work that most prominently 'distilled the essential anti-modern and counter-cultural sentiments of the early 1960s and directed them against the rationality of the Enlightenment culture of literacy'.[26] McLuhan saw in the technologies of radio, computing and television precisely what Brooks, Warren and other New Critics wanted for literary culture: the belief 'that the unifying networks of electronic communication might restore mankind to a state of bliss not unlike the one said to have existed within the Garden of Eden'.[27] This self-conscious romanticising of a non-existent past and rejection of the authority of the written word was shared up to a point by Walter Ong's notion of 'secondary orality' which resembled the past 'in its participatory mystique, its fostering of a communal sense'.[28]

It is little wonder then that Milch, from his first writing efforts at Yale in the early 1960s – even with the legacy of Warren's powerful commitment to the written, book-led value of culture as a balm or mitigation of the worst excesses of capitalism – was unable to commit – beyond two poems and the same twelve pages typed out like a penance – to writing down words on paper in the traditional manner that prepares for their final realisation as books. Milch's career could only flourish in the context of an evolved television industry with strict demands, deadlines, and a necessity for regular, communal (if not always happy and friendly) talk. In a sense Milch is a historical accident caught between two modes of striving for an utterly romanticised communal past that were essentially incompatible. None of this would be of great moment given high pay cheques and regular recourse to gambling, heroin and alcohol, as well as the glitter and glitz that Hollywood made available on a daily basis. However, once he was sober – and for a few weeks suicidally depressed[29] – and heading into his late fifties, such matters needed more than a rationale as an obsessive-compulsive tic. This period followed the failure of *Big Apple* and Milch's first teaching gig overseas, and finally, but not least, the national trauma of 9/11, which came *within a week* of the beginning of Milch's oral classes about how to write (presumably how to write 'for television').

What is remarkable about these five sessions is that almost every example, exercise, analogy, quote, joke or ghastly story from Milch's past that he was to repeat over the next decade makes an appearance in the nearly 150 pages of transcripts. The final sessions included a contribution by Bill Finklestein, a producer and writer who had worked with Milch on *NYPD Blue* and *Brooklyn South*; Milch also used extended clips of the Mooney–Lois moments mentioned above from *Big Apple*; there was some limited audience participation, initially about the impact of 9/11, and then more about the exercises that Milch set for the participants each week. As ever Milch was entertaining, self-deprecating and confessional as well as impeccably polite; but he would be the first to admit how intimidating he must have been to the audience, even one entirely made up of seasoned staff writers. The classes have, even on the page, the sense of the shadowy good manners of an AA session, with 'trust' floating somewhere between truth and bad faith.

I summarise Milch's key points in the five sections below; these are issues that he returns to again and again over the next decade; they are a mixture of 'rules', 'guidelines', hints and tips as well as general musings about the nature and origins of storytelling:

1. Do not believe in anything you think about writing when you are not writing, sometimes expressed as do not think about writing when you are not writing. Here is Milch early in week one:

> if you take nothing else away from this whole conversation, the big thing to take away is that nothing we say here has anything to do, finally, with the state of being that you occupy when you actually write. And the corollary of that proposition is that you must not believe anything that you think about writing – about what it means to write, about what's entailed in writing – you mustn't, as it applies to your writing, you mustn't believe in anything you think when you're not writing.

There are a lot of – some might say simply impossible – parental injunctions about what one can and can't think about, especially since this assumes that one has some kind of choice in the matter. In part this may allude to a fragment that Milch sometimes attributes to William James: 'absent action, all animals are sad ... and whenever you are not writing you are going to be sad'.[30]

2. Writers are ambivalent towards form because it is a kind of authority. '[T]hat ambivalence usually has its roots in experiences which cause the aspiring writer to be both in an experience and stand outside an experience. And oftentimes, that doubleness is caused by a traumatic association with the idea of form.' The notion sometimes develops into a strange riddle that Milch seems utterly convinced of, which is that 'content finds and tests the form in which it is expressed'. It is strange not least because form is precisely the aspect most hostage to industrial conditions, limitations and constraints. How this law becomes operationalised, or not, will be clear when we come to look at Milch's practice.

3. Turn problems of spirit into problems of technique. Again, this seems to derive from the pragmatism of William James ('how to play the hand you are dealt well'). But it may also refer to James's assertion that habit is 'the enormous fly wheel of society' and that repeated behaviour helps the spirit (or the ego) get into the right mode, a kind of version of 'the muse should know where to find me'.[31] Milch's favourite example, as we have seen in an earlier chapter, was one told to him by Warren: the example of August Kekulé, the organic chemist who discovered the structure of benzene after a reverie or dream of a snake eating its own tail (itself an ancient symbol). He had been working on this for several years before the vision arrived; the lesson is: 'Visions come to prepared spirits.' Being sober for a couple of years is not the equivalent of a 'prepared spirit' (whatever that might be). It does, however, sound inspiring, but it is also necessary to have the time, space, quiet and therefore money to get oneself into a position whereby one's 'spirit' can get along with the business of prepping itself. Milch glosses it this way:

> As an example of 'I had no anticipation before I sat down that that would be what the story would be that I was going to tell.' I would suggest to you that that is more typical rather than less of a writer once he or she has sort of entered into the world of his imagination.

Milch's initial instructions in the first session to the audience are rituals designed to stimulate this kind of mood. They are minimal and evoke late Beckett:

> Two voices. No names. No description. Voice one and voice two. The setting – don't say what the setting is. Write for not less than twenty minutes, just follow, just hear what they say. Not more than fifty minutes, put it in an envelope, seal the envelope, and shut up. Don't talk about it.

These 'techniques' are hardly new or foolproof: if we consider the account that Mason Currey offers of many writers in his book *Daily Rituals*, there is much to be said for being taken by the mood of the moment, as there is for writing in the morning before the complications of the day add up, or for drinking quite a lot of alcohol or taking amphetamines or other drugs.[32] Milch's advice to write for no longer than 50 minutes and no less than 20 is an arbitrary invention of form to allow some way in which to overcome resistance to these kinds of rituals. But as in *The Sopranos* storyline involving aspiring writer Christopher Moltisanti, who murders his AA sponsor J. T. Dolan (Tim Daly) after the latter does not have time to be supportive because he has to deliver a script for a *CSI* episode by deadline, we do not always have the luxury to decide on form or the time in which to practise it.

Apart from the time constraint (which Milch later admitted was the addition of a mystical aspect to give the exercise some ritualised magic), the other key part of the exercise was its public nature. The following week each participant was expected to drop his or her sealed envelope into a large glass container (although anonymity was an option). Milch promised to read each one and meet with each person. The technique, of course, tends to produce conflict between form and creativity – one voice, for example, is likely to be parental – either nurturing or critical – the other defensive, much like the internal voices we often replay in our heads.[33]

4. All writing, all art, is a reaching out beyond ourselves: Milch's favourite example in the lectures are sporting events, where camaraderie between strangers is expressed through the mutual celebration of the success of their team on the field: 'What do all those moments have in common? They begin with an individual and culminate in the individual finding the deepest meaning of his individuality in a going-out to something outside himself or herself.' Part of this is about making the distinction, following Coleridge, between fanciful (private) associations and imaginative ones.[34]

5. Finally, Milch peppered his talks with his favourite moments from poetry, mostly three poems from Warren: 'Homage to Theodore Dreiser', especially the last stanza; 'Audubon: A Vision', again the last stanza; and most crucially for Milch, 'I Am Dreaming of a White Christmas: The Natural History of a Vision', which in its final stanza suggests that the past can be wiped clean by art's process in the present. As Milch puts it in these lectures:

> And what the narrator is talking about is this process that we are embarked on, this is the process in which every form of pain in its pastness, in its seeming irrecoverability, is once again brought to life and converted, in the process of signifying into the future tense of joy. And that's the only proper function of art.

There are also practical tips that are actually useful and we can see them already at work in *NYPD Blue* and especially *Big Apple*; for example, using the resource of the viewer's imagination rather than endlessly piling on exegesis or lines that merely clarify plot or character moves that are already evident:

> the work of the writer is always to gain access to the imagination of the viewer and then get the hell out of the way. Do the minimum that invokes the image or the experience for the reader or the viewer, and then your work, your work, is done, then the characters start to take over and the reader or the viewer's imagination takes over. That's an exercise in humility.

Milch also reveals some aspects of his literary tastes. Throughout the lectures he references *The Brothers Karamazov*, mainly because of the Inquisitor's insistence on 'Miracle, Mystery and Authority';

> When I read Samuel Beckett, I finish and I said, '*That's* a great writer.' When I read Dostoevsky, I say, 'What a great story.' And that's why, in two hundred and fifty years, nobody's going to know who Samuel Beckett was, because he was incapable, with all his gifts, of the final humility, of submitting himself to the story.

And there is a favourite example from *King Lear* in which Gloucester has his eyes gouged out by Cornwall, and the latter's servant challenges him:

> the little guy – just in terms of sinking roots deep – the thing I found so wonderful about that guy who called his wife and said they were going to rush the cockpit [on Flight 93]? That was the guy whose mother said to him, 'Do not come home dirty. Do not play in the street.' And, uh, probably a little meek, and he married a girl a little bit like his mom, and so once they made the decision, before he rushed the cockpit he called home ... now why do we laugh when we sink the roots a little deeper? Because we just expanded our idea of bravery, didn't we? That it's not only the property of someone whose heroism is instinctual – you know in *Lear* when things have gotten just as bad as they can get...

Milch goes on to describe the intervention of the hitherto anonymous servant as a groundling who, like this 'little guy', finds his moment and destiny in the face of absolute evil.

These points, hints, observations and quotes will be familiar to anyone who has seen series DVD featurettes for *Deadwood* or *John From Cincinnati*, or heard Milch speak at any point over the past fifteen years. What is very different and timely at this point in his career is his concentration on the writings of St Paul. Milch had become close to Father Ellwood Kieser, who set up the Humanitas prize in 1974, shortly after he was on the podium to receive it for the third time for *NYPD Blue* in 1999. Recalling the event during his writers' strike sessions of 2007, after going into detail about his sexual abuse at Camp Paradox, Milch gives the following account of what happened as he accepted the award for the first time:

> I won the Humanitas prize, which is given by the Catholic Church. And I look at the guy who's a Catholic priest who runs the Humanitas award, and I say to myself, 'This guy's a paedophile.' He may not know it. I may not know how I know it, but this guy's a bone smoker, he's a sexual degenerate. And, inexplicably to myself ... when I'm expressing my thanks, I said I just want Father Kieser to know that I'm gonna take this money and buy a racehorse. Apart from whatever may seem to be – and everyone says, 'Oh you know Dave, he's such an iconoclast, he just fuckin' around!' That's what I thought. I mean I did buy a racehorse. And I won it again the next year, and I'm really kinda confronting this guy. And he's looking back at me with love. I'm thinking, sure, he loves me because he wants to cum on my face. And I had had some experience with authority figures doing that ... So now I teach myself about horseracing. And the racetrack is ... a nest of vipers. The best thieves in the world ... In that environment which was of course an effort to reconstruct the environment in which I [mimics his father's injunction], 'Don't let me see you sneaking out here!' I have owned the horses that have won two Breeder's Cups ... I taught myself to swim in those waters. And then simultaneously I lose as much money as necessary to fulfill my father's prophecy. I was a busy boy.
>
> And this priest is looking at me the whole fuckin' time with this smile on his face. And so I win the Humanitas award again about ten years later but by now I had gotten sober. Not the time I was just dry. Now I'd been able to let God's grace work on me a little. And so I win this prize and I think ... am I gonna break this guy's balls again? But there he is sitting next to me so I say, 'You know I've never liked Father Kieser. I don't know what it is that fucking irritates me about him.' I said, 'It's like he's got this look on his face like, "I know something about you that you don't know about yourself."'
>
> Now *I think* I'm gonna accuse him of being a paedophile. And the next words that come from my lips are: 'I'm grateful to have lived long enough to have discovered that the shadow in which I believe that I and my characters must always move was in fact cast by God's protective

hand.' And that is the thing that Father Kieser has known about me that I didn't know about myself.[35]

Kieser was dying of cancer at the time, and a few weeks after the Humanitas ceremony he sent a message to Milch asking to talk with him at his hospital bed. Kieser was a Paulist Father and Milch describes him coming in and out of the painkilling drugs to hold his hand and beg him '[t]o do the story about Paul'. And, Milch said, 'He blessed me.' By this point Milch had not only remembered that he had been abused and that his abuser was a regular friend of his father's who adored gambling at the racetrack: he must also have known that his own addictions and obsessions did not, as it were, *belong* to him in the way that he might have imagined – as most of us do – that we *author* our own actions.

It is also likely that Kieser reminded Milch of conversations he had had with Warren about the existentialist theologian Paul Tillich, when he makes the claim early on in the 2001 lecture series that the impulse to write is a reaching out to God:

> It's a reaching out to God though ... the ... words are symbols of reality but they are symbols which partake of the reality that they represent ... and in that paradoxical doubleness is the explanation of how writing is a reaching out to our fellow human beings but also a reaching out to a larger spirit.[36]

Kieser's inaugural Humanitas keynote, delivered in 1974, also stressed television's capacity to 'unify the human family', which would have appealed to Milch's emergent, sober sense of unity under the surface of chaos. This not only confirmed the deeply held theoretical and practical understanding of his professors and mentors at Yale but offered a healing sense of the potential of a medium that for Milch was 'fallen'.[37]

During the second lecture (or talk or session – the genre of these events is hard to define; they partake of the 'happening', something akin to the Ken Kesey or R. D. Laing happenings in which gurus dispensed their wisdom to the flock), Milch began reading from the Bible, specifically St Paul's epistle to the Corinthians, chapters 12–13, the reading that the Revd Smith in *Deadwood* uses in his eulogy at Hickok's funeral – every part of the body is part of one body: a unity. While this develops the theme of being something larger than oneself, it does not abandon the Brooks/Warren insistence on unity in the face of the shattering, shredding and alienating forces of modernity; that storytelling on television (or in any other art) might have the power to address this is clearly a passenger that missed its train. Terry Eagleton and Roger Scruton, almost opposite poles of the debate, both agree that culture was a failure as a substitute for religious unity. But Milch's fascination with St Paul is a thread that does not go away over the remaining four sessions. Father Kieser died on 15 September, three days before Milch began the lecture series. The show about the life of St Paul drew upon Milch's experience with the cop genre, with justice and the law. Paul was arrested in Jerusalem but sent to Rome for trial since he could claim to be a Roman citizen and thus make an appeal to the emperor, Nero. Nero on the other hand, was insane, and the law was effectively an matter of whatever occurred to him at the time. Paul lived in Rome under house arrest for several years before either being executed by Nero or dying of natural causes.

As Milch is fond of pointing out, St Paul, apart from being one of the most read writers ever, is a classic instance of one of his characters. He commits a hideous crime in the service of the bosses, then finds redemption through good works. According to some Pauline thought, Paul followed the Sadducees rather than the Pharisees, with the former believing that the holy texts are 'kind of frozen', whereas the latter believed that there is room for interpretation, that there is a permissible continuing commentary as events unfold in the present (Milch makes a comparison with Sunni and Shia traditions in the session). Paul was working for the Sadducees, and feeling, in Milch's terms, an 'outsider', never part of anything. According to this telling, Paul eventually realised that the Christian belief in a Messiah who came, died and was resurrected should have meant the 'end of days', as predicted by Jewish eschatology. But since this did not happen, the continuation and evangelisation of Christianity was sheer blasphemy. Paul therefore took particular interest in becoming the main enforcer for the Sadducees, and it was he who organised the group who stoned St Stephen to death. The Sadducees, somewhat embarrassed by Paul's violent enthusiasm, sent him away to Damascus to deal with the Christians there, and this is where his conversion happened. This is Milch towards the end of the second lecture:

> I can share with you that – let me hasten to say I'm not comparing myself with St. Paul – but I know what it is to do, what you never dreamed of doing, what you never thought you'd be capable of doing [reads from the Bible]: 'We know that the law is spiritual, but I am carnal. Sold under sin. I do not understand my own actions, for I do not do what I want. But I do the very thing I hate. Now if I do what I do not want, I agree that the law is good. So that it is no longer that I do it but sin which dwells within me. For I know that nothing good dwells within me, that is, in my flesh. I can will what is right but I cannot do it. For I do not do the good I want but the evil I don't want is what I do.'

Milch goes on to describe Paul as a temporal lobe epileptic, foreshadowing the Revd Smith's seizures in *Deadwood* (although these are caused by a brain tumour), and then describes Kafka as 'every bit as crazy as Paul'. Being 'crazy' – the way that Milch describes himself is 'crazy as the day is long' – is a passport to insight, to working unencumbered by the self and its ordinary distractions. It is aristocratic in its choosing. These sessions offer a clear sense that Milch is somehow on the edge of things in his sobriety, in the days after 9/11 and the death of Kieser, facing a series of psychological or existential forces that his use of narcotics had previously dealt with or mitigated.

Shortly afterwards, Milch pitched the St Paul story to executives at HBO. As is well known, since Milch never tires of repeating the story, he made an amazing pitch, but HBO had already commissioned *Rome* (2005–07), a co-production with the BBC that, like *Deadwood*, was cancelled in 2006. The premise of Milch's story had been the survival of Christianity in a city without laws (since, in this version, Nero's powers were absolute), centred around St Paul's survival and work there; according to Milch, his response to the news that HBO already had a show 'about Rome' was 'OK let's make it a Western.' If this is true, then there are a large number of gaps – mostly unexplained – in the process of swapping from a costume drama set in the ancient world to one of the most iconic American genres.

Since Milch was on the payroll and HBO was positive about the idea of a Western series, he went away for a long while to research the show. He settled on the history of the town of Deadwood, perhaps because after the discovery of gold there it was settled by whites on what was Indian land. Hence, like Rome under Nero, there was no law, since US state or federal laws did not apply. It was a place, therefore, thirsty for social, moral and lawful organisation. As such it was similar to the St Paul idea: a story of the foundation and flourishing of spirituality, despite the fact that once the mining town was exhausted it was also virtually emptied of any population. More importantly, it was an American story set in the late nineteenth century at precisely the time when Milch's favoured writers were at work: Twain, Dreiser, William Dean Howells, Henry James and, of course, Melville. Milch spent some time in the town, working with local historians; he also wanted the 'scent' of what it would be like to be a full-time, hard-working, hard-playing man, and to that end he chartered flights to bring rodeo stars and workers to stay in Santa Monica hotels while Milch observed their drinking and other antics.[38] To watch and not to participate, to be proximate without contamination, would have seemed like, perhaps was, research.

I have written a detailed monograph which provides a critical account of *Deadwood* and its multiple achievements: without wishing to repeat myself or short-change the reader of this book, I want to offer a different take on the show in terms of how Milch talked about it as he was writing it.

Like *Big Apple*, *Deadwood* is both the name of a place and a choice of title that has a double resonance. Compare 'Deadwood' to Henry James's lively character in *Portrait of a Lady*, brimming with charisma: Caspar Goodwood. 'Wood' as an emblem of vitality and fecundity is in Milch's title associated with death. Indeed, the rugged coupling of Alma Garret and Seth Bullock that kicks off the beginning of season two of the show is explicitly associated with the self-annihilation that couples can provide one another, and directly threatens the stability of the camp, eventually causing mortal combat between Al Swearengen and Bullock. Apart from its obscene meaning, 'wood' is also the material that Christ was nailed to, and that most of the town is built from (the show was shot at Gene Autry's ranch, familiar to any connoisseur of Westerns, including appropriately enough *Westworld* [HBO, 2016–present]). So the title of the show both hides and shows its doubleness: a place of death, of reverence towards the figure or symbol of death.

The doubleness hides a further uncertainty: HBO, unlike broadcast networks at that time, required entire seasons to be shot in advance before the first episode was aired. In the past, Milch and other staff writers could adjust during the 22-episode season of *NYPD Blue* according to critical, popular and rating responses. There was no possibility of that here. On the plus side there were only twelve episodes to a season, which meant something like a 12-day shooting period per 50–60 minute episode – a considerable luxury for television. But this made Milch's notorious last-minute writing even more extreme than it had been on *NYPD Blue*. Actors would get emails with their lines mere hours before the shoot, or sometimes at the point of arrival on the set. The writing expanded to fill the available time. HBO wanted an *auteur*, indeed sold itself as 'it's not TV it's HBO' on precisely that basis, and Milch was uncomfortable with the responsibility and spotlight that this notion conferred. In an augury of the conditions that faced the production of *Luck*, the company hired the veteran director of Westerns Walter Hill to direct the pilot episode of *Deadwood*. An early cut of this effort remains in which Milch refused to intervene, perhaps out of respect for Hill. It resembles the final pilot in some scenes, but is mostly different, and badly so. Milch either let it fail deliberately or hoped that his writing could communicate itself without him being there. Either way they had to reshoot, and the result was a stunning pilot of such visceral force that it created the momentum that propelled the show well into its third season.

However, the price to pay for this was Milch's method; it is described by Bochco as:

> the Art of Performance Writing. He would lie on the floor, surrounded by his adoring followers, and dictate his scripts to a script typist at the computer. A monitor would be in front of David where he lay on the floor, and he would dictate, then re-write, then re-write again and again, all verbally, for the amusement and edification of his adoring audience. Personally, I couldn't watch it. It was a display of narcissism that I found impossible to be witness to. This was his paid audience.[39]

Ted Mann, who is credited with writing most of the scripts of *Deadwood*, refused to be in the trailer while Milch wrote like this. Mann told me that typically Milch would come on set, go to the trailer and begin a monologue in front of the writers, effectively mirroring the lectures he gave in late 2001, except in this case he was talking about themes and characters and the associational patterning of the episodes. The writers would then go off and have the opportunity to write the scenes, enough for the day or the next day's meeting.[40] Milch would sometimes talk for two or three hours about what he was thinking about these characters; he would assign scenes to particular writers, or interns. There is no record of who was assigned what, but there is an almost complete transcript of Milch's talks (for a sense of its length, an A4 single-page printout of these talks for the entire three seasons of *Deadwood* measures over half a metre in height – with the drafts it is over 2 metres). Often the actors would be there and would even get a writing credit for contributions they made. Other staff writers would be given scenes to work on, but Milch would do the final revisions for everything right up to the last moment. The draft script files are colour-coded so each actor and crew member knew which version they were working with – it is fair to say that Milch used the full palette range of the scriptwriting software.

Deadwood can be summarised fairly succinctly in terms of plot. It is set in a town in the late 1870s shortly after the discovery of gold. Hordes of people pile into the region looking for easy money and ways to steal from those stupid enough to actually look for the gold itself. From Milch's point of view this was the equivalent of alcoholics doing a 'geographical', moving territory but taking their problems along with them. Since the area is built on what, by treaty, counts as 'Indian Land', there was no law or authority. The alternative to the law is the Gem saloon, a brothel run by Al Swearengen (Ian McShane), who also controls the opium economy through his contact with Mr Wu (Keone Young), who runs the Chinese part of the settlement, and disposes of those whom Swearengen murders by feeding their corpses to his pigs. Swearengen also runs a pair who rob those families and settlers fleeing the violence and disorder of the town. The show begins with the arrival of two good men, one a former sheriff from Montana, Seth Bullock (Timothy Olyphant), and the other his Jewish business partner, Sol Star (John Hawkes), who open a hardware store. Arriving too are 'Wild Bill' Hickok, accompanied by Charlie Utter and 'Calamity' Jane Cannary. Swearengen also has to face the arrival of a swankier brothel outfit, the Bella Union run by Cy Tolliver (Powers Boothe), a vicious misogynist who is in love with his chief whore Joanie Stubbs (Kim Dickens).

Among the new arrivals are well-to-do husband and wife Brom and Alma Garret (Timothy Omundson and Molly Parker). Swearengen 'salts' some land with gold nuggets and sells it at an inflated price to Garret who, on discovering that he has been swindled of his fortune, threatens to call Pinkertons (who are already after Swearengen because of an outstanding warrant for a Chicago murder). Swearengen has his henchman Dan Dority (W. Earl Brown) kill Garret by throwing him off a cliff edge on his own land, only to discover that it *does* in fact have substantial gold seams. Inheriting the land, Garret's widow Alma seeks the protection first of Hickok, and then, after Hickok is killed by a degenerate drifter Jack McCall (Garret Dillahunt), Seth Bullock. Eventually Bullock and Alma develop a relationship as her wealth accumulates; in the meantime (in season two), mining magnate George Hearst (Gerald McCraney) sends his chief geologist Francis Wolcott (Garret Dillahunt again) to spread rumours that the mining claims are illegitimate and should be sold to him at knockdown prices. Wolcott recruits Tolliver's help in spreading these rumours. Swearengen takes a beating from Bullock and is seriously ill while this is going on, but once he is back on his feet he finds an opportunity to neutralise Tolliver's advantage with Hearst (through violence), and the second season ends with marriage celebrations as Alma, for the sake of her adopted daughter (a survivor of one of Swearengen's attacks), marries the crusty miner, Whitney Ellsworth (Jim Beaver). This is probably the high point of the show, the moment when dance and storytelling come together in a kind of Yeatsian celebration of art.

The third season, however, offers a far darker storyline. Hearst himself has arrived (his geologist was also a serial sex killer, who hanged himself at the end of the second season) and stamps his imprint on the camp by buying the town's hotel from its weaselly owner, the self-appointed mayor E. B. Farnum (William Sanderson), and pressuring

Alma to sell her gold claim. Hearst murders at will, recruits dozens of mercenaries to do his bidding, and effectively outpowers Swearengen's attempt to bring the town under the law of fair elections – which Hearst himself has fixed. The season ends with a mixed tone of resignation: evil has gone (Hearst leaves for another claim in the Anaconda copper mine in Montana), but the town has been violated; the engine of capital and its less-than-human commanders have devoured the law that the town attempted, with much pain and argument (and violence), to establish organically. The final shot is of Swearengen alone, talking to himself, cleaning blood from his office floor.

Writing *Deadwood*

My account of *Deadwood* will consist mainly of tracking Milch's thinking about these seasons in those monologue sessions and how this matched up to the extraordinary achievement we see in the final version. Most of the time what Milch is trying to establish is less to do with narcissism, despite what Bochco says (although it is easy to see why it might appear that way), and more to set an emotional climate in which the writers can proceed with the scenes. As Milch puts it in one session: 'This is the right ground of experience out of which the present themes are to come. That's what's shadowing this behaviour.' Milch's conversations, his revisions, his talks with the actors on set – all of these things have some remainder or presence, are felt if not spoken or seen in the final product that we watch. Anne Enright suggests that this might be a rule for writing fiction, that 'your story must contain the remnants of former drafts, whose original meaning is lost, but which now make an odd kind of sense'.[41] Milch talks about being 'true to the original intuition of the tension in the scene, and then just sort of let it happen', but this demands going back to the dialogue and revising again and again so that 'the speech ought to be able to test, if your emotional connection with the revision is healthy, it ought to be able to withstand that ... revising'.

These sessions are about what counts for Milch as writing, but of course he does not put pen to paper or finger to keyboard. The writing is manifested through the actions of his amanuensis typing into a computer what he says, or through transcriptions of his conversations (by interns or others) that transform them into shareable material, and, secondarily, via archival records that constitute the source of much of the material in this chapter. This captures more than the materiality of words handwritten or typed on paper; rather, it captures the living sense of words in formation and action as they emerge from Milch's mouth. Some of them end up on screen coming out of others' mouths, but more are kernels of ideas of speech or mood or character that gradually firm and coalesce into action, speech and character. It is important not to misunderstand Milch's repeated claims that he does not do outlines or think about writing when he is not writing. As we shall see, this does not mean that he is not planning scenes, episodes, entire seasons in advance. His 'writing' is anything he is doing or saying when in the mood, the work, the job of writing – including plans, dialogue, notes for the actors, consultation with others in the room, recalled memories of other conversations and reading as well as random thoughts, fun and teasing. When Milch says he tries not to think about writing when he is not writing he means he is trying, as many of us do, not to bring his work home with him, and therefore cultivating the habit of regular opportunities for his muse to find him. Finally, I should prepare the reader for the presence throughout this chapter of extensive quotations from these sessions. Milch is a skilled monologuist who carries his audience across a vibrant landscape of ideas, memories, dramatic tactics, false starts and sudden insights, and it can take some time to get to a stopping point. What follows is a representative selection of some of that writing while working on *Deadwood* and *John From Cincinnati*. In this way we can observe how Milch paints a picture in words of the drama.

Early on in the planning for the pilot Milch was concerned to create a picture of the chaotic and unrestrained criminal appetites of the Deadwood camp. Take this account of the Gem saloon's rapacious mixing of characters:

> All the news in the fucking bar, all the gossip is about the arrival of Wild Bill. For many of the layabouts and drunks, Hickok's presence is the excuse for grandiose, alcoholic character-assassination (use [Jack] McCall's soliloquy). But Swearengen perceives Hickok as a potential source of danger – i.e., Hickok becomes the object of Swearengen's paranoia. Filter this through Swearengen's other paranoid constructs – his reaction to Merrick's benign inquiries about the Trick. His concern about other gambling outfits ... Integrate Swearengen's personality dynamics ... with Farnum's re the town's legal situation and jeopardy at the hands of the Indians and the U.S. Government. Filter through also the New York dilettante [Brom Garret] and his wife, who become the object of the venality and greed which is the predicate of the settlement. Bullock and Star making friends, especially Star. Calamity Jane comes in, starts blowing guys for free. It's how Swearengen makes a connection with Hickok and Utter –

Swearengen: I'll do whatever you want because she's a friend of yours, but I prefer her not sucking pricks in the corner, because it undercuts my whores and sets the wrong tone.

The final event does not happen; Milch finds in Jane something more compelling to substantiate her wildness, and the dialogue here becomes more developed later on in the process. But this block of words already has a deep core of what the early parts of the first season communicate to us, in particular Swearengen's paranoia about the government and about Hickok.

It is common for Milch to talk his way into dialogue like this, so that the other writers in the room have a sense, alongside the metabolism of the drama he paints, of how the characters speak. This dialogue can run for pages, or be interrupted by Milch underpinning why they are saying and doing what they are. There are many dead ends in terms of solutions to the dramatic problems he is setting up, but those issues themselves tend to remain on track, however finessed the final dramatic outcome. Here is the moment when Milch settles on a prologue for the pilot in order to establish audience engagement with Bullock:

> Bullock's credentials as a character worthy of the viewers' attention and as a focus of the story are less obvious than Hickok's or Swearengen's; he'll be an instrument of the ordering or civilizing process but will enter into this identity only slowly and in a sense reluctantly.
>
> One way to establish him is through a prologue which shows him in Montana in late June of '76 – i.e., at the time Hickok and Charlie Utter and Calamity Jane are arriving in Deadwood, and Al Swearengen is establishing his primacy as lord of Deadwood's underworld.
>
> There is a story about Bullock, when he was a deputy sheriff in Helena, facing down a lynch mob, hanging a convicted man himself so that the mob couldn't do it, i.e. fighting off vigilante justice not to prevent a hanging but to defend the idea of law. That's a pretty fine distinction, and to a practical man like Bullock it might be an argument for suppressing his lawman's instinct in order to function more successfully as a private citizen.
>
> It might frighten him to recognize that 'noble' instinct in himself which could fuck him up to a fare-thee-well as far as making money, being popular, etc. The idea of starting over in Deadwood, where he wouldn't be saddled with his reputation – in Montana his nickname was 'Bishop' – might have appealed. If we played such a prologue, then the absence of heroic behaviour in Bullock, or its slow-surfacing, would be understandable to the audience, more-or-less the equivalent, in terms of dramatic structure, of the Gary Cooper character at the beginning of *High Noon* renouncing his larger responsibilities to the community in order to pursue a life as a private citizen and husband.

Milch draws on the local history he has read, as well as biographies of Bullock, but his core intuition about the *character* rather than the historical personage is in formation. As if fitting the character with various costumes (it's not clear, for example, whether Olyphant has been cast in the role when he speaks here), Milch tries out various kinds of scene, moment, speech on Bullock, looking for further ways that that core might be discovered, as well as revealed to the audience.

Once established, the mass of characters thicken in relation to one another, all dancing to their various core drivers, but also developing in relation to the beat of global as well as private movements in the plot. This is Milch now well into season one, talking about Bullock showing his wife, Martha (Anna Gunn), who has just arrived in Deadwood, the house he has built for her. He quickly segues into a plot that involves Alma Garret's father Otis Russell (William Russ) trying to extort from her on learning about her successful gold claim.

> The idea of the house, the plot of land, the house on the plot of land, for Bullock, is that duty accommodates and protects him from the chaos of emotion.
>
> What's going on with him is he's pre-sexual in his defense mechanisms; he was so angry at his father for beating him all the time – he protects himself with the idea of order – he more or less had it worked out except for sex, so when his brother dies, the idea of marrying the widow, beneath the veneer of piety, that's, 'Well I'll be safe there, too.' Safe from whom? From the father. Well, here's the father of the girl he's attracted to [Alma Garret (Molly Parker)] saying, 'I will negate any idea of order or duty or legality or truth. I'll put her at absolute risk unless you give me everything that I want.' Now Bullock's going to be in panic, which he will show as rage.
>
> Star, as the Jew who is like the eunuch – as perceived culturally, he's got to listen, he's a merchant, a salesman's got to listen to anything. At this level, Bullock wants to tell him this fucking story – wants to scream at him in effect, and know that Star has to listen and have no opinion. Because as a Jew 'If I can sell you something I can have no opinion about anything.' And then here Star is with the same fucking ... now Bullock's got no place to go. Probably the end of the scene, he goes back out to smoke again, which is what he was doing with Russell, which at some level acknowledges a phallic symbol, he's doomed, he's going to have to live into it rather than have any refuge from it.
>
> This accommodates the arc of it from Bullock's point of view. From Star's point of view, there is something he's experiencing deeper than floating on the surface of the mercantile identity, which is the Jew's relation to culture; 'I will ape the culture and have my own secret life, but the way I'll survive is to ape the mores of the [dominant] culture,

> and the deal there is that I never complain. I do my complaining behind closed doors, and I never have a need that I express to a Gentile.' But now he's so fundamentally wounded, he wants to tell Bullock the story, and in that process there flares up Bullock's [recognition] that he's been guilty of a betrayal. The one thing he was sure of is that he'd never betray anyone; he'd so bind himself to duty that he'd never betray anyone.

The speaker is an artist with a command-view of the nation and culture in which his characters move, agree with it or not. It is comprehensive and understands what moves his characters inside and out.

How this is cashed out in scenes across the seasons is complex. We start with a picture of the house that Bullock built for his wife and brother's widow Martha, something we don't see until season two. What Milch is building here is a story that enfolds Al Swearengen, Alma, Bullock, Star, Trixie, Martha and William (Bullock, her son). Bullock begins building the house at the same time that he and Alma are on the first steps towards becoming lovers. Alma's father arrives in camp in the penultimate episode of season one and it is quickly established that he is a con man (*Farnum*: 'the man's a charlatan ... a cheat, a broad tosser and a clip'); more deeply we might sense that he has used his daughter – turned her out – in order to access wealthy society, the better to exploit their resources. The death of Alma's husband Brom in suspicious circumstances has alerted his rich family to Russell's ruse, and he sets about blackmailing his daughter in order to extort from her. Bullock, ever the cop, instantly knows this. Their post-prandial walk along Deadwood thoroughfare, as transmitted, carries the kernel of Milch's idea of Bullock as trapped by his nature, not in the dialogue but in the way Timothy Olyphant plays his infuriated restraint:

> *Russell*: Understandable, her late husband was so taken with my daughter. I didn't know him very well, but I certainly recognized his doting infatuation.
>
> *Bullock*: I didn't know him at all.
>
> *Russell*: I admit that I had hoped she might find a man who would dote on her and more, perhaps had a surer sense of what the world was. And, apparently, I'm entitled to hope that again.
>
> *Bullock*: My wife and son will be joining me soon.
>
> *Russell*: I'm long past judgment, Mr. Bullock, and I've learned that, no matter what people say, or how civil they seem, their passions rule. I see no reason why your wife and son's arrival need alter my hopes for my daughter's happiness or security or the security of her holdings.
>
> *Bullock*: I'll say goodnight, Mr. Russell. With thanks, for dinner.
>
> *Russell*: That will disappoint Alma. I'm sure she didn't think she was saying goodnight when we left for our walk.

Bullock: She'll be alright.
Russell: If I have offended you Mr. Bullock, I've accomplished the opposite of my intentions, which would not be an unprecedented result.
Bullock: I just want to say goodnight.
Russell: Of course. Goodnight Mr. Bullock.
Bullock: Goodnight then.
Russell: Trust me to explain to Alma, I'm a practiced and inveterate liar.

Olyphant has Bullock desperate to escape, knowing full well that he *needs* to beat Russell to a pulp, which he does in the next episode.

In the meantime, Trixie has visited Star in his hardware store and they begin to have sex when Bullock interrupts; embarrassed, he walks to Swearengen's Gem saloon and on discovering that Con Stapleton has been installed as sheriff (itself a product of Tom Nuttall's distraught confession to Swearengen that he is losing touch with the camp), blurts out that Trixie has given Star a 'free one'. Swearengen confronts Star with a demand for payment ('You pay or she pays. No home visits. Five, seven for an ass-fuck'); that is the 'betrayal' that Milch is talking about, and the 'wounding' that Star receives. Star and Trixie have to live their romance secretly, although enabled by Swearengen.

Bullock and Alma eventually couple in the final episode of the first season, and by the beginning of the second they are both absorbed in sexual rapture. Swearengen sees this as a threat to the camp (putting it succinctly, Alma's gold claim needs to be secure in Deadwood to attract commerce and political clout for him; Bullock has to handle that side of things – but neither can work if they are fucking their way into oblivion while the political centre of the South Dakota region, Yankton, is sharpening its knives to carve the town up). After humiliating him in public Swearengen is caught up in Bullock's 'cunt-struck' rage and the two fight to the death in the thoroughfare. Both are saved only by the arrival by stagecoach of Martha and William, which distracts Swearengen from cutting Bullock's throat. Shortly afterwards Bullock takes his family to the house he has built for them.

We can see in these few paragraphs that Milch compresses a great number of intuitions that span across seasons and characters; his sense of the direction of character is impeccable, even if the details are not locked in tight. Sometimes Milch is dead on target all-at-once with a character. This is an extract from a long account of Hickok's 'psychological makeup': '[He] ... can't find a way to live other than moment to moment. So, he drinks and gambles to intensify the moments when his instincts have no use, and to accommodate his despair.' And there are other times when Milch is stuck, but not blocked, seeking out the correct calibration of the polarities of characters and their relationships:

> I keep bumping up against the similarities between Charlie Utter and Sol Star in their respective relationships to Hickok and Bullock. There's some way I don't understand yet to use these similarities. Maybe the point to make dramatically, in showing the similarity of the relationships, is some fundamental difference between Utter and Star.

This leads to the idea of bolstering Star's independence in the prologue scene, and having Utter leave the camp after Hickok is killed by Jack McCall – the difference is that Star can live independently without Bullock, but Utter cannot remain in the same way without Hickok. He has to find another identity through which to enter Deadwood's community. What is powerfully evident in this example is how *fast* Milch's thought was able to handle and partially solve difficult dramatic problems, evident in this case in the finished work. He works by drilling into binaries, finding the necessary association between them and exploiting their dissonance: it is a breaking apart and coming together of fictional elements anchored at psychological depth to his sense of how and why a person speaks and behaves and thinks in the way they do.

The problem with Milch's writing voice is that he writes indeterminately. As he notes at one point during the discussion,

> the first course I ever taught was called Strategies of Indirection ... using words that seem to be instruments of direct communication and in fact you're using them in a different way ... the electricity that words carry that allows them to make us feel them as real experience rather than simple signs.

This means that the words he uses can have four or five axes of alignment for the actor. Take, for example, this monologue delivered by Swearengen from the balcony of the Gem saloon in the first episode of season two ('A Lie Agreed Upon, Part One'). Dan and Adams are at his side as he watches Bullock in the thoroughfare, fresh from fucking Alma:

> *Swearengen*: Self-deceiving cocksucker I am, I thought when America took us in, Bullock would prove a fucking resource ... look at him, striding out like some randy maniac Bishop. Sheriff! About his duties to the camp, huh? Luck trouble didn't jump out earlier, huh, Bullock? Might have found you mid-thrust at other business. *(Seth stops and looks up at Al.)* What is it? Taken by a vision? You would not want to be staring like that – at me.

Consider the ways an actor could deliver that final line by emphasising just one word or phrase:

> *You* would not want to be staring like that at me.
> You would *not* want to be staring like that at me.
> You would not want to be *staring* like that at me.
> You would not want to be staring like *that* at me.
> You would not want to be staring like that – *at me.*

The final emphasis is the choice made. This is partly because italicisation and underlining are discouraged in the craft of scriptwriting, since it would appear that the writer was directing too much; hence the emphasis on 'at me' is given by the pause inflected by the dash and assisted by an edit that cuts back to Swearengen on the final two words, and the swelling of ominous music on the soundtrack. The problem for Milch is that if his other voice isn't around to tell the writers, the director, the editor and, crucially, the actors, what his writing voice *meant*, then someone else will do it, because tick-tock – production time is expensive. A decision *has* to be made when one's writing voice produces indeterminate lines. Milch's affection for actors goes beyond the fact that they necessarily lead a double life, lying, pretending for the camera, occupying fake or fictional identities, much as Milch's persona was of a successful student/writer/husband on the one hand and a junkie/degenerate/gambler on the other.

While Milch is around he needs to tell his colleagues everything he can. In the case of the Bullock/Swearengen fight, that means what he thinks of the actors, Timothy Olyphant and Ian McShane:

> Ian likes to think of himself as working class, and Tim's dad is rich, and so all the surface differences between them, that's what they think they disagree about, and the truth is they recognize each other absolutely. And it's dangerous. It's dangerous. The danger, for example, is that Ian's going to lead Tim right off a cliff. It's why Powers [Boothe] wound up in second position in the billing. Because Powers knew he could out-act Ian any day of the fucking week ... I never thought much of Ian as an actor, but Ian's got balls. He's a fucking fighter. And so that kind of stuff, which is really pre-verbal, needs to survive when you get familiar with characters ... You have to keep it dangerous. There is something Swearengen knows that Bullock gets out of being with that woman that is somehow equivalent to what he gets out of being with Trixie. And while he could never admit to getting what he gets out of being with Trixie, whatever the fuck that is, he can see it in Bullock, and Bullock can't stand that he sees that in him, that he is ... what St. Paul said, sold in sin, he is carnal, she does it for him. I just know you need to keep that edge of genuine danger, that these are two guys that could accidentally kill each other.

Milch's familiarity with the actors and their lives and their abilities gives him an edge when writing their lines because he has access to the on-set rivalries and calibrations of talent that also feed into any staging of competitive force. And, given that he knows that any good actor can give a *wrong* reading of one of his lines and make it look brilliant, it is mission-critical that he gets to talk to them in detail. (This issue will return when we come to *Luck*.) Indeterminacy is of the essence for Milch's alloyed characters since they, too, are caught between competing drives, a public voice and their private voices. And this gets at why, in interviews, talks and lectures, Milch's communicative social voice tends to dominate the space: he is paranoid, with some justification given the history – and his experience – of production in Hollywood, that someone else will give a public reading, hence interpretation, of his work that is as likely to be wrong as right. This is what happened with the 'racism' incident mentioned in the previous chapter during the seminar he gave for writers while working on *NYPD Blue*. Once his words left the orbit of his communicative protection they could be adjusted by others to mean the contrary of what he meant. Communicating his intention, his meaning, is vital to a successful Milch production. The industrial conditions of *Deadwood* provided a perfect opportunity for him to ensure he was able to do this effectively with minimum interference.

Milch's writing indicates that he is rehearsing for what he needs to tell the actors:

> Swearengen's boys should be on the eye and report to him what they see. And also how he hears about Hickok. Trying to digest all of this and to synthesize the information in various scenarios would obsess him. Somehow, show the equivalent process in Bullock and Star – that is, they evaluate the same data in terms of what it forecasts for the settlement, its nature and staying power. What's important here is that Bullock not be passive as he synthesizes the data.

Or:

> Swearengen is not unconflicted about killing Brom – know this can bring outside heat. He'd much prefer it if Brom leaves the settlement without realizing it at all that he's been duped.

This is all inside Swearengen's head – all private, *we* don't know what he is thinking – but Milch is telling his colleagues what is inside the character's head, giving them an inside view of what will only be seen on the outside in the show. This allows the crew to angle things a little more one way than another and get closer to Milch's intention.

Milch knows that when any material gets on the air it has to have some kind of clarity, it has to lean one way or the other. Total indeterminacy would not get beyond a pilot, if even that far. How then, can he move from a script zone that does not have that clarity to a performance zone in which that clarity is necessary? The answer is by talking. Words and speech constitute his bridge to the world. If Milch cannot talk he has no bridge. Milch is cheating the script one way rather than another way by surrounding his dialogue, at these formative stages, with interior intelligence about what is driving the characters to do and say what they do and say. He *needs* everyone on the team to collaborate with him in doing that cheating, in shifting the script *this* way rather than that. When Milch says a character 'would' or 'wouldn't' do this or that, he is speaking from inside the character, interpreting his writing voice for the crew. When he says 'we', as in '[i]f we're not going to show Hickok's murder until the end of the third episode', he means the camera, and Milch is more widely thinking about the *sequence* of the display of data to the audience. Part of this is additive, piling on scenes and moments into the sequence that paint a particular tone:

> Intercut during this sequence with Swearengen as the events of his evening culminate: these would include his efforts to contact the new rivals; his frustration compounded at the distraction caused by word of the Metz massacre, as he hears its details increasingly, privately convinced the murderers aren't Indians at all, observing to Dority 'that's Persimmon Bill's act, that cocksucker must be back from Wyoming, get word to that cocksucker I want to see him, if these boys from Wyoming and Chicago want to play rough they'll have him to deal with.' Add to this mix his uncertainty as to whether Hickok is allied with new arrivals, if he isn't his resolve to buy him.

Imagine an analogy with Dr Jekyll and Mr Hyde: Hyde is Milch's writing voice, and these words, this guide to interpretation, is Jekyll. Jekyll knows all about Hyde, is his closest friend, and he knows that when he is transformed into Hyde he cannot stop that transformation. So, Jekyll has the job of telling everyone what is inside Hyde, what he actually means. Why? Why can't Milch as Hyde tell us what he means? Because, perhaps, he does not want, cannot be, so explicit when he is Hyde. He has to be indeterminate Hyde in order to be Hyde. He has to hide. Something about his training at Iowa, something about the power of having a secret so deep one cannot remember what it is or what it means, something about having a father who says one thing but *means* something quite different, something that any intelligent, intuitive five-year-old can detect and interpret, something like that may be at the heart of a start of an answer.

And there is a further problem. Perhaps Jekyll is not as clear as he thinks he is. Perhaps when Milch *does* try to explain what he means to the crew and to the actors this is only partially successful. He would then have to build into the script itself something more determinate while holding on to the spirit of its intuition; perhaps mix up the words, make them ornate, difficult to deliver, in order to stimulate the actors to continually ask for clarification. There are hints in the discussion about season two that some of the crew did not: 'If that director had gotten any aspects of the performances in that show, we would have a much more focused Alma, a much more focused Bullock ... one forgets how far away from the intentions... [tape malfunctions]'. For example, in the conversations about the pilot episode the familiar language of *Deadwood* has not arrived. Here is the first version of Swearengen's speech to the patrons of the Gem, after discovering that news of the (fake) Indian attack on the Metz family might disrupt his evening's business:

> *Swearengen*: Let me tell you something. Fuck the fucking Indians. What did they ever do with this fucking land? They had these hills how many fucking years and did they find gold? No, because they're fucking savages and they live like fucking pigs. Did you ever see a fucking Indian saloon, or where you could buy pussy, or play a game of cards. No, because they're too busy riding around naked on their fucking horses. This camp is safe. This camp is safe. What happens outside the camp may be a different story, now you're playing the Indians' game, and I can't make any guarantees. But I'll do this: I'll pay fifty fucking dollars to anyone that brings in one those motherfucker's heads cut off from their fucking bodies ... So, everyone, fucking, the next drink is on the house, and don't worry about anything.

In the final transmitted version this becomes:

> *Swearengen*: Now, I know word's circulatin' Indians killed a family on the Spearfish Road. Now it's not for me to tell anyone in this camp what to do, as much as I don't want more people getting' their throats cut, scalps lifted or any other godless thing that these godless bloodthirsty heathens do. Or even if someone wants to ride out! In darkest night! But I will tell you this. I'd use tonight to get myself organized. Ride out in the morning clear-headed. And startin' tomorrow morning, I will offer a personal fifty dollar bounty for every decapitated head of as many of these godless heathen cocksuckers as anyone can bring in. Tomorrow. With no upper limit! That's all I say on that subject, 'cept next round's on the house. And God rest the souls of that poor family. And pussy's half price, next 15 minutes.

In both versions, Swearengen's aim is to discourage his customers from riding out in righteous drunken vengeance by reminding them of the dangers ('they're fucking savages'; 'throats cut ... in darkest night'), but the first version sounds as though it was spoken by a white supremacist in the twenty-first century and the second does not. The first version has a racism that is Swearengen's personally – in the second the racism is pointed towards ensuring that his speech is effective – 'godless heathen cocksuckers' has a musical vulgarity that 'fucking savages' lacks. In addition Swearengen is careful to pretend in the final version that he has no right to tell anyone what to do, that is, he has an awareness of the sensitivity of drunken egos that is absent from his direct assertions of authority in the first. Milch found his way into this character by revising up his intelligence and moderating his racist vulgarity, such that it is manifested in a ploy to 'assay' or calibrate his opponents and friends. Intelligence here stands for socialisation: Swearengen rounds out as a character, finds depths, even though in terms of plot the effect is exactly the same. But from the actor's point of view this is much harder to understand. It demands more explanation from Milch-as-Jekyll, it demands his presence on set, moment by moment. And this is how the rest of *Deadwood* developed, through Milch increasingly complicating the locutions of characters such that only Jekyll's presence on set could ensure the correct interpretation.

Sobriety also means God-talk. As we have seen, Milch was drawn to writing about St Paul, but it is also clear that his time at Alcoholics Anonymous segued with some kind of religious devotion. What that means remains obscure, but even early on in the planning this kind of talk emerges:

> Where's God's hand in Swearengen? Why does he let Trixie live when he's strangling her in her room? He sees in her eyes just before she is about to die a child's wistful fear. In Trixie's last moment of extremity, is Swearengen able to recognise that same primitive uncertainty out of which his own savage cunning and brutality have grown? Does that recognition prompt an instant's compassion for her? Is that God offering His hand? And having God's hand for a moment, how quickly does Swearengen seek to loose its grasp?

The Revd Smith is the most obvious remnant of the St Paul script, and Milch spends a lot of time with his back story, and then with his relationship with Swearengen:

> Swearengen feels in Smith's camaraderie Smith's assumption that he and Swearengen are fellow sufferers and sinners redeemed by Christ's sacrifice. Al doesn't like any person thinking he knows him that well, especially with a fucked up idea like that. And then, as this feeling moves toward consciousness, it might express itself, 'What does that fucking

guy think, that I'm the fucking devil?', which is actually what Al is afraid of, he feels so separate from God...

By the time the pilot was written Milch had already planned out many of the character arcs for the rest of the season. Most of the plot events were also established in broad strokes: the fact that Swearengen does not kill Trixie, the smallpox epidemic, the killing of Hickok, the relationship that forms between Alma and Bullock. Each episode is written fairly conventionally for dramatic television, even one without commercial breaks, in three acts. The more Milch talks the further the details of setting, character and motive are honed. Characters who don't appear until the third season, such as Jack Langrishe, are already in place before the first has started shooting. Swearengen's paranoia and Bullock's searching for settlement eventually coalesce into the abstraction that Milch calls an 'organizing social force', something that protects the survival of the camp. Beyond the paranoia he finds other mechanisms for this:

> Efforts by other characters to find organizing principles other than paranoia for getting through the day – (a) the mercantile identity; (b) staying high; (c) the constructive social impulse (domestic relations ... custodial or parental relationships, involving the child; friendships like those between Cochran and Merrick, Utter and Hickok; pets, like Ellsworth's taking over the care of Driscoll's dog).

Critically this leads Milch to build the character of Alma Garret as a junkie rather than a literary journalist as he had first envisaged; Doc Cochran is her 'dealer' initially.

By mid-2003 much of the plot of the first season of *Deadwood* was in place, and they were well into writing the second episode where the dialogue is settling into something familiar. Cochran's warning to Jane not to tell Bullock where the survivor of the Metz massacre, Sophia, is hiding, for example, is complete:

> *Jane*: Why hold out on him? He formed the party that found this Little One, among all the dead of her family.
>
> *Cochran*: Didn't he? And didn't he shoot a man he suspected in the murders? And if I confided, would he circulate my optimism? Wouldn't he say, 'When the little one speaks you'll find out I was right – not the Sioux killed her family but road-agents.' And s'pose it was road-agents, and they hear his talk. Where does the Little One stand then?
>
> *Jane*: You got a dark turn of mind.
>
> *Cochran*: I see more misery out of them moved to justify theirselves as them that set out to do harm.

Milch is also sectioning off parts of his talking for specific episode writers to handle, as well as developing characters not in the pilot (which was shot the year before). For example, his account of Cy Tolliver, rival pimp to Swearengen and owner of the Bella Union brothel, accesses the knowledge we see on display in his early poem about the gamblers at Haskell Levine's:

> You are willing to embrace the idea that there is some force operating stronger than the percentages: 'I'm feeling lucky today, Pittsburgh always wins when...' People want to feel that they can choose whenever they want to do it. These are the legitimate prey to those who know that, ultimately, the percentages win but the price that those people pay is that they never feel as if they're in action; they're detached from the world. That's the choice they make, for one reason or another. They're voyeurs, because the thing that you never get is to be 'in action'. If you're going to side with the percentages, there is something fundamentally inhuman about the percentages. What's human is: you risk, you win, you lose, and you die. You feel your humanity in the state of contingency of uncertainty set against the backdrop of doom. The percentages are eternal; to the extent that you allow yourself with the percentages, you win except what you lose is your humanity ... This is the backdrop to what Tolliver is now living into, that his passion for having been unacknowledged or subsumed or subordinated and absorbed into the percentages: 'Honey, all you got to do is keep the trim in shape and...' – he has not acknowledged the fundamental impulse in his relationship [to Joanie Stubbs], which is that he would like to love her. Something in him is saying, 'You should've wanted to love her.'

At the same time Milch is building something that he, too, wants to protect and to survive. After the success of season one, there is no break in their planning for the next season, although now there are other voices transcribed, however briefly. For Milch the issue was to highlight the continuing organising force, beyond the pursuit of gold:

> No-one has yet settled into a public identity as a source of happiness. One way or another that's going to be the organizing force in the second season; the discovery that whatever separate piece you think you can make as an individual, unless it has some sort of expression in a civic identity it doesn't hold (civic identity including marriage) and isn't adequate as a source of happiness. You have to take some sort of responsibility.

Bullock is now sheriff, Tolliver is in league with the mining magnate George Hearst via his intermediary, the geologist Francis Wolcott. Milch is also interested in Pinkertons as a corrupt protection force and confects the plot in which an undercover Pinkerton agent infiltrates the camp and seduces Silas Adams; he talks about Joanie Stubbs opening her own high-end brothel elsewhere in the camp, and the arrival of the Nigger General and his friendship with Hostetler. There is also a lengthy talk about the arrival of Mark Twain and his conflicted nature as the risk-taker Samuel Clemens and the literary figure, including a scene with Swearengen and Twain telling each other tall tales.

Although Milch is voluminous in his talking, we also hear from Ted Mann, Jody Worth, Regina Corrado, Elizabeth Sarnoff and producer Gregg Fienberg. Before the second season began writing the problem they all faced was the status of Swearengen. By the end of the first season he had been established as a character who could overcome any challenge, even a standing military army in the town. The dramatic issue was to bring in a complication that would disable that dramatic advantage and offer the audience another view of the town beyond the grasp of a pseudo-benign but godlike organising figure. Eventually, after many dead ends, they focused on the arrival of the telegraph as a disruptive force for Swearengen that is aggravated by his knowledge that Bullock, 'cunt-struck' with Alma, has taken his eye off the ball. They hit upon a fight between the two; it is Milch himself who intuits some of the elements of the scene:

> One good image ... is if Swearengen knows that Bullock, in terms of Swearengen's sense of the simultaneity of everything that's going on in the camp, if Swearengen knows that Bullock's up there banging Alma ... if Swearengen hears the gunshot ... We talked about ... the way form inevitably dictates content, and if you start with, in his eyes, if he's treating the whole town as if it were a stage set and he's showing where the people are fucking moving ... I don't know if that argues for starting with him up on the balcony...

As with the pilot there are very lengthy discussions about the opening sequences, since these put in place much of the momentum for the season that follows. As Milch says:

> This is one of those regrettable situations where the first piece of writing is going to take an awful long time because it is going to contain so many things it's going to generate so many different storylines but we just have to be patient with it, and whatever contributions each of you can or chooses to attempt, that's great. And anything else in terms of what you think should go into the show, just don't wait is what I'm proposing to you. Be busy.

Each of the writers is instructed to do an outline for a scene they want, and more often than not they deliver on time and with exactly the kind of dynamics that Milch is seeking. Where he loses control, on set, especially when it comes to the technical *direction* of shots – the composition, camera movement, positioning of the actors – then we begin to see deviations from the spirit of the script, despite his wholehearted efforts to see them off. In one sense it is the sheer ambition of Milch's vision that cannot be encompassed by a television show, its seriality keyed in the medium to the paced sequential delivery of packets of character and plot data, often impeccably performed, but vulnerable to the deadening effects of multiple viewpoints alternated segment by segment. Milch incorporates this aspect of the medium as an aesthetic *of* the show:

> Last year I talked once about the fact that invariably form in a story predicts content to the extent that you have a story whose form embraces multiple points of view. Which is what this one does. You're jumping from place to place. The very multiplicity of the points of view demands that the deepest source of reality is in the apprehension of community. That you can only understand experience from multiple points of view and to the extent that the individual accepts the necessity of the multiplicity.

'Multiplicity' in the naturalist confines of the nineteenth-century camp meant collective, community organisation. To fail to see the necessity for this would doom the camp to violence and privatised experience. For example, here is Milch thinking about why it is that they have been struggling with Bullock and Alma's sexual relationship:

> It seems to me that the mistake I've been making may have to do with focusing on the sexual component of the relationship and its being flaunted because it may be that simple it's so uncharacteristic of Bullock that he just wouldn't do it. The offense that Swearengen has nothing to do with the sexuality of it. It's the anti-social aspect of Bullock's behaviour, which Swearengen attributes to the fact he's banging her, but I think that Swearengen's fundamental intuition is that Bullock is making a separate peace, he's trying to find happiness [in] a purely private or familial relationship.
>
> One idea of western storytelling or whatever the fuck it is, or one idea of the dominant theme is the individual's discovery of his proper context of his activity in loyalty to the state or the fucking community, as opposed to the purely personal, which could be represented, say, just by family. Something is rotten in the state of Denmark. What's rotten is a mother fucking an uncle, a kid is fixated on the betrayal within the family, rather than the common welfare of the country.

But this knowledge is complicated by the way the characters recruit the world and nature to their own purposes. Swearengen, in Milch's view, is effective as a community leader because that role fulfils a view of himself that is ultimately 'romantic': 'He believes the world is dependent upon his energy for its survival. It's another version of what they call projection, if you feel like you can't control what's going on inside you have to believe you can control everything that's going on outside.' And, of course, nobody can do that. The Deadwood camp is particularly vulnerable to external control because its riches make it so: the story of seasons two and three is the gradual wresting of all control from Swearengen and his making peace with what remains after Hearst leaves with the town under his financial and political thumb. More than that, dramatically, Swearengen can do too much – there is an expectation among the audience that things will go sour in the camp until Al comes along with his secret plans and cunning in order to make it right. That was essentially his role in season one. Late in the 2004 planning for season two Milch observed: 'I think that Swearengen's personality continues to be too overwhelming to the material and that it gives you very effective scenes but it deprives the other characters of anything to play.'

The team began to think about ways of neutralising Swearengen's force, confecting a new Swearengen who emerges after the fight with Bullock. The crucial scene, one of the most important in the entire show, occurs after the two of them fall from the balcony of the Gem into the muddy thoroughfare. Bullock struggles to get up, and as he does so Swearengen pulls his knife and makes to slit his throat from behind. He does not, however: instead he sees the stagecoach, just arrived, carrying Bullock's wife Martha and his son William. The son smiles at Swearengen who stays his hand: 'Welcome to Deadwood', he shouts to the carriage, '... can be combative.' The puzzle here is *why* Swearengen does not kill Bullock. According to Milch, we get 'a new Swearengen being analyzed by the old Swearengen ... It's like when a guy's going to turn into Mr Hyde; when he's still Dr Jekyll he says, "Put the wax in my ears..."' The solution was to have Swearengen partially live into his decision to spare Bullock, and then return his guns and sheriff's badge in public. However, the fight brings to a head a medical condition – impacted kidney stones – that nearly kills Swearengen. While he recovers the rest of the camp develops without him: 'different kinds of parasitic things ... go on when someone is dying or dead. [People] start to reposition themselves; they start to affiliate with different characters.' Milch was particularly concerned that taking Swearengen out of the action had to be long term or it would feel like 'a fucking cheat'; he deliberately wanted to frustrate audience appetites.

Swearengen's return really is a remarkable transformation:[42]

> when he comes out he's going to see the beginnings of the New World. He's going to have the telegraph operator there ... You have Swearengen at the end of the second episode, paradoxically, although he looks like he's beat to shit, it's really the apotheosis of Swearengen's power because he discovers his deepest power in a gesture of concession to Bullock. In terms of the way the audience experiences it, he has the capacity to grow. So, he does not need to prove himself any longer by killing people; he also proves himself by handing the power over to Bullock ... Swearengen demonstrating his adaptability.[43]

This was a commercial and political risk for Milch as well as the rest of the crew. Swearengen was a key emblem of the show and putting him on a shelf for several episodes required the support of HBO. For Milch, it was an attempt to get back to the spirit of the original writing in 2002 and 2003 before the show was aired and became such a success:

> we have to let the characters sorta find their own ways, even if the ways that they find diverge from or contradict what we have seen about them up to this point. In that way you give the characters back their volition which is where you began. When I began imagining the series I tried to let the patterns ... be dictated by, for better or worse and with whatever defects of my own imagination, was the reality that I experienced in the characters and [you want to] give them back their free will as you're thinking about the plot lines.

The literary heroes that Milch went back to – beyond twentieth-century figures such as Warren, Fitzgerald and the poet Stanley Kunitz – were all nineteenth-century novelists: Melville, Dreiser, Twain. (At one point he remarks that *Deadwood* is 'like an old 19th century novel, big sprawling cocksucker'.) When Milch also had actors in the writing room he would draw on these enthusiasms. Anna Gunn, who began her stint as Martha Bullock in season two, and had worked with Ted Mann and Milch on an episode of *NYPD Blue* eleven years before, is treated to an extemporisation on Martha's history as well as the history of naturalism in literature (Crane, Zola, Dreiser, Norris, Maupassant) that dealt with 'historical forces operating that were just too powerful for the individual will to deal with, so you keep seeing people, the circumstances of those lives overwhelmed any opportunity they had to make choices that could govern their lives'. The point of the reference was to demonstrate that women like her character had, historically, very little choice in how the world was run, 'they'd been overwhelmed forever by, among other things, men'. So what it means to be that woman was 'lower your expectations', 'train yourself not to be bitter'.

One of the clearest examples of a character being changed by 'his own volition' was Francis Wolcott, Hearst's geologist, who comes to Deadwood to buy up the gold claims on behalf of his employer. At first Wolcott is a nerd-like figure, unfamiliar with women or sex, and somewhat lightweight. However, his association with Cy Tolliver allows Milch to calibrate the differences and similarities in such a way that we see Wolcott develop into a savage serial killer, one of the most evil characters in the entire series. Here is the thought process half-way through the thinking about the character, beginning with thoughts about Tolliver:

> Something about his mother terrified him and he is a misogynist because he is so afraid of all women, but because he is so successfully misogynist he becomes uninteresting ... If you allow his misogyny to transmute itself into racism and he becomes the architect of the suppression of the Chinese now that character has a whole different dimension ... And Wolcott is at the centre of all of it. The thing about Wolcott is that he's like Albert Speer ... [the] Nazi architect. He wasn't one of them, he wasn't a bad guy because he was an aesthetician of evil. He wasn't compelled to evil. That's Wolcott. Wolcott is so handsome and so gifted and it appears to him that [if] there is no God then it's all a tawdry fallen show. And there's nothing else for it but to be very good at manipulating it.

Wolcott brings Chinese prostitutes into the camp to be run under the supervision of Tolliver via Mr Lee (Philip Moon), a rival boss to Swearengen's ally, Mr Wu. Milch continues the comparison with the evil of the Nazi regime through their arrival in improvised prison wagons, 'the effect to be [Jews] in cattle cars going to Auschwitz'. For Milch, Wolcott is an example of the schism between religion and rationality, that once alchemy is split by science into medicine and geology, we start to see human subjectivity affect the split. But in his understanding, no such split can hold – Wolcott may *affect* disinterested scientific distance when he kills the whores in Joanie Stubbs's brothel, but he suspects there may be something more; as Milch puts it, imagining a conversation between Wolcott and Doc Cochrane (unfilmed):

> 'There seem to be certain vestigial attributes which my science has not accommodated. I pretend to myself that it's a mere intellectual disinterest which persuades me to watch the way blood spurts for example, from a severed jugular, but I suspect something else is afoot. Is it possible doctor that there is some subterranean stream still flowing in us?' What he's talking about is the Faustian idea of what seems to be a disinterest in the pursuit of knowledge, is in fact a desire to grab the infinite by the balls.

It is typical of Milch to discover his way into a familiar icon or genre through complicating another kind of off-the-peg character; in doing so he transforms that character into a strange, unsighted figure – Jack the Ripper with a PhD in geology.[44]

Wolcott hangs himself in the final episode of season two (Milch recounted, several days later, his finding a young man who had hanged himself), a tiny moment of justice for a character whom Milch equated with figures such as Robert Oppenheimer and the bureaucrats who managed capitalist affairs and in doing so had become dislocated from their own humanity. For Milch, in a foreshadowing of some of his concerns in *John From Cincinnati*, the two were intimately intertwined:

> The fundamental disrespect that allows the movement of people in groups, in pursuit of whatever symbol of economic gain or of any of that shit, makes possible anything else. And it's of the essence. I'm not passing any moral judgment on it, it's of the essence, it is what we do as human beings. That's what distinguishes us from other species. We are capable of that kind of abstract thinking which will then express itself in the inflictions not only on the environment but on other people. The rule in the human experience is not peace, it's war. It's the murder of hundreds of thousands and the more effective we get – the kind of genial folksiness of a guy like Hearst cloaks the truth which stands out in bold relief when you are just slitting people's throats. It's the same aberration. I try to be a responsible leader. My behaviour organizes behaviour of a lot of other people and unless I pray constantly, it occurs to me to hurt these people all of the time, just because I can. That's the essence of being a human.

Wolcott is a beta male to Hearst's alpha, but that makes him at least as dangerous on his own scale of power; by introducing both figures to the camp – Wolcott in season two, and Hearst mainly in the third and final season – Milch slits the envelope of a show that had established its own medium-specific ways of doing and being in the world for its characters, and revealed a deeper, darker truth and the reality in which they had to move. As with *NYPD Blue*, the accessibility and familiarity of the genre was a portal for his imaginative work.

All great artists use genre and familiar figures in this way – think of the great directors of the twentieth century (Nicholas Ray/*Rebel Without A Cause*, Alfred Hitchcock/*Notorious*, Max Ophuls/*Letter from an Unknown Woman*, Orson Welles/*Touch of Evil*) or novelists (Cormac McCarthy/*The Road*, Philip Roth/*The Human Stain*, Scott Fitzgerald/*The Great Gatsby*), and the remarkable way they are able to use genre in terms of what Stanley Cavell calls 'a medium'. In *Deadwood*, the benign circumstances that HBO offered – a closed set with a cast available to meet Milch's strange, last-minute revision process – combined successfully with Milch's appetite for innovation, his deep work ethic and what was clearly a realisation of his ambitions as a writer to become part of the tradition that he had helped assemble in *American Literature: The Makers and the Making*. Like Bullock, he is 'taken by a vision', but at a stage in his life where he was experienced and wise enough not to squander it.

After Tolliver clears up Wolcott's mass murder of the prostitutes in the Chez Amis, and Stubbs – isolated among the bodies – sees him off (as she failed to do with her father as a child), the next major plot pivot is the death of Bullock's adopted son, William. For the viewer, this event comes out of nowhere, anchored to three axes of dramatic action that envelop it – Tom Nuttall's purchase of a bicycle (a penny-farthing-type 'boneshaker', poorly adapted to the muddy thoroughfare), and the bet that he cannot ride it through town; the murder of one brother by another, Mose Manuel (Pruitt Taylor Vince), on the encouragement of Wolcott and Tolliver; and the castration of a stallion at the livery by Hostetler (Richard Gant) and the Nigger General (Franklyn Ajaye). While there was no hesitation among the writing team about the rightness of this event, there were moral qualms. Milch comments:

> Speaking personally, there's a tremendous taboo in dramatizing the death of a child. One feels like I'm putting my own children at risk. An audience takes every opportunity to try and dissociate emotionally from a series on that basis, by making the argument that it's not credible, that it's manipulative. What they're really saying is, 'That's too tough for me.' The truth is, as a parent, that is a contract you've signed on for whether or not you're willing to admit it. That we all know at some level when you become a parent you're admitting that life can absolutely destroy you. That if something terrible happens, you feel as if there is no resource in you to deal with that. In a sense, that isn't the question that life asks you – do you have the resource to deal with it? Okay, you don't have the resources to deal with it, you're still alive, now what? You don't survive, you endure.

That is the situation that they confront Bullock and Martha with – how to endure. For one of the writers, Elizabeth Sarnoff, the question was would they stay together once William was dead? Milch sees it this way:

> You know to me, if I had to make a bet I would say the only chance that they would ever have of staying together is that kid dying [...] In a way I should think she would be more dependent on him without a child ... [for wives] ... it's the children who are the organizing principle of the woman's behaviour. And, therefore, for her to lose the child and to be out in the fucking world that outrages her sensibility. And not to have the man she loves. If he lets her go then, then he's a bad guy.

Martha does stay with Bullock into the third season, but in the second half of 2005 when they began writing it, there comes a realisation that it would be a lot darker than anything that had come before:

> A contrast between the third season and the second season is it gets rough, its gets physically rough in the third season. Those things – it's like a virus – those things are usually self-limiting in some way – but when you see a fight that's motivated by economics and you see someone getting beat and realize this beating isn't going to stop with one getting knocked out, this beating's going to end with somebody being dead. When you're watching that, when you become aware of that, there's a real sea change [...] It's not that these people are more evil. It's just that they have given themselves over to an organizing principle which includes death, which includes murder, in the same way that's why I wanted Swearengen to have that Indian head. When they took the land from the Indians, until they made their point, they had to go ahead and kill them and that just became an accepted approach. Then they stopped killing them as long as they stayed out of the camp. Once you've crossed that line, that hangs around your neck no matter what – if you're capable – that's a living option for you always. I remember burying this guy in Mexico and I remember saying, 'I'm not really this kind of person, this is a fucking exception. This is a big fucking exception.' And the truth is that's not how that works. There are no exceptions.

This season sees Hearst dominate the town, bringing in armed forces to intimidate its people, murdering Ellsworth to prompt Alma to sign over her gold claim, mutilating Swearengen and inflaming Bullock's sense of injustice. But in a sense the entire season is a holding off of a final confrontation with Swearengen and the rest of the town; when it comes it is also avoided at the last minute, again by an act of murder, this time Swearengen killing one of his whores to substitute her for Trixie, who wounded Hearst in a fit of rage after Ellsworth's death. It is not that this does not matter, but that Milch begins to find other interests beyond this one. It's as if the fact of what humans are under capitalism's organising principle is less interesting than figures, characters and their impulses that push back against it.

For example, early on in the season we are introduced to the theatre impresario Jack Langrishe (Brian Cox), who brings his team of thespians to the town in order to make money and to enliven its cultural dimension (not much in evidence up to now). Like Hickok, Bullock, Swearengen and Calamity Jane, Langrishe was a real historical figure who toured the mining camps, running shows such as an adaptation of Rip Van Winkle that had a strong moral message (in that case a temperance one). The stage was a reminder to the camps of the culture of the East, however unruly the performances and the audience. Langrishe may have been gay, but in *Deadwood* his love of theatre is one aspect of the civilising impulse hitherto neglected; in any case Milch makes a surprising decision – although never cashed out because the show was cancelled too soon – to make his homosexuality something of an act that he puts on for the world. Milch eventually has a young woman move to the camp, in secret, who Langrishe meets and hopes to introduce to the rest of the troupe. This girl is the product of sex with a woman married to a homosexual: the daughter is Langrishe's but she is used by him as a 'beard' to protect his public status. But these complexities are never resolved, merely hinted at in the final output.

Langrishe is also friends with Swearengen, who is, in Milch's words, 'a great producer', and he provides a sounding board for Swearengen's strategic planning, as well as a bridge to Hearst whose bad back he treats. This latter role was originally designated for a character called Dr Summerland, who was also a real historical figure, John D. Rockefeller's father William, a con man, rapist and snake oil salesman who lived for a time in North Dakota, as well as in Deadwood, after abandoning his family. Milch was drawn to him because he illustrates his belief that 'the fundamental impulses toward monopolistic acquisition is [*sic*] an effort to control the absent father'. But some time during the writing of the sixth episode came wind that the show would be cancelled. There are no more notes available.

Whatever the reasons for the cancellation, what is clear is that Milch was not running away from the Hearst–Swearengen conflict but finding innovative ways to bounce plot matter around new elements in the mix, such as Langrishe. Some of the most touching scenes in the third season have seemingly little to do with the assault on the spirit of the camp by Hearst. Notably, the death of the ageing actor Chesterton, played impeccably by the British actor Aubrey Morris, is a staggering avoidance of sentiment at precisely a moment – they are rehearsing the Gloucester–Edgar mock-suicide scene from *King Lear* – when the drama most risks indulging it. Cox brings to Langrishe something that had always been a distinctive dimension of the show, its capacity to misdirect the viewer while beguiling them in a fresh undefined way. More than that, Milch is daring the viewer to appreciate the force of acting and performance – culturally, politically and economically – in a context that appears extremely inhospitable to it. The episode 'Amateur Night' introduces Langrishe's troupe to the town, providing the denizens with an opportunity to show off their skills – Richardson, Farnum's long-suffering 'pet', is a fine juggler – but also allowing the viewers to reflect on what it must take to get in front of people with one's creative or any other kind of skills.

There is another reason why Langrishe is critical to this season and this writer. Swearengen is stuck in an impossible impasse facing the machine-like Hearst. He knows that he must respond to Hearst's provocations, that he must act, but he does not know what to do. Hearst – in Milch's theory of monopolistic individuals – has 'something missing', some aspect that would humanise his activity. He has no sense of proportion or scale; *everything* – the entire planet – 'speaks to me'. Swearengen on the other hand, by genetic accident or strange brain wiring, *has something more* than his selfish criminal desires, and that is the thing that allows Sophia and Trixie to live, that refuses to include the 50,000 dollar bribe in Deadwood's founding document, that sees in the camp the possibility of democratic community. It is precisely this that inhibits him from making a move, much to the frustration of the other camp 'elders'. It is Langrishe who talks Swearengen through his problem, rather than offering a solution. As Milch puts it, 'it takes the artfulness of Langrishe to raise to the level of consciousness what Swearengen's own strategy is':

> *Swearengen*: If that cocksucker hadn't shareholders you could murder him while you adjusted his back.
> *Langrishe*: Serpent's teeth, shareholders. Ten thousand would rise to replace him.

It is tempting, if reductive, to think of Langrishe as Milch's avatar, whispering wisdom to Swearengen, the one man in the camp with a taste for art as an organising principle, hoping that some part of his knowledge of it will make the world better, halt its rapacious capacity to destroy itself. Milch is motivated by many things, but one of the many personal stories that he tells in the writers' room is the one about winning the Humanitas prize in front of Father Kaiser, and imagining while making his speech that he will call him a paedophile. Instead, as we have seen, Milch said something beautiful and touching; something arose in the moment of saying it but stayed like the revelation of an idea one had already thought but forgotten, a truth one knew and hid away until the moment it most needed to be heard. Perhaps writing itself is, for Milch, the time when opportunities for this kind of revelation are most ripe.

Langrishe tries in his talk with Swearengen to cultivate a similar understanding about how an antagonist might be seen as something else, someone who provides the occasion for a better choice, another path, and perhaps he succeeds. The final plan we see Swearengen enact is to dress the prostitute whose throat he has cut in Trixie's clothes so to fool Hearst and his men. If the deceit fails, he will be killed. It is a theatrical manoeuvre that is steeped in all the violent and abusive history that Swearengen brings, and yet it is taken by him, his allies and us as an act of nobility, of courageous self-sacrifice. The stakes are very high, and the motivation alloyed, doubled, sold in sin. It is a fitting ending to the show that most clearly realised Milch's vision of a world facing a social and economic destination that formed the vantage point for its reception.

Notes

1 David Thorburn, MIT interview with Milch, www.youtube.com/watch?v=MDT-VIP8bvE8 (accessed 24 April 2018).
2 Denis Dutton, *The Art Instinct* (London: Bloomsbury, 2010).
3 More has been written about *Deadwood* than any other Milch show: see, for example, Ina Rae Hark, *Deadwood* (Detroit, MI: Wayne State University Press, 2012); Paul Stasi and Jennifer Grieman (eds), *The Last Western: Deadwood and the End of American Empire* (New York: Bloomsbury, 2013).
4 Bernard Weinraub, 'The Demons That Have Driven *NYPD Blue*', *The New York Times*, 18 June 2000, www.nytimes.com/2000/06/18/arts/television-radio-the-demons-that-have-driven-nypd-blue.html (accessed 31 December 2016).
5 According to Bochco, 'it was a real, not a studio definition of profits'; Steven Bochco, *Truth Is a Total Defense* (self-published, 2016), p. 97. *NYPD Blue* made over a billion US dollars in foreign sales alone.
6 I am grateful to Murray Pomerance for clarifying this for me during his visit to Brisbane in April 2018.
7 Susan Sontag, *Illness as Metaphor* (London: Picador, 2001).
8 These lectures were originally available at http://theideaofthewriter.blogspot.com.au/2008/07/1997-lecture-series.html, although the link has been inert for some time. For a short clip, see http://mediacommons.futureofthebook.org/imr/2012/04/23/reaching-out-milch-s-teaching-voice-genius (accessed 26 December 2016).
9 Not all actors appreciated this or made much of it. Timothy Olyphant, in one of the *Deadwood* DVD Extra featurettes, makes it clear that he just let Milch talk above his head and then delivered his lines when the time came.
10 One has to pause and wonder at the extraordinary oddness of the character names so far (and those about to be mentioned): Trout, Mooney and Maddock connote some kind of mutated night-time fish disco.
11 Dickens and Welliver both had ongoing roles in *Deadwood*; Dickens has maintained a fine career in shows such as *Sons of Anarchy*, *Fear the Walking Dead* and *House of Cards*. She virtually steals the show in the film *Gone Girl*. Welliver – the son of the painter Neil Welliver, who Milch had met through Warren at Yale – found later success as the lead on the Amazon show *Bosch* (2014–18).
12 As was clearly the case in US hospital dramas of the 1990s; see Jason Jacobs, *Body Trauma TV: The New Hospital Dramas* (London: BFI, 2003). US movies and television display such a fascination with the destruction of *things*, often in slow motion, that one wonders if there is not simply a cultural desire to pull it all down or, at least, to experience what that would feel like.

13 Cormac McCarthy, *Blood Meridian* (New York: Random House, 1985); it is little surprise in this context that McCarthy spends a lot of his time at the Sante Fe Institute with friends such as the physicist Murray Gell-Mann, whose work on fundamental quantum particles won him the Nobel prize. The need to anchor one's work to a fundamental immovable point is especially strong in US literature, and postmodern, postcolonial fiction offered merely a dead end, however entertaining it was for a time. That is why Roth's trilogy, *The Human Stain*, *American Pastoral* and *I Married a Communist*, dwarves his earlier attempts to deal with the ongoing problems of narrator, narration and point of view that Mark McGurl tracks in *The Program Era: Postwar Fiction and the Rise of Creative Writing* (Cambridge, MA: Harvard University Press, 2009). They are realist accounts, inflected by genre to a strong extent, and anchored to amazing granular details. David Shields, who was one of Milch's students, cites the description of glove manufacturing in *American Pastoral* as one of the reasons he gave up on fiction altogether.

14 Amy Hungerford, *Postmodern Belief: American Literature and Religion since 1960* (Princeton, NJ: Princeton University Press, 2010), p. 55.

15 Hungerford, *Postmodern Belief*, p. 56.

16 Hungerford, *Postmodern Belief*, pp. 132–3.

17 Hungerford, *Postmodern Belief*, p. 136.

18 Hungerford, *Postmodern Belief*, p. 136.

19 Stanley Cavell, 'The Fact of Television', in *Themes Out of School: Effects and Causes* (Chicago: University of Chicago Press, 1984), pp. 266–7.

20 http://news.bbc.co.uk/2/hi/uk_news/wales/1517665.stm (accessed 29 April 2019). The report says that he was commissioned by BBC Wales to give the class. The institution has subsequently changed its name.

21 McGurl, *Program Era*, p. 230.

22 McGurl, *Program Era*, p. 232.

23 McGurl, *Program Era*, p. 233.

24 Frank Furedi, *Power of Reading* (London: Bloomsbury, 2015), p. 186.

25 Furedi, *Power of Reading*, pp. 186–7.

26 Furedi, *Power of Reading*, p. 187.

27 Lewis Lapham, quoted in Furedi, *Power of Reading*, p. 189.

28 Quoted in Furedi, *Power of Reading*, p. 190.

29 In 2006 Milch admitted that he was taking a large amount of medication, adding that his doctor believed it was 'nowhere near enough'. See *An Evening with David Milch* (moderated by Paul Brownfield, published as a DVD by The Writers' Guild Foundation, 2006).

30 Like many of these sayings, I suspect that Warren is the source: this one appears to be a version of the James–Lange theory that physiological changes counter-intuitively precede emotional states.

31 William James, *Habit* (New York: Henry Holt, 1914).

32 Mason Currey, *Daily Rituals* (New York: Knopf, 2013).

33 Some of this sounds suspiciously like the fad for Transactional Analysis made famous for a while in the 1960s and early 1970s by Eric Berne: there the critical 'pig parent' would attack the 'adapted child', all, as it were, in the adult psyche. How such archaeophysic entities assist creativity, if they do, is a mystery, but I suspect that Milch had encountered something like this in AA. Berne later developed the idea of the 'life script', a story about oneself that is created in childhood and played out to the very end. See Eric Berne, *What Do You Do After You Say Hello?* (London: Corgi Books, 1975).

34 M. H. Abrams, *The Mirror and the Lamp* (Oxford: Oxford University Press, 1971).

35 David Milch, 'The Idea of the Writer', Day 2, part 3/3, www.youtube.com/watch?v=P-SaoBQNDwQ (accessed 29 December 2016), around 25 minutes into the clip. The prize was for the *NYPD Blue* episode 'Hearts and Souls', the fifth season episode in which Simone dies. This suggests that Milch had become sober by 1999 at the latest.

36 Milch has never declared himself to be a member of any Church: as he says in these lectures, 'I'm not a member of a church or anything – that probably doesn't shock you – I'm also not a member of a synagogue...'

37 http://humanitasprize.info/welcome/?page_id=1011 (accessed 29 December 2016).

38 For example, Watson Parker's many books on the town, in particular *Deadwood: The Golden Years* (Lincoln, NE: University of Nebraska Press, 1981).

39 Bochco, *Truth Is a Total Defense*, p. 97.

40 Interview with Ted Mann via Skype, February 2010.

41 Anne Enright, 'The Genesis of Blame', *London Review of Books* 40.5 (8 March 2018), p. 7.

42 I discuss this transformation in detail in *Deadwood* (Basingstoke: Palgrave/BFI, 2012), pp. 111–16.

43 As does Bullock; according to Milch, 'he has to surprise us. Which is another way of saying you have to have faith that the character can develop, and the audience will come with him rather than sort of freezing him...' He then mentions that George Lucas 'started out making a wonderful movie and then because he was afraid to let anything develop he just kept making the same movie in a different time frame'.

44 By 'unsighted' I mean the way that word is used in racing to indicate a turn or corner that cannot be seen on approach.

Luck

4

> [I don't think that] ... there's some sort of equivalency or a kind of grid that you can impose and say this equals that and this is what's going on. I don't think that's how symbols work. I think that what happens is various events generate certain resonances in the viewer's imagination. To the extent they are recapitulated, those earlier associations kind of attach themselves to the new event and give it additional reverberations and the temptation is always to try and find in those reverberations some kind of magical form of explanation. That's how religion happens, you try to infer some sort of pattern in life. What makes a symbol vital is its absence of specific correlation or identifiable meaning. Not the fact that it has a meaning but its refusal to mean in any literal or specific way ... The point is having said this as writers the trick is to forget it and just sort of go ahead. And that's the kind of doubleness that is very difficult to sustain. You have kind of an intellectual intention and then the creative intention is a separate or parallel process. So almost inevitably what I've said has cancelled itself out.
>
> David Milch[1]

When *Deadwood* was cancelled in mid-2006 Milch faced the full artistic consequences of a commercial and corporate decision that was almost entirely out of his hands. In working on the character of George Hearst he had tried to personalise, individualise someone with 'something missing' – a sense of scale and proportion and debt to wider humanity that Swearengen had discovered in himself. The reasons for the cancellation mixed personal and industrial forces in a similar way: Milch's contract with Paramount gave them the rights to overseas sales, denying HBO a lucrative revenue stream (according to Milch the Europeans liked the show because they 'think it hates America'); Chris Albrecht, head of original programming there, may have been vulnerable to internal political struggles of the kind later dramatised in *John From Cincinnati* at the surf product company Stinkweed. Without

Steven Bochco to smooth diplomatic relations with the bosses, Milch had to rely on his own skills and sense of compromise, and he was unwilling to go with the shorter, six-episode season that was suggested. The play by HBO was to allow him to 'stay in the action', similar to the way Alma Garret explains to the young foundling, Sophia, her decision to sell her gold claim to Hearst. At a seminar given to a class of students at the University of Southern California in 2008, Milch dramatised the moment in a typically self-critical fashion:

> For an artist to see a world begin to generate itself seemingly autonomous from one's own imperfections – that's good. You dream about that, you dream about getting involved in some such thing maybe once, twice ... But *Deadwood* was a fully complicated kind of world, all different kinds of stories, all resting transparently in the spirit which gave them rise ... Be careful what you wish for. You keep looking for gold, you might find it. And if you find it and you do not realise that you are a creature of God, you are going to start committing some horrible, horrible crimes ... For a series of complicated reasons, having nothing to do with the series itself, the series is cancelled. Arbitrarily, no notice, no chance to get it shaped for a finish, nothing. But ... the good news is [in the voice of the bosses]: 'We love you Dave. You have a gift. You.' What that is, is an appeal to my vanity, to separate myself from the spirit which gave me rise. It's an invitation to go to hell. And the only price that I will have to pay is, every person who is participating in that series will feel betrayed – I was a heroin addict for thirty years, certainly that was a good chance to explore the resources of consolation of narcotics again. Five hundred people immediately employed who weren't actors out of work. Like that. But, 'We love you Dave!' And, *carte blanche*. 'Anything you wanna do. *Anything* you wanna do ... How would you like to do a series about surfing?' I mean look at me, I'm the guy right? I hate water, I hate sand, I hate swimming ... But I have to believe that starting from there I can get to the spirit ... So I went to work.[2]

John From Cincinatti

Milch had a number of project ideas that had been outlined, scripted or discussed. One was a history of the 'Big Four' founding professors of medicine at Johns Hopkins Hospital, in particular William Halsted, who was addicted to morphine and cocaine.[3] Another was a script called 'John From Elsewhere'; this concerns a loser called Tex, about to be thrown out of his apartment when he meets a new neighbour called John who seems to know everything about him; John has no idea how he got there but his pockets are full of cash and he has an American

Express Platinum card with the name 'John Monad' on it. An even stranger figure then arrives at Tex's door, designated in the script as Zenon of Nyack; he tells Tex that he would like to hire him to work with John, and condones the fact that Tex has already spent a large part of the cash that John found on suits and DVD players, and has engaged in activities as anyone might (or 'would') if they discovered what appeared to be unlimited amounts of money. When a suspicious Tex asks Zenon what his act is, he recommends that he watch Stanley Kubrick's *2001: A Space Odyssey*, paying particular attention to large black monoliths – John is the same kind of thing, and Zenon is his 'placement officer'. They are tasked with daily 'jobs' and Tex is warned to '[t]reat John as if the fate of the planet depended on it'. But it becomes clear in the third act that Zenon has no idea what is going on either; as he says to Tex,

> Obviously you're the main performer in whatever's going on here. I have a paranormal experience that nearly kills me, turn my life upside down trying to honour the message I've received, and my reward is playing water-boy to a street-level con artist.

The way the jobs are allocated is to have an address printed on the back of an ATM receipt; Tex and John head out to a maternity hospital where they witness a sad man watching newborns through a glass screen; Tex realises that it may be his father looking at him as a baby – his mother died in childbirth. Zenon appears later and tells him that he had a vision of Tex's mother dying, as well as discovering that he can levitate. Somehow both Tex and Zenon appear to have been chosen by – what? extraterrestrials? – to look after John. At one point the latter tells Tex, 'I'm from Cleveland or Cincinnati.' The script ends with Tex tracking Zenon to his motel room where he sees him levitating: 'I'm up.'

The script is undated, but it reads as if it was written before *Deadwood*; the cast is small (apart from the three central figures, there is Tex's love interest, Jane, an aspiring fashion designer who works at Prada), and there is only one axis of action throughout. The script features Milch's standing interest in the lumpenproletarian, degenerate con artist who has the opportunity to find grace and redemption through the circumstances in which he finds himself. And some of the events, names and motifs find their way into early episodes of *John From Cincinnati* – the levitation, John's encounter with a low-life figure at the end of his existence, the unexplained somewhere-in-between-supernatural-and-extraterrestrial entity that has an undisclosed plan to save humanity from itself. The 'John From...' notion was taken from the Pacific cargo cult phenomenon, in which natives exposed to advanced modern technologies would fetishise aspects of their initial encounters with the colonising groups. One such cult originated on Vanuatu in the early twentieth century when 'John Frum', a kind of spirit vision, began appearing before the villagers dressed in Western clothes and promising to bring them clothes, housing and other goods. Entire religious systems evolved from such encounters, along with rituals and symbols (such as an aircraft landing strip), some of which continue to the present day. As Milch tells the writing team:

> a primitive people and a coke bottle falls from the sky and they elaborate a whole cosmology based on worshipping a coke bottle. And the reason is that the impulse to spirituality at some root level is to control what we experience as the uncontrollable, which explains things that we can't explain rationally. So if a coke bottle falls, they develop a whole religion around a coke bottle. Now quite literally the cargo cults, the John From cults are based on in the second [world] war when American planes began to land in the islands of the South Pacific, the indigenous culture was so fucked up by the experience they began to build airfields, not that they knew what the fuck airplanes were, but in an effort to control this phenomenon. And the pilots would say, 'I'm John from America.' And so these cults were called 'John From' cults ... when I first did this I called it 'John From Elsewhere' ... Now here's the difference between spiritual materialism and spirituality; spiritual materialism is the effort to control through spirituality.

John From Cincinnati blends these ideas with two other elements that have a decisive effect on its drama. The first is the importing of a number of people from *Deadwood* – actors such as Austin Nichols (Morgan Earp/John Monad), Jim Beaver (Whitney Ellsworth/Vietnam Joe), Garret Dillahunt (Jack McCall/Francis Wolcott/Dr Michael Smith), Dayton Callie (Charlie Utter/Steady Freddie) and Paula Malcomson (Trixie/Jerri) – and writers, notably Ted Mann, Regina Corrado, Alix Lambert and Zack Whedon. The latter two had joined *Deadwood*'s writing team in its final season alongside Kem Nunn, who had made his name writing 'surf-noir' novels such as *Tapping the Source* and *The Dogs of Winter*. Just over two years younger than Milch, he too was interested in the dramatic resource of the unlucky, degenerate underclass, and like Milch was not averse to weaving mystical elements into naturalistic, gritty settings and events. On the face of it, to a corporate manager of creative artists, matching Nunn and Milch seemed a good plan. And *John From Cincinnati* is highly effective in terms of its resolute commitment to an ineffable, weird mysticism. What it lacks, however, is a fluent capacity to make good drama with the imaginative riches that both artists brought with them.

Even subtracting the sour note that lingered after the cancellation of *Deadwood, John* had a problematic gestation. The casting mixed experienced actors, such as Bruce Greenwood, Rebecca De Mornay, Ed O'Neill and Luke Perry, with newcomers such as Keala Kennelly (a professional surfer), Emily Rose and Greyson Fletcher (also a surfer), and this seemed to lead to a visible unevenness in the performances. Some of it was shot in San Diego at Imperial Beach, just north of Tijuana, which proved to be expensive but necessary if they wanted the surfing spectacles required by the script. Milch made little effort to hide his contempt for the sport and its culture, but did commit himself wholeheartedly to the project even if he later suspected that it was a failure. The show was cancelled early on in production and only ten episodes were produced.

John is about a community of surfers who are visited by a being (perhaps an extraterrestrial, perhaps a prophet sent by God), John Monad (Austin Nichols). What Milch added to Nunn's surf-noir *mise-en-scène*, and 'John From Elsewhere's' conceit, was an idea he had voiced during his monologues writing *Deadwood*. This was based on his belief that it would only take one or two more attacks on America following 9/11 to convince the nation to agree to a genocide, to, say, bomb Pakistan with nuclear weapons. The prophecy that John brings to the surfers is that in the wake of another 9/11-style attack, the public, narcotised by the media, will give their assent to the nuclear destruction of all followers of Islam. In order to prevent this, God – or something – sends a miraculous agency in the form of a young boy; this is the 13-year-old surfing prodigy Shaun Yost (Greyson Fletcher), the grandchild of Mitch (Bruce Greenwood) and Cissy (Rebecca De Mornay), and the son of Butchie Yost (Brian Van Holt). Both Mitch and Butchie were surfing stars of the past, but have lost their way, Mitch in his crumbling marriage to Cissy, and Butchie to heroin, while his former wife and the mother of Shaun, Tina Blake (Chandra West), has departed to work in the pornography industry.[4] The setting is a depressed border town, and the Yosts are a working-class family whose generational gift for competitive display surfing has marked them out in the community as celebrities. Shaun lives with Cissy and Mitch, while Butchie spends his time shooting up in his filthy room at the decrepit Snug Harbour motel. Mitch and Butchie were managed by Linc Stark (Luke Perry), the CEO of a major surf merchandise corporation, Stinkweed. As the back story unfolds we discover that Stark betrayed father and son by over-exploiting them, and now intends to do the same with Shaun, aided by his young assistant Cassie (Emily Rose).

The Yost family form the central hub around which a constellation of others orbit and, as in *Deadwood*, they eventually form a community pitted against the rapacious powers of capitalism and human gracelessness. The Snug Harbour motel is owned by Barry Cunningham (Matt Winston), a recent lottery winner, who has bought the place in order to confront his memory of being abused in one of the rooms there as a child; he is assisted by the manager, Ramon (Luiz Guzman), and a lawyer, Meyer Dickstein (Willie Garson); watching Butchie nearby is his Hawaiian dealer, Steady Freddie (Dayton Callie), and sidekick Palaka (Paul Ben-Victor – the latter two actors had memorable bit roles in *NYPD Blue*). A retired policeman, Bill Jacks (Ed O'Neill), still grief-stricken after the death of his wife, is a friend of the Yosts; finally, Garret Dillahunt plays the doctor who treats Shaun after he breaks his neck during a surfing competition in the first episode. The group of ethnically defined characters at the periphery (Mexican, Jewish, Hawaiian) exist as a kind of emblem of friendship without family, a club; family is in a sense where you find your companion's home to be. This is a strong part of the charm of the show on subsequent viewings, once the distraction of the plot is done with. When Shaun miraculously recovers from what should have been a fatal accident, the entire group is energised. Cassie seduces Mitch in order to destabilise the Yost family, but after meeting John, she commits to documenting 'His Visit' (as each episode is named, followed by its number); arriving mid-way through the show, Tina Blake also threatens to destabilise the family, but she becomes the opportunity through which both Cissy and Butchie discover their capacity for grace and forgiveness.

On the face of it, the show is a melodrama, drawing on the conventions of secular realism; but that genre demands a potent unseen that is often bound up with the past of its characters. The show balances this against an obstinately visible series of supernatural events. John's appearance in the first episode is the beginning of a series of miracles, with Mitch finding himself levitating a few inches off the ground after surfing in the morning. These miracles begin as private moments witnessed only by the individual or the family, but as the show continues they gradually become public. Bill's parrot, Zippy, comes back to life when Shaun touches him, and returns the gesture by 'kissing' the near-dead Shaun in hospital, after which he suddenly returns to full health. John, who has an earnest, pleasantly confused demeanour, has his own paranormal talents: he can make money appear in his pocket, and he is impervious to mortal injury. He seems less of a subjectivity than an entity that channels other, mysterious forces – he is a kind of medium. Like a parrot, he repeats the words of characters back at them, but he can also repeat things he cannot have heard and mimics events he could not have witnessed (such as something spoken by Bill's late wife). According to Milch:

> I think he is capable of echoing stuff, of recombing stuff, but mostly it's to reinforce the emotional position of the previous speaker. Essentially what he is saying is, 'Jump in. Whatever you say it doesn't matter, just keep going. You're absolutely right. Whatever the fuck you said.' Which is simply to say energy begets energy.

The question that eventually occupies all of the characters as they puzzle over the miracles and John's odd behaviour is what is his intention, his mission among them? In this way the characters mediate and model the viewer's own puzzlement at the indeterminate nature of the events we see. Like us, they are forced to account for events that they experience outside the realist, secular domain of explanation. As V. F. Perkins was fond of saying, 'clarity is the enemy of suggestion', and this was the rule in the writers' room in early 2007 as Milch and his colleagues worked to develop the show's script:

> that is the storytelling challenge that you will encounter over and over and over again with these materials, because of the absence of a stable convention to accommodate and shape the viewer's expectations ... You have to examine the kind of secret currents that ultimately express themselves as aesthetic positions. And realize that they aren't necessarily aesthetic positions.

This does not indicate that Milch was on the kind of firm artistic ground that his monologues in the *Deadwood* writing room demonstrate. Perhaps the impact of that cancellation had driven him into far more abstract terrain, and, given that *John* was neither anchored to the conventions of a familiar genre such as the Western nor to historical events, this penchant for abstraction led the show 'off the cliff'.

We can see in the talks that Milch gave during the 2007 writers' strike, and the USC seminar, that he had been reading a lot of Kierkegaard, in particular *The Sickness Unto Death* and *Purity of Heart is to Will One Thing*; in his induction talk to interns at the Red Board offices in 2008, he instructed them in the thoughts of the nineteenth-century founder of psychopsychics Gustav Fechner, whose *The Little Book of Life after Death* is often referenced in *John* writing room discussions. This was not a big shift for Milch: William James wrote the foreword to Fechner's book and Milch had certainly read *The Varieties of Religious Experience*. What he wanted to do was square the circle between the concrete – the body, the nation, the individual, the chemistry, the physics – and the universal, the abstract. In applying this to art he would use Coleridge's distinction between the fanciful and the imagination, that is, the private associations we have to symbols, sounds and other things, and the imaginative-universal that socialised and made accessible one's private creativity to all. As Milch says in the writing room:

> There's this German Romantic philosopher named Fechner who says that the idea that you go from humans to the Absolute is obviously part of the pathetic fallacy. He said there are like 9000 intermediate states of being. We're thinking Don Rickles could play him (The Controller), but he ain't getting any younger, so if the series goes seven years, we're kind of fucked.

Also in the mix was Miguel De Unamuno's 1912 book, *Tragic Sense of Life*. We can see some of the appeal of Fechner in particular to an imagination of *John* as combining the particular, quantum abstraction of the beginning of the universe with the chaotic fluid mechanics of waves in the sea. Take this obscurity:

> All life circles of the higher spirits intersect each other, and you ask how it is possible such numberless circles can intersect without disturbance, error, or confusion. Ask rather first, how it is possible that innumerable undulations in the same pond, waves of sound in the same air, waves of light in the same ether, pulses of memory in the same mind intersect, that, finally, the countless life circles of man, bearing their great future, already in this life intersect without great disturbance, error, or confusion. Rather a far higher plane of life and growth is achieved through these vibrations and memories reaching from this present life to the one beyond.[5]

Whatever this means, it is close to the sense we have when watching *John From Cincinnati*: human awareness is nested in an infinite regress of beings and consciousnesses that stretch before and after the present moment.

This animistic and vitalistic sense of the universe is combined with the apocalyptic stylistic visual rhetoric emphasising end times for America that is the superb title sequence. The music, 'Johnny Appleseed' by Joe Strummer, suggests the exhaustion of natural systems and the death of the soul. The combination of despair and hope indicates that Milch was operating in relation to the tradition of the nineteenth-century American jeremiad in its literature, as outlined by Sacvan Bercovitch:

> The symbol of America magnified the culture into a cosmic totality: hence the euphoria of its adherents. But the same process of magnification carried a dangerous correlative: if America failed, then the cosmos

> itself – the laws of man, nature and history, the very ground of heroism, insight and hope had failed as well. Their European contemporaries, for whom democratic capitalism was one of several traditions, could be disillusioned in society without descending into despair, just as they could espouse the middle class while exposing the limitations of its ideals. Our classic writers tended to uphold those ideals even when they most bitterly assailed their society. Their very radicalism, we might say, forced that upon them, since they identified America, symbolically, with the ideals of art and the self. Hence their quickness to condemn and the hyperbole or desperation we sometimes feel in their condemnation. When they abandoned their faith in America, they had no other recourse. The result was what we might call the anti-jeremiad: the denunciation of all ideals, sacred and secular, on the grounds that America is a lie. I use the term anti-jeremiad to recall the ubiquity of the national symbol. In this country, both the jeremiad and the anti-jeremiad foreclosed alternatives: the one by absorbing the hopes of making in the meaning of America, the other by reading into America the futility and fraud of hope itself.[6]

Bercovitch goes on to note that it was Herman Melville whose early writings exemplified this 'cultural schizophrenia', trying later to resolve those tensions in *Moby Dick,* where the America of Nantucket is criticised but the values of self-reliance are celebrated. The problem is that the charisma of Ahab, his disenchantment with the abstract universe (the self, evil), is so powerful that it colours our sense of Ishmael's disenchantment with the real world: both reality and abstraction are negated.

Milch never gets as far as Melville in that respect, and in some ways *John* is a reaffirmation of the value as well as the origins of communal symbolic communication in order to sustain a world where the human spirit is cultivated as a notion for transcending the real rather than as a mystical social and historical construction. The problem is the volatility of the tone and spirit of the series itself: John is able to speak like a therapist or AA group leader, as he does to Cissy when he convinces her not to commit suicide. So this is a ghostly material world channelling currents of Fechner, James (both novelist and psychologist), Leibniz, the Bible and the other Big Book. The overall effect is *Four Quartets* (Eliot) meets *The Shining* (Kubrick): what we experience is not uncertainty regarding the reasons why supernatural things happen but an assertion of their indeterminacy, while at the same time it is suggested that there is a reason but not one we can know fully. The insistence on the materiality of visions, their concrete presence before us, means that realism, the uncanny and the marvellous all occupy – impossibly – the same stage at the same time.

This is exemplified in a sequence that comes at the end of the sixth episode, when Ramon prepares a 'cookout' at the Snug Harbour motel courtyard facing all the rooms. All of the show's major characters are there enjoying his barbecued food. As they eat, John begins a lengthy monologue that appears to hold important information about the nature of his work on earth. His audience is made up of people who are really there, those who could not possibly be there, and those who may only be there in a supernatural sense, like, but not exactly, ghosts. We also know that John himself is in at least two other places at the same time. The indeterminacy of the sequence is further reinforced by the odd reaction of John's audience to what he says. At times they appear to be listening and hearing his words, but at others they seem oblivious. And because the content makes very little literal sense, as the audience of the show we experience this too: the *sounds* John makes with his mouth form words, but their association to anything concrete is largely obscure. What we sense is that there is something important, with ultimate stakes, being spoken, rather as a member of the congregation at Mass who does not understand Latin might feel.

Props can also be there and not recognised by others as there: Mr Rollins, the man who sexually abused Barry, is there but 'dead' and unmoving, although he is clearly a human actor, not a cadaver or a special effect, crudely painted grey. Bill Jacks ascends the spiral staircase that we have seen connects his living room to his late wife's bedroom. We are shown brief 'snaps' of what appear to be groups of people posing for a photograph: in one Rollins is central, smiling wickedly at the camera; in another the character is in two places at once. Hence, we have a fundamental diegetic indeterminacy in which the laws of physics, particularly those concerning the location and stability of matter, as well as memory, are available to be reshaped and contradict one another simultaneously.

What Milch is trying to get at, following the intuition at the heart of 'John From Elsewhere', is a figure who is a medium, or transmitter, for a larger, inscrutable and unknown intending spirit or consciousness; in the struggle to understand we become humanised, ready to face the world together:

> what John has been describing in a kind of disconnected telegraphy, this is part of the story, this is all that stuff, you should see almost a pastoral enactment of in the courtyard, what they used to call Arcadia. Except, the prism or the refraction of each of the character's consciousness articulates Arcadia in a very strange way.

The show internalises the issue of its legibility. John's Snug Harbour address is not intended to make much sense on a conscious level for the Yost family and their associates; instead John is trying to move their spirit in the same way that the show hopes to move its viewers. 'Where's that guy *from*?', asks Cissy about John in the third episode; 'Cincinnati', replies Butchie. 'Cincinnati' is an answer as good as any, but it is not the answer we want. By presenting characters as surrogates who model and anticipate positive and negative responses, the show brings to our attention our desire for meaning and clarity. It does not dismiss this desire as problematic, but recruits it to a larger, if obscure, project of spiritual tutelage.

The problem is that Milch characterises contemporary media in much the same way as he figures John as a prophet:

> as I'm watching the planes going into the building, over and over and over and over again, I'm thinking, 'It's enough. It's enough with the planes going into the building. I want my old programs back' ... so the President says, 'let's give them a twelve episode mini-series; we come up with the villains, we're going to go in, at the end we'll pull down the statue, we'll give them a whole different program. And they are so sick of the planes going into the buildings, they'll love it.' So we stage the invasion of Iraq really as a change in programming for the audience so narcotised by their addiction to television that all of their frustrated patriotism ... we can solve your problem with better programming, what's going to happen the next time there's a terrorist attack? There's going to be a charlatan who says, 'do we want to kill every Muslim in the world?' Absolutely not. But by the same token they are fucking up our programming.'

This is not a compelling argument, but it does suggest that suggestibility is the cost of the American Dream, an appetite for entertainment that negates universal human morality, or at least the possibility of cultivating it. John's audience is 'rendered unconscious' in order to listen to his sermon, but the content, where it is legible, seems once again to return to Milch's pet theory of social organisation based on the 'need of the human spirit for mystification' and the abstract symbols (gold, money, crucifixes et al.) that stimulate that need on a mass scale. That need to mystify, for Milch, 'is what calls us to try to shape the universe in a moral form, even if we're wrong'.

Eventually, in partnership with Stark, the Yost family and John design their own symbol – a circle and a line – itself a modification of a human stick figure that evokes the binary code of computing, and it is promoted by Stinkweed under the cover of a series of lies and distortions about the miracles we have seen. The circle and line refer, according to Milch, to man's capacity to signify, communicate and worship, 'or to indicate a sense of one's place in the universe, so essentially what it stands for is art', and in his discussions with writing staff and the cast his reference was to palaeolithic cave paintings or other early attempts at symbolic depiction.

For Milch, storytelling rather than making 'television art' is of the essence; this is why the digital camera Cassie uses, or the internet that Shaun uses to promote himself, are as good as any other vehicle for the telling of stories:

> The universal spirit is the state of grace, and it is the state of art. The telling of a story is nothing more or less than the process of the view coming to experience separate entities as informed by a single unity ... [making art is] ... every kind of human behaviour which presupposes our unity as transcending our seeming separateness.

Like Fechner, Milch is interested in the persistence of originating energies in human experience, but as with Eliot he is alive to the deadening aspects of human culture, especially the mass media. But Milch needs long-form television in order to tell that story with the characters he creates, and that means breaking bread with commercial forces that he is only partially skilled at handling effectively. More generously, with *John* Milch found himself instructing writers relatively new to the job in his art, and this seems to have been rewarding. Nonetheless, the difficulties in conception, production and realisation intruded and the room was not as fluent as those of *Deadwood*'s seasons. Part of the reason for this was that Milch's tendency to indeterminacy in his writing had no external control; as he said, he was given *carte blanche* – from genre, history, or much by way of studio expectations. But this freedom also meant that the expanded edge of his imagination caused artistic congestion and confusion: at one point Freddy and Palaka were going to 'appear' in costume as Osama bin Laden and Ayman Al Zawahairi.

There was also some confusion over how to handle the 'notes' generated by Milch's monologues; as he says to one young writer:

> It might be that I may be impeding somehow that process in you, staying second to second, that you're trying to think too globally about honouring some overall intention. And I think Ted tries to take it moment to moment. And he's got the courage to be wrong. In a fair-minded fashion, I'm always ready to re-examine and change any fucking thing. The point is, when we talk about it, it seems as if we wind up agreeing but, if you make the case on the other side of the ledger, I'll swing with that...
>
> [*Ted Mann*] If you're on the page, and you're trying to execute those notes, and those notes don't seem to be playing, then you fucking gotta throw those *notes*, rather than the page...

This recognises how hard it must seem for a new writer to write alongside Milch, with the kind of creative authority that he wields. But the apocalyptic gestures of the show's opening titles are also indicative of Milch's waning sense of the authority of the medium itself to deliver the kind of experience to the audience that he is after. *John* both reflects this creative ennui and tries to engage with it:

> if your heart is open enough, when you walk from set the trailer, if you're lucky enough you'll see fifty different people, and every one of those lives is as full and complicated as yours is, and if you're lucky and the sun is shining right, you'll have intuitions of that, and that's why I reach out. If I see a sign that says Avon sold here, I buy some Avon products from that woman, because I want to meet her, because just seeing the sign I feel as if she's become a part of my life, and I want to act to bond with that instinctive feeling. And it's the reason why people go to entertainment in the same way they used to go to church, it is responsive – you know nobody watches an hour of television anymore. Everybody surfs, and in that process of surfing, they are making an entirely different story for themselves. Stimuli coming from all different directions, and they're experiencing that as a unity, and the unity that they're experiencing is, 'Why am I so depressed when I go to sleep?' It's because they're eroding their sense of community by the exercise of technology in the absence of any overall [ends].

In this thought, the crisis for Milch and his writing is that the everyday world of modernity, already freighted with transactional commercialism (the Avon woman), has opportunities still for the 'reaching out' that prefigures the acknowledgement of a social bond, the commensurability of human experience and thus our modern dependency on one another for meaning and sustenance; and this is vanishing in the face of new technologies that rush so swiftly into view that sleep itself, the realm of irrational rest, has been invaded by dissatisfaction. How does one establish a bond with a viewer, with another person, using this very technology? And how does one motivate a writing team, let alone oneself, to deliver something in a context that only acknowledges its failure?

The subject of *John From Cincinnati* is the regeneration of belief. To the extent that it is shared by the viewers as they watch the collection of mostly working-class characters as they gradually exhibit kindness, faith, mutual support and build a community together, it is a difficult, often painful, experience. There are few other examples of an accurate account of working-class family life over several decades in American television: the shadows, currents and flows of resentment, shame, fear and regret that occupy faces and spaces like spectres; the shining emergence of love disguised as attack, or hate that blooms into intimacy and companionship; the secret shared knowledge, fiercely revealed together, of a world ranged against them; the awfulness of officialdom, and the necessity to band together against its dehumanising, self-righteous, bourgeois viciousness. In this respect, *John* shares with *The Shining* an acknowledgement of the epic mediocrity in which some lives are caged: but in the latter this is played out in a specimen glass for the delight of others; *John* is far more generous and inviting for its audience, but like the film, it trades too much on our willingness to forgive the irritating uncertainty about the status of the supernatural. This means that what is merely a plot matter keeps intruding on our experience of the world the show depicts.

That is until we see, in the final episode, the manager of the Cherry Oldies used car lot (credited merely as 'Car Salesman'), played by Peter Jason, talking with John, Linc Stark and his assistant, who are there to hire a Chevrolet El Camino at John's request ('camino' is Spanish for way or road). Jason's character is a craggy, duck's-ass haircut car salesman, an 'Orange County, right wing, former shitbird surfer' who occupies the role of Zenon in 'John From Elsewhere' – a kind of middle manager between God (or whatever) and John. Early drafts have him more clearly as a repugnant racist hater of Muslims, which buries his function far too deeply and distractingly. This was the final scene to be shot, and Milch and Mann worked carefully together to hone the character into a blend that is both enigmatic but concrete and vivid. By the time the final episode was shot and cut, it is fair to say that the audience could take him as God himself.

When Stark rudely cuts him short, boasting that they own more cars between them than he has on the lot, he replies:

> *God*: So I got to know what I mean before I can have a feeling? Do I have to know you're going to understand me? Do I have to know you'll understand before you'll listen? Twenty-five cars between ya? You should've let me sit down before you told me. I got that many dealerships in each of that many sectors, and brands on goddamn franchise. *I've* gotta boogie, me?
>
> *John*: He feels you're ready for the Camino.
>
> *God*: You're off-line now, Country.
>
> *John*: I don't know Butchie instead.
>
> *God*: How's he for high-performance? And he ain't who's worst-underpowered. Intrusions, evanescences – I am a shepherd without crook or understanding. Fits and stops and starts. Waves-ripples-and ramifications. Busted knee, mother-son handjob ... *Christ.* Jesus Christ Jesus Christ. Crosses and shoulders to bear 'em. You and

your twenty-five cars. Circle and line on the wall, and zeroes and goddamned ones, is what to turn the both of your gifts to – and not one damn minute to waste.

John: Ragheads are going to get themselves eradicated.

God: Country. I took you off-line.

God's middle-manager salesman knows all about the generational ripples after Mitch's career ended with a busted knee; his withdrawing from family life left his wife Cissy adrift, fixated on her son Butchie, to the extent that she assists him on one occasion to masturbate; that is the end of that generation until Shaun is born – and even then his father's drug habit and his mother's stardom in the porn industry seem ill suited to future growth. But 'intrusions and evanescences' are the non-rational elements that get in the way of apparent social and individual trajectories. The thought is that one has to get in the El Camino and just drive, in the faith that the machine's logic is not in the end a determining factor. This is what prevents a catastrophe, and the method is commerce.

The car salesman is perhaps the most iconic 'groundling'-level figure. 'The resources of the internet, of soulless mercantilism, if we brought the right heart to it, could stave off genocide', says Milch on the DVD commentary for the final episode of the show. But having faith that a mercantile figure will offset human self-destruction is a hard sell, and flies against most people's experience of contemporary modernity, where the benefits of capitalist organisation come hand-in-hand with alienation, a high frequency and higher intensity of suffering without meaning, and an unbidden yearning for something deeper in social relations (call it the ready everyday manifestation of the human spirit) that is constantly being blocked. One cannot will oneself out of this or confect a faith against a structural and systemic organisation by avoiding a fight with those who benefit most from it. Milch does not want to go there because that would imply a binary logic of Us and Them. Without binaries, however, we cannot have transcendence; if it is *already there*, unseen but reachable, then there is no effort or work demanded beyond 'showing up' for the next day. Milch describes it in the writing room as 'spiritual materialism' and in that sense Stark is an internalisation of the commercial forces that make television and writing television shows such as *John From Cincinnati* possible at all. 'Last time I looked capitalism was winning. Nobody's come up with anything better. Let's not be showing that we're better than Linc. Let's show the tremendous energy that is at the disposal of a sensibility like that to bring everybody around.' This does require a kind of blind faith and an availability to the solace and sacrament of the present moment (the 'Quotidian Plural' as Milch puts it), the ready miraculousness of it and its transient charismatics: fine notions, perhaps, but not exactly the engine of restless dissatisfaction with things as they are that has underpinned at least some of the beneficial human progress in material comfort, ethics and morality that has been achieved. There is more inspiration there, at least, than in the experience of consumption or the spectacle of Luke Perry. It was naive to imagine that either John or *John* would have the fictive persuasive force to reverse the entirety of disenchantment with Western modernity, however many genocides were waved in front of the viewer as moral bait. Worse, Milch recruits a tired counter-cultural rejection of technology as inherently corrupting of the everyday pastoral – 'if the sun is shining right' – at its best a Thoreau-like fantasy of communitarianism, at worst an avoidance of real social and cultural divisions that need to be fought out in order to be resolved.

The leaning towards mysticism that necessarily accompanied this theme led to some problems in the writing room. In order to be an effective showrunner, or an effective leader – an effective anything – one has to be clear about the nature and scale of the work and communicate that regularly to the rest of the group. Milch was always dazzling and 'brilliant' in the room, but that is a different thing from being understood or leading in a way that can be followed. At one point Kem Nunn notices a moment of clarity in Milch's description of a scene:

> *Nunn*: You can see the season in this approach on this thing. And I've never been able to see the fucking thing, the whole season, I've got to admit. And I'm co-creator.
>
> *Milch*: I am glad you kept that to yourself. And that argues, and I would say with no malice, if you've never been able to see it, you've got to say 'Big Wave [Dave], I don't see it.'
>
> *Nunn*: I tried to say that to you once. I said to you, I think this is kind of a one man job. Because it's the working out of a very particular vision, because it's absolutely what writers and artists ought to do. But it's sometimes hard to enter into somebody else's vision.
>
> *Milch*: ... this is not one person's vision ... The fact is that we had lived into the proof that no one works by themselves.

Nunn counters, referring to *Moby Dick*, that 'great writing carries its own sense of authority', but that there is no way to tell the story in one continuous moment; Milch responds:

> So to tell this story in one continuous moment in time would be the most elegant way to do it. But it ain't going to work. So I was elegant the

> first 61 years of my life. Needless to say, I've been a slob my whole life: why pretend to be different?

A film or a novel or a play would offer the prospect of a continuous story, but it would remove the option to gradually build up story and characters, layer plots, assemble actors and find a voice that matches them – all aspects of the television drama industry that Milch had benefited from in the past. Which is what he means by 'why pretend to be different?' – there was no way Milch was willing to entertain a mode of thinking and writing outside of the television episodic format, and this was beginning to hamper his capacity to communicate effectively with the writing team. This was also because the method that Milch had found was one that required a lot of time and indulgence on the part of the supporting people and industry around him. As he claimed at one point in the production:

> [I]t's not that I wouldn't plan ahead if I could, it's just that I understand that when the student is ready, the teacher comes. If I'm the student of my materials and I am available to the materials, they will teach me what's next, but I have to believe it. I show up every day, I submit myself to the materials, I am the student, I say, 'teach me. Teach me what's next.'

There are scenes that stand out as emblems of what the show might have been, had it kept faith across all its means of realisation in Milch's vision. In episode seven, Barry Cunningham walks into the bar of the motel he has just purchased, conversing with his teddy bear about his plans to convert it into a community theatre, a place for the 'building up of the spirit'. Suddenly the jukebox begins playing a tune and we hear a disembodied voice – in fact Milch himself, in a parody of his own over-polite attempt at social grace, which soon develops into the malicious criticism of the self-loathing internal 'committee', the judge and jury of one's own critical invention:

> Mr Cunningham, Mr Cunningham, good evening to you sir. Mr Cunningham thank you so much for letting me run a tab. That's so kind, that's very gracious of you. All right, have a good evening sir, thank you ... You faggot cocksucker. Look at him. Look at him walk over there like he's a normal fucking person. Don't go out and suck a fast prick in the alley pal before you can ... Mr Cunningham good evening. Good evening. How are you? You look very well – you almost look like a human being. Congratulations on imitating a human being Mr Cunningham. You fucking faggot.

Matt Winston's performance as this hateful speech is delivered is pitch-perfect, and there are many other gems to savour. However, late in production it was clear that the show was not being well received. Milch kept faith with it:

> By the time ten episodes are seen, I think it'll be hard for any fair minded, or someone with a fair access to his or her imagination, not to experience this as an extraordinary, extraordinary show ... By putting us after the [finale of] *The Sopranos* was setting us up for a knockout punch. There's no way that people are not going to mourn *The Sopranos*, in terms of the juxtaposition with whatever follows it.

Last of the Ninth

Milch had a number of projects on the boil as part of his agreement with HBO, but after *John From Cincinnati* vanished from the screen he spent the rest of 2007 and some of 2008 working with Bill Clark on a historical cop show, *Last of the Ninth*. The show was based on aspects of Clark's life, particularly his work as an undercover cop infiltrating radical movements after he returned from service in Vietnam. The show takes the buddy cop trope of *NYPD Blue*, but tunes it much more explicitly around mentor–student roles: the show begins in April 1972 with veteran Detective John Giglio (played in the pilot by Ray Winstone) and a young partner Joe Dalton (Jonah Lotan) caught up in the immediate aftermath of the murder of two uniform cops on the street who have been ambushed and shot many times by a group of black assassins. This was based on the real-life shooting of officers Rocco Laurie and Gregory Foster, colloquially known as a 'salt and pepper' team,[7] and themselves Vietnam veterans, by the Black Liberation Army in January that year. The shooting, putatively in revenge for prisoner deaths during the Attica prison riots the year before, was excessive in its brutality, with the victims shot repeatedly in the head and genitals. The show demonstrates how the shooting was also political in several other overlapping dimensions: the Knapp Commission, set up in 1970 by New York Mayor John Lindsay to investigate police corruption, has created paranoia across police precincts (and former undercovers like Dalton take the brunt of the suspicion as potentially 'wired' moles); but Lindsay's dependency on the black vote means that investigations into the violence of militant groups like the Black Liberation Army and the Black Panthers are hampered. The Deputy Police Commissioner, who has an eye on the movie rights to the story of police corruption, runs interference on the case. Giglio is under pressure at home too: his wife has left him to raise their disabled boy alone (with Giglio's Catholic mother), but an electronics wizard tips him off that she wants to get back in contact. Amid this thickened historical context, Dalton and Giglio bond over their shared love of German Shepherd dogs.

The script for the pilot and the audio conversations between Clark and Milch, as well as between Milch and the pilot director Carl Franklin, are incredibly rich and detailed in their excavation of the historical moment and their ongoing relevance to American race relations. Both Milch and Clark lived in New York City in the early 1970s and both were close to the events they attempt to pattern in the fiction. Clark was an undercover and then rookie cop, dealing with the intense friction and paranoia of squad life; Milch claims to have dealt acid to Eldridge Cleaver and the Black Panthers, but whatever the truth of that he certainly knew them, in particular Cleaver's wife, Kathleen. Franklin was working on a documentary for HBO about the history of the Black Panthers (never completed) and also had a strong investment in the story; Milch interviewed those with contemporary experience of the events, such as journalist and writer Jimmy Breslin; Clark drew on his NYPD contacts, in particular the Police Commissioner at the time, Ray Kelly.

Unfortunately the pilot was not picked up by HBO; once again one tends to think that this was because Milch had set a number of hares in motion, but none of them was enough to secure the interest of his backers. What remains is a decent script and hours of conversation between Milch and Clark that drill into the minutiae of the cultural, social and political moment. The conversations are dramatic, thrilling and always fascinating: but *Last of the Ninth* did not sufficiently embody those qualities on screen. One can never doubt Milch's total commitment to his projects, however: during an intake session for interns in late November 2008, during which Milch introduced his writing 'exercises' and swept his audience through the works of Fechner, James and Warren and the nature of fiction itself, he took a call from Michael Lombardo, president of programming at HBO. After he put the phone down he said: 'Cocksuckers. Those are the people who didn't pick up the show. Now they want me to tell them it's great. "Oh it's just my heart and lung machine – go ahead and unplug it, what you got an electric razor you gotta use?"'

Luck

By the time Milch finally landed his horseracing pitch on fertile ground, the television industry was undergoing a radical change in size and scale. As on-demand television services such as Netflix expanded, the competitive urge to extend television fiction programming in quantity and scale ushered in another wave of high-quality episodic drama in the 2010s. *Luck* was an appropriate title for Milch's project, which both benefited from this expansion and suffered because of it.

Luck is the last Milch television series to have been produced at the time of writing – although the *Deadwood* movie is, finally, in production as I finish this book. Both *John From Cincinnati* and *Last of the Ninth* suffered in their conception from Milch's unerring faith in the value of his work, such that each laboured hard to set up wonders that might only be cashed out in later seasons, which were never produced because the labour put into the first negated any corporate, commercial appetite for more. *Luck* was released in 2012 in nine episodes, one less than *John*, before being cancelled shortly into the pre-production of its second season apparently because of concerns about animal welfare. Whether or not it stands as the final sustained work that Milch produced, it provides an opportunity for a fitting ending to this book: much of his life is folded into what we see on screen but, equally, much remains enigmatic, indeterminate, hidden in shadow.

It is that shadow and its impact that dominates my consideration of *Luck*. This is a provisional, almost gestural, attempt to point to broad dimensions of the piece as an effort to face and negate a creative and industrial impasse that it was impossible for Milch to avoid, given the medium in which he chose to continue working. Even more than *John*, it is an uncompromising vision with very little connecting appeal to the contemporary world. Instead we get Milch's world, his memories, his life, as it is refracted and fragmented across another ensemble, multi-narrative fiction.

The plot is complex and hard to track at times, though at others it is seemingly conventional and legible; this is paralleled by the often thickened but also at times sparse and bare dialogue. Both work in tandem to court opacity and indeterminacy. Even more blockage is introduced by the casting of star talent, notably Dustin Hoffman and Nick Nolte, as well as second-tier familiars Dennis Farina, Michael Gambon and (very briefly) Joan Allen. These players are given an outstanding supporting cast, in particular Kevin Dunn, John Ortiz, Jason Gedrick and Ian Hart; even so-called minor roles are populated with actors of considerable talent such as Patrick J. Adams, Kerry Condon and Ritchie Coster. Not one of them is a Milch regular: there is no Titus Welliver, Kim Dickens or Dayton Callie. W. Earl Brown turns up for a fine cameo, but otherwise the casting itself tells a story of how radically Milch's vision was overcome by other forces. This was to be the story of the production, and it shows in various ways in what we see on screen. Nonetheless, without Hoffman, who was confirmed in 2009/10, it seems unlikely that the show would have attracted the talent it did. This includes the directing talent: Michael Mann, who commanded joint authority over the show with Milch, as well as luminaries of the film and television industry such as Philip Noyce, Allen Coulter and Mimi Leder. The icing on this expensive cake was the soundtrack, provided chiefly by Massive Attack and their track 'Splitting the Atom'.

Four groups intersect throughout a story anchored to the activities and perfidies associated with the Santa Anita racetrack in Los Angeles. Chester 'Ace' Bernstein (Dustin Hoffman), an elderly gangster, is released from prison after serving three years, the result of his being framed. Reunited with his lieutenant Gus Dimitriou (Dennis Farina), Ace plots revenge on those who we are led to understand were responsible for his imprisonment when they framed his nephew for drug possession and Ace took the rap to protect him: Michael Smythe (Michael Gambon), Isodore Cohen (Ted Levine) and Nick DeRossi (Alan Rosenberg). It is never quite clear how Ace is going to do this – partly perhaps by introducing casino gambling to the track via an alliance with Native American partners, partly by buying and running a racehorse, Pint of Plain. Ace and Gus recruit a young business hotshot, Nathan Israel (Patrick J. Adams), to negotiate and gather intelligence from Smythe and his associates, but Smythe murders and dismembers Israel. In the meantime, Ace has become – almost – romantically close to Claire Lachay (Joan Allen), who uses rescued racehorses to rehabilitate ex-convicts; in a remarkable scene he also seems to find some kind of spiritual bond with Pint of Plain. Eventually, Smythe hires a hitman to murder Ace, but this is thwarted.

The show ends with Pint of Plain eventually winning a race. It wins by a nose from Gettin'Up Morning, which is trained by Walter Smith (Nick Nolte), who also has thoughts of revenge, even more obscure than Ace's. Somehow the success of this horse will deliver redemption, since its lineage is that of a former winner, also trained by Smith but brutally destroyed. Smith interacts with several jockeys: two youngsters, Rosie (Kerry Condon) and Leon (Tom Payne) – who provide something of a generational contrast in an otherwise emphatically middle-to-old-aged drama – and Ronnie, a veteran played by Gary Stevens (in reality an experienced jockey) who is struggling with addiction. The jockeys are handled by Joey Rathburn (Richard Kind), a neurotic, suicidal agent with a stutter, clearly making his final moves on the track.

The third group are The Degenerates (Milch's term): four gambling addicts – Marcus (Kevin Dunn), Jerry (Jason Gedrick), Lonnie (Ian Hart) and Renzo (Ritchie Coster) – who band together in the first episode on a multiplier bet that wins them a fortune. One of them buys a racehorse with his cut of the money, and the rest of the series shows their anxieties about losing the money through either bad luck or poor impulse control. They are the most lively and legible group in the show, and Milch clearly had fun writing their parts, which sing with a vitality characteristic of his depiction of working-class figures.

Finally, the figure who interacts with all three groups is the enigmatic horse trainer Turo Escalante (John Ortiz), whose management of the care, feeding and training of the horses gives him a special but mysterious authority over their form. Escalante is involved with the track vet, Jo (Jill Hennessy), who becomes pregnant with their child; she eventually miscarries, but there is also a hint that Escalante may adopt a Mexican boy he has befriended. His rivalry with Walter Smith is professional and fierce but respectful.

As should be clear from this crude description, once again, as in *John From Cincinnati* and *Deadwood*, we have several clumps of character groups that evolve in their inter- and intra-group interactions as the drama progresses. That much is fairly standard in most long-form US dramas of the past three decades. And, again familiar to Milch viewers, there is the depiction of a kind of grace found among them, especially when they share the drama and spectacle of a horse race. Hence, Milch finds opportunities to stage the unity of consciousness, to use a Jungian term, in external ways. The vibrant and innovative depiction of the racing itself, taking its cue from Mann's exuberant direction in the pilot, assists the audience in being caught up in the excitement whatever their experience of racing spectatorship. The race spectacles provide a kind of cleansing rest for characters and audience alike, even when plot elements rely on the outcome, and are similar in that respect to the public communitarian spirit underpinning the 'amateur night' and wedding scenes in *Deadwood* and the cookouts in *John*. The ordinary joys and despair of The Degenerates are another resource for the staging of this kind of event, evident for example in the barbecue held on the patio of their motel.

What is different is the underlying tone and vitality of both dialogue and performance. There is, for want of a better phrase, 'something missing' in almost every scene that neither the *mise-en-scène* nor the structural organisation can compensate for. This is true for scenes that are straightforwardly opaque to anyone not familiar with the minutiae of gambling at the track – a clear decision to keep the audience at a distance but build their loyalty through something else, say, the commitment and pain evident in the anxiety of The Degenerates, or the cool but ruthless way Ace organises his takeover of the track. It is also true, however, of scenes that are thoroughly legible, such as the brittle but romantic back and forth between Escalante and Jo. *Luck* exhibits a kind of woodenness despite its evident faith in and commitment to the story and characters it depicts. There is the elaborate carpentry and baroque ornamentation of plotting and language familiar to *Deadwood* viewers when The Degenerates discuss what to do to avoid losing their winnings; but there is also the spare and sparse dialogue, almost Beckett-like, that we have at the end of each episode when Ace and Gus reflect on the events of the day as they fall asleep in Ace's comfortable hotel room; old men at the end of things, full of wisdom and experience yet unable to resist nature's slumberous pull on the elderly body. One of the best moments of the entire show is its first shot of Hoffman/Ace: a close-up frontal shot of his face: inscrutable – determined? haunted? – but clearly and somewhat brutally naked in its display of the ravages that age has inflicted upon the *The Graduate*. What I am presenting as a binary oscillation between a density of language and purpose, and the sheer emptiness, the flatness, of the very same things at other moments is quite striking, and might lead us to assume that mistakes have been made. But there is no mistake once a shot has been filmed, printed, scored and transmitted: *that was* what was intended.

Some of the dialogue is hard to understand, but that does not mean it is hard to follow. This is hardly a hymn to narrative complexity: there are people who own horses, who ride them, who bet on them, who win and lose at the races. That much is clear even if we can't track the nuance of jargon and accents. As we watch we do get a sense of a larger design which might or might not get clarified – Bernstein's plans may or not be something to do with revenge; and the show as a whole conveys a sense of obscurity, as if it wants to discourage us from the usual forms of involvement. In a later episode we get an 'audience surrogate' moment when the young financial hotshot, Nathan Israel, is quizzed by Bernstein in an obscure way, but we can tell that he likes him. It's as if the show is telling us it is OK, but you have to have faith.

This raises another question connected to legibility which is to what extent we have to live into an artwork before we can appreciate it, or before we realise the game wasn't worth the candle. Maybe that time is never. This is an enormous risk, especially in television; it is almost doing things in reverse. The discordance is striking; we are frequently misdirected and thrown in new and surprising ways. We are encouraged to think the show has a plan, as Bernstein has a plan, but then we are led in various ways to doubt its coherence or its importance. The soundtrack is part of this: the show uses music insistently in nearly all its scenes to remind us of – of what? – of the kind of momentum or mood we should follow, or attend to? Or is it a distraction, something to lull us into mistaken certainties? Is there such a thing as patient teaching without a coherent plan, a desire to take us up into a world that is not part of a settled view?

I am not suggesting, as some reviewers have, that the point is to refuse clarity or definition in a kind of modernist gesture. I think the show is trying to discover and articulate something about human beings, in fiction that believes it knows more than the rest of us and yet is still obscure to its makers. As those same reviewers have noted, the idea of a fundamental concord or unity underlying the universe is an important Milch theme that seems to be put under quite a lot of stress here. Part of that may be connected to the mismatch in the mediation between 'inner' and 'outer', especially involving those desires that we have but do not want to have, as if we are haunted by aspects of ourselves. This theme is most prominently figured with those characters who are compelled by addiction, but it goes to a deeper place concerned with the relationship between appearance and essence, past and present. Take the most apparently legible character, Bernstein's villainous British nemesis Smythe. Like us, he just wants to figure out how Bernstein is trying to fuck with him, and he shares with Bernstein a ferocious attention to the detail of self-expression and appearance, as if reading mood, reading that relation between inner and outer, is the source of all true power. Being able to read that discrepancy or concordance between inner and outer is of the essence when it comes to gambling, especially horseracing, where the divination of form is itself an art.

Unlike *John From Cincinnati*, which wanted to preach or at least speak to the nation about the destructive nature of technology and media, or *Last of the Ninth*, which yearned to find in the clash between race, between cop and terrorist, some commonality of mutual exploitation in history, *Luck* is utterly unconcerned with social and historical forces, the founding of civilisation, or the utility of abstraction in the upbuilding of the human spirit. What is missing?

Milch. He is certainly 'there' in the sense that this is, and was sold as, a highly personal project. During promotional interviews Milch would recount the story of the first time his father took him to the racecourse, and how the persona that was granted him that day – a degenerate gambler who knows the way the world's cookie crumbles, who can swim with and beat the sharks that inhabit the track – has lived with him ever since. And Milch had rehearsed his idea for the show at the 2007 writers' strike series of seminars, linking it to an image of hands passing money over a counter at the track that he was blocked on for years. He observed:

> If I stopped working my first thought is I have to go to the racetrack. And I hate it. In other words the idea of freedom to me is shameful because it is so unfamiliar. And the reason it's shameful is because that is the way you rationalize – I have to punish myself for being glad I'm free ... gambling [for me] is I've got to get out there to get into trouble and therefore justify my shame.

He kept trying to pitch the show during his time at HBO in the 2000s, an elaborate hour-long pitch made to various stars, drawing on the history of the track, the famous story of the neck-and-neck competition between the stallions Alydar and Affirmed in the late 1970s, and the former being tragically killed in the culminating (or almost) catastrophe of the Calumet Farm saga as depicted in Ann Hagedorn Auerbach's chilling book, *Wild Ride*.[8] One of the problems with the pitch was that in order to be as gripping as *Wild Ride*, some depiction of animal suffering was inevitable. Although we see a horse snap its leg on the track and subsequently be euthanised in the first episode (thanks to CGI effects), *Luck* was extremely coy about the kinds of practices and abuse that Milch, in his pitch, was quite open about, and which gave the drama-as-pitched a grim but compelling edge (possibly not to the taste of squeamish actors).

Furthermore, it seems likely that Milch had continued his gambling despite overcoming other addictions; indeed, in a typical exhibition of his 'deficits', he appeared on the *Late Late Show with Craig Ferguson* twice (in October 2009 and in March 2012), claiming that he needed to make $25 million from *Luck* to break even for his 'research expenses'. This meant, among other things, that Milch had 'stayed in the action' throughout his television career, abandoning alcohol and heroin, but maintaining what was outwardly a successful career breeding champion horses. Milch recounted to me the time he bet a large amount on his horse at a prestige race; after it failed to deliver he immediately left the track and drove home, only to find his wife Rita calling from the track to remind him that his family were still there. His long-time trainer would wear a heavy parka overcoat that Milch would stuff with wads of $1,000 bills for betting. His involvement with the sport was not merely compulsive or artistic but existential: without it, or its promise – call it the freedom to indulge unincorporated shame – Milch was unhappy. It made sense to try to engage the track with the resources and reputation he had established in Hollywood in order to somehow bring it under the authority of artistic ends.

The problem was that, after Hoffman was confirmed in 2009 and his gravitational pull attracted a high-calibre cast, including the attachment of Michael Mann to the project, *Luck* became a product in size and scale that outgrew Milch's creative authority. There were, to put it crudely, too many high-status creative entities involved even before the first few scripts were completed. It might be instructive to track this via my own encounter with Milch, since it is coincident with this period. I interviewed Ted Mann via Skype in February 2010, when he talked about Milch's writing process and the great amount of material generated by his practice of talking about characters and themes for hours in the morning before moving to writing in the afternoon with the team. He also mentioned that Hoffman had been cast in *Luck* and put me in touch with Scott Willson, Milch's assistant at Red Board Productions in Santa Monica. Later the next month, when in Los Angeles at an academic conference, I called Willson, who invited me to the offices, although he could not say if Milch would be there or not. When I arrived, Willson showed me some of the printed materials I have referenced in my discussion of *Deadwood*. As I waited in the front office for Milch to arrive, I got into conversation with Bill Clark; Clark was a dynamic, expansive talker, a big charismatic man with an interest in everyone and everything, even me. The conversation among the young assistants, Clark and Willson was dominated by the prospect of *Luck*'s first shooting days, scheduled for the following week; Willson showed me a framed photograph of a visit by some of the crew and cast (including Hoffman) to the Santa Anita track. At one point I heard Clark mention something about 'our people' and 'Mann's people', which I took to indicate the hurdle of two creative support teams who had to establish, or further evolve, diplomatic relations. It was clear therefore that creative authority was still to be cashed out, and what was no more than an aside from Clark was to become one of the big stories during the production of the show.

Milch did not turn up that day, but I did meet him the next as he walked into Red Board. He was characteristically generous with his time and in allowing me *carte blanche* access to the materials stored digitally, mostly comprising transcripts of his monologues and lectures. He also invited me to attend the shooting of the pilot of *Luck*, but I had to decline as I was returning to Australia the next day. Over the course of the next year I went through the materials he had provided and also kept an eye on news about the production of *Luck*. As with *Deadwood* (but not *John*) the pilot had been shot, but it would be many months before the other eight episodes would be written and filmed. Indeed, when I returned for a longer visit to Red Board, in April 2011, episodes were still being written as the production of completed scripts continued.

The first day I was there I had lunch with Milch; he mentioned that he was seeing Hoffman the next morning and that I was welcome to join him; he also let me watch the pilot in his office (twice); this version had not been scored and there was some minor post-production to complete, but it was clearly very nearly ready. The next day I met Milch for breakfast, at 7 a.m. at my hotel, and it was clear that something had changed. The prospect of my meeting Hoffman was off, and Milch expressed himself puzzled and frustrated that he was not allowed to give the actors notes (brief advice on how to play a scene or adjust the performance), let alone visit the set and talk to them. This was clearly a great contrast to his work on *NYPD Blue, Deadwood* and *John From Cincinnati*; it is clear to anyone watching the DVD extras that show production scenes that Milch's presence on set is an integral aspect, and something of a lifeline to actors not to mention directors wanting to know the meaning of his often indeterminate dialogue. Milch's puzzlement was the one time I saw him at a loss, unable to explain why he had been shut out so completely. As my discussion of *Deadwood* in the previous chapter indicated, Milch's 'Dr Jekyll' knows all about what his 'Mr Hyde' writing persona means, and it was Jekyll who was used to visiting the sets in order to communicate this vital information.

Breakfast over, I went outside with Milch to the hotel forecourt where the valet would bring his car. A peculiarity of that hotel (Shutters on the Beach) is that it does not have its own car park – a multi-storey building nearby is used instead, so there was some delay before his black Mercedes 600 arrived. It was a sunny, crisp Los Angeles morning, and while we waited I remembered that I'd wanted to ask about his evident love for dogs (the Milch family has several), and mentioned the poem by John Updike, 'Dog's Death', which had been referenced in one of his monologues. Milch remembered this right away, with a gasp, perhaps because the poem is somewhat Milchean in its mixing of primordial drives, shame, love and family tragedy (propelled by love and habit, a dying family dog drags itself to some newspaper on the floor in order to toilet). But it was clear that Milch was irritated; he was heading to his meeting with Hoffman and the valet was slow in getting his car. He questioned the woman at the kiosk as to the delay. 'I could have got it myself', he said, before telling me a story about historical criminal activity at a nearby hotel. Then the car arrived and he left.

It was only later that I realised the importance of this event. If Milch was going to see Hoffman in order to shoot the breeze then a minor delay would not matter (perhaps even a hanger-on professor would not in those circumstances); but if Milch was meeting with Hoffman in secret, against the wishes of Mann and his people, in order to coach him, to provide the big star with the kind of guidance that Milch was used to dispensing, which, indeed, now seems to be central component of his writing technique, then any delay risked diminishing his work. He had *something to say* to Hoffman before he went on set that morning (hence the early breakfast). In other words, the critical work that Milch does with his writing is to communicate its meaning to the actors; if he is unable to do that, then, in a very real way, his writing is not fully *there*. Could this be one source of the 'woodenness', the flatness of the performances we see in *Luck*, ones that had the characters behaving like, as Milch had said to me a few minutes before, 'automatons'? And given that he had noticed this and the fact that the scripts were still in production, was there an adjustment to this unwelcome reality in the later episodes? It is hard to say with certainty, since the evident fluency and clarity of those episodes could equally be a product of our greater familiarity with the shape and pace of the plot and the nature of the characters.

After breakfast I went to the Red Board studios and sat in an office shared by two of the people writing episodes, the sports columnist Jay Hovdey, and Robin Shushan. I wandered around a bit, and found myself back in the front office just as Milch's horse trainer, and clearly the model for Escalante, Julio Canani, walked in, carrying what I took to be a large framed painting; in fact the frame contained a collage of photographs and images taken from magazines. He looked at me and pointed at it: this is a portrait of Hillary Clinton, he said. Later, Milch took us all to lunch at LA Farm restaurant, part of the same building where luminary showrunners such as Steven Bochco, Dick Wolf and Larry David, who worked in the same complex, often ate. As usual it was taken for granted that Milch would pay for everything, and we were joined by the champion jockey Julie Krone (who is married to Hovdey) and Milch's son, Ben. Canani regaled the table with his story of coming to America in the 1950s, after skipping school to train horses in his native Peru, and working as a gardener in exclusive suburbs (and enjoying the opportunities provided by the housewives nearby). Milch recounted the story of when his horse Gilded Time damaged its leg, and he drove a hundred miles back home only to be called by his wife: 'At what point were you going to take us back as well?' Or when he took fifteen minutes stuffing wads of $5,000 bills into Julio's French army parka: 'When a guy like me hears "bet all the money you have"…' Later Milch invited me to the writing room where Krone, Hovdey and his long-term amanuensis Caleb Bacon were working; they were writing a scene with Walter, Rathburn, Rosie and Leon in a bar, which we see in one of the later episodes. While that was a relaxed session, Milch told me later in the car park as we said goodbye that he had kept me out of the room, even though he knew that was what I really wanted to see, in order to shield me from some 'stupidity' that had been going on earlier.

Perhaps it was the case that, in the midst of the turmoil created by his exclusion from the actors, not to mention his proximity to the racing world and its people, Milch's gambling intensified; certainly there was never a sense that it had stopped, despite his very public claims that his other addictions were behind him. While the first season was still being broadcast, *Luck* was cancelled amid claims of animal mistreatment. The irony – one of many – is that the good and bad treatment of horses and their power to heal the human spirit is a theme that the show was developing, and which is now removed from our screens. Indeed it seemed to want to balance a pastoral view of horses (as aids to the rehabilitation of prisoners) with the dynamic expression of their full breeding and training as athletes, which implicitly, and somewhat mischievously, asks us which we prefer – Dustin Hoffman's polite jogging next to a pony or the majestic competition of racing beasts.

Almost instantly, reports began to circulate renewing the narrative about the intensity of the rivalry between Mann and Milch, even to the extent of potential violence.[9] There seemed to be some good-natured relief shared between them once that rivalry had ended, and it is evident to anyone listening to the commentary over the final episode provided by Mann and Milch that any conflict was over creative authority and practice, rather than a deeper artistic schism. Mann was certainly a major contributing force in *Luck*. As an aesthetic technician of surface, he was able to articulate the hectic energy of the track and its spectators, especially in the dynamic, carefully composed racing sequences, which convincingly convey a sense of thoroughbreds able to punch holes in the wind. The race that crowns what is now the ending of the show is tremendous. One review mentions *Luck*'s horse races as implying the earth's rotation, and certainly when Gettin'Up Morning and Pint of Plain compete for the win in the finale, that cosmic sense of planetary motion is conveyed by the beauty of the San Gabriel mountains in the background, and our knowledge of its location as straddling a fault in the crust of the earth.

What thickens the excitement of the spectacle is that the race is itself a beginning, the discovery of true rivalry between two great horses (their story is based in part on the legendary rivalry between the thoroughbreds Affirmed and Alydar in the 1970s). After the result is known, competition becomes unity when the two trainers Walter Smith and Turo Escalante acknowledge that they are participants in that rivalry: that their luck is to be caught up in some part of the world's excellence. 'Next time more of the same, huh?', says Smith. Sadly this was not to be. Milch might have been satisfied that even without his close guidance, *Luck*'s peculiar flatness-in-motion also produced compelling television. But, again, it was unfinished, incomplete like all of Milch's work. It survives as a series of longer or shorter fragments, a Romantic aesthetic interest that aligns him much more with nineteenth-century artists on the cusp of modernism than even his mentor Warren.

After *Luck* was cancelled Milch continued to work on and promote other projects. He had been commissioned to adapt the PlayStation game *Heavy Rain*; with his daughter Olivia he had purchased the rights to adapt some of William Faulkner's novels. He told me about his plans to start with *Light in August*, mentioning a high-profile Hollywood star in the lead role of Joe Christmas.[10] Olivia would later establish herself more securely in the industry as screenwriter and director of the Netflix original *Dude* (2018), earning a writing credit on *Ocean's 8* in the same year. Milch gave a number of seminars and readings of his work at the University of Pennsylvania in 2010, and in 2014 worked on a new show, *The Money*, about a media mogul clearly based on Rupert Murdoch, continuing his fascination with the flaws of individuals who wield enormous power.[11] As with *Last of the Ninth* the pilot was shot, with Brendan Gleeson in the lead role, but not picked up for a full series. He was also working on an adaptation of Peter Matthiessen's novel *Shadow Country* about the outlaw Edgar 'Bloody' Watson, with Jeff Bridges reportedly interested in the lead role. Milch would also appear as an interlocutor at literary events in Los Angeles – for the publication of Oliver Sacks's book *Hallucinations* (2010) and Peter Whybrow's *The Well-Tuned Brain: Neuroscience and the Life Well Lived* in 2015, appearing on stage next to somewhat bewildered authors. Perhaps it was thought appropriate to place Hollywood's most brilliant writer next to intellectuals with a public face, but one can see Milch out of his depth when discussing matters beyond his own experience or view of art and work. Milch would also appear alongside other television showrunners as the appetite to hear from *auteurs* was magnified as the expansion of streaming television brought a glut of original episodic drama to public view. In 2008 he appeared at an event in New York called 'Outside the Box: Television Masterminds', alongside the creator of *Weeds* and other contemporary shows such as *House* and *Battlestar Galactica*.

Finally, in February 2016 Milch appeared on the cover of *The Hollywood Reporter* above the headline, 'The Spectacular Fall of a TV Genius'.[12] It was a photo of Milch unshaven, dressed in denims, looking back at the camera from the stands at the Santa Anita racetrack, clearly a picture taken in 2011 around the time of the shooting of *Luck*. In smaller font under the headline most of the full story was summarised:

> [t]he story of how David Milch, a gambler and beloved four-time Emmy winner behind *NYPD Blue* and *Deadwood*, blew through $100 million in earnings, gave up his homes, was put on an allowance of $40 a week and owes the IRS $17 million. Still, his supporters stay close: 'He's brilliant.'

The story would have surprised nobody who knew Milch, who, in any case, had never kept his spending on the track concealed. The article frames Milch's losses in terms of nationwide gambling addiction, and includes a lot of praise for him from the industry and friends, but it had the air of a gruesome tale of sudden loss. Instead, it is better to think of Milch's descent from the super-rich to the merely rich as akin to most of his writing output since *Deadwood*: a gradual lessening of power. *The Hollywood Reporter* could reference a 'TV Genius', and Milch is one of the few who might be called that: not all works of genius, however, are works of art. Given the history of his work that this book has tried to outline it is probable that Milch is indeed a genius. However, it may be that the medium itself has not yet found a genius who can make their mark as indelibly as those working in film or literature or the fine arts have done. Milch was fond of pointing to William James's test of pragmatism as being the 'cash value of an idea', the generative capacity of it. In these terms the word 'genius' has little to offer beyond a casual statement of status; a better description of Milch is as a virtuoso speaker, a man who could weave worlds with his words, and persuade those in his immediate audience that they were dealing with brilliance.

It is this quality that is Milch's advantage, his gift, his luck, but also one that has consequences. Appearing to be the most brilliant person in the room is fine as long as one is able to connect with its other occupants; otherwise they are merely spectators at some performance, as Steven Bochco believed. It is apt then to leave this audience with Milch talking. During the writing of *Deadwood*'s first season he was at the height of his powers, and during a discussion about character and plot – specifically Alma Garret's addiction to laudanum – he recalled his attempt to write a novel as an undergraduate at Yale. This was the one – the only one – about the death of Judgy when he was sixteen. By now Milch was nineteen, then twenty, then in his final year. Whatever he thought he was doing, being a writer became an option once he had met Robert Penn Warren, but in order to be one he had to write. However, Milch's real skill is in speaking, talking, not writing down, not forming words on a page. The catastrophic tale he tells would chill to the bone any aspiring writer:

> My friend had died and I didn't know what the fuck I was doing so I was just fucking around with this stuff. And I had a really good ear

> and I wrote a bunch of these chapters which were essentially just very good dialogue. And I was drinking a lot and taking the normal fucking drugs, so I guess a couple weeks before graduation, I said, 'Let me deepen my research a little bit.' I'd been up for a number of days and I took a bunch of acid, or something I was told – God only knows what it was. I had been working on this chapter – I was working exclusively through dialogue pretty much. And this last chapter was Judgy Lydell's mother when she finds out that he's been killed. And she's by herself. She don't have anybody to talk to. And all she's doing is scrubbing this fucking floor. As an obsessive. And so I was writing the same thing over and over again, about these ten pages. 'Mrs Lydell picked up the chair. She moved the chair. She took the rag. She scrubbed the floor four times.' And I'm thinking, 'You know this is going to be a rather dismal conclusion to this writing exercise.' I didn't know how to write at all. She's by herself. She's got nobody to talk to. She's not going to talk to herself. I'm fucked.

It did not occur to him to add characters to the scene; instead Milch knew that 'This is what I started, this is what I have to finish. The only trouble is I can't.' And then somehow he writes in Mrs Lydell's voice:

> I got the phone call that my son Judgy is dead, and then I felt that I should clean the floor, so I was cleaning the floor, I tried to scrub in multiples of four and then my mind went away. And then a voice said to me, 'Don't you understand what I have been trying to explain to you in secret code.' And I said I don't understand the secret code. And he said, 'Well, how many times did you scrub the floor?' I said four times. 'And why did I make you scrub the floor four times?' And I said I don't know. And the voice said, 'Because the first three parts are night and dawn and day.'

This is 'fucking gibberish' thinks the young Milch, and he decides to 'get fucked up' on whatever cocktail of drink and drugs he is able to ingest in two hours; eventually he finds himself in the Law School library where he starts writing again, trying to nail the multiple of three scrubs with something for the fourth one. Finally he has a revision where the voice says to Mrs Lydell: 'And the fourth part of all these three things is your son Judgy dead. And that's what I was trying to explain to you, that he's alright and I was trying to show you.' Eventually, Milch stops writing and tries to get home, but passes out in the middle of Elm Street, not far from Whitney Avenue where a few years later he would shoot out the lights of a cop car. He goes on, now, in 2003, telling the room:

> So I had gained access to my imagination in terms of the patterns of things and the recurrences and the parallels and all of this shit in a very

unnatural way, but I sort of persevered through it and came out with this thing that was quite compelling and then it fucked me up for about ten years. And I think if I had worked normally for ten years I probably would've produced just what was produced that evening. I guess what I'm trying to suggest is that in this behaviour of hers there are so many sins you commit once you have committed yourself to a lesser truth. And even aesthetics are a lesser truth in the absence of some sort of humane predicate to the aesthetic. And I had started with, I felt like I had not grieved my friend and so I wanted to find a way to say goodbye to him that was better than I had done when I went home and went to his funeral and everything. Life doesn't just give you one moment to make a decision and then you got a pass – every day you have to find the right way to be. If you're a junkie you just want to get fucking loaded. But I do think that trying to portray the moment of art is next to impossible.

Notes

1 David Milch, 2005, when writing *Deadwood* final season.
2 David Milch, USC seminar to COMM426, 'Religion, Media and Hollywood', 24 January 2008, www.youtube.com/watch?v=ans3AJVBIe4 (accessed 29 April 2019).
3 This history is detailed in Milch's 2007 writers' strike talks, 'The Idea of the Writer', https://www.youtube.com/watch?v=85FYtguoxEs (accessed 16 April 2018). He later encouraged his brother, Robert, and nephew, Mike, to develop this script. Eventually something similar was made into the drama series *The Knick*.
4 West is married to Mark Tinker, long-term director on episodes of *NYPD Blue*, *Brooklyn South*, *Deadwood* and the pilot of this show.
5 Gustav Fechner, *The Little Book of Life after Death* (Cambridge: Little Brown, 1904), pp. 77–8.
6 Sacvan Bercovitch, *The American Jeremiad* (Madison, WI: University of Wisconsin Press, 1978), pp. 190–1.
7 A pairing of a black officer and a white officer.
8 One of the pitches was made to Sarah Jessica Parker.
9 '*Luck*: Angry David Milch Brought Baseball Bat to Edit Bay?', *Los Angeles Times*, 14 March 2012.
10 'David Milch Will Tackle William Faulkner's Works for HBO', *Los Angeles Times*, 25 December 2011.
11 http://writing.upenn.edu/wh/people/fellows/milch.html (accessed 29 April 2019).
12 Stephen Galloway and Scott Johnson, *The Hollywood Reporter*, 26 February 2016, pp. 44–9.

David Milch filmography

This covers merely the shows on which Milch had a significant creative influence and writing input, and does not include his work as executive producer on other shows, or his uncredited contributions to film scripts. As detailed in this book, Milch had considerable creative authority over the following series, which included in many cases the final revision of scripts. I have therefore listed the major shows that he was responsible for overall (and dates indicating the period of his influence), rather than individual episodes that he is credited with.

Hill Street Blues (1982–87)
Beverly Hills Buntz (1987–88)
Capital News (1990)
NYPD Blue (1993–2000)
Brooklyn South (1997–98)
Big Apple (2001)
Deadwood (2004–06)
John From Cincinnati (2007)
Luck (2012)
Deadwood (movie, 2019)

Bibliography

Abrams, M. H., *The Mirror and the Lamp* (Oxford: Oxford University Press, 1971)

Affron, Charles, *Cinema and Sentiment* (Chicago: University of Chicago Press, 1982)

Arendt, Hannah, 'What is Authority?', in *Between Past and Future* (New York: Penguin, 2006)

Arnott, Peter, *Public Performance in the Greek Theatre* (Abingdon: Routledge, 1991)

Bailey, Blake, *A Tragic Honesty: The Life and Work of Richard Yates* (New York: Picador, 2003)

Barr, Charles, '*Straw Dogs, A Clockwork Orange* and the Critics', *Screen* 13.2 (1972)

Bercovitch, Sacvan, *The American Jeremiad* (Madison, WI: University of Wisconsin Press, 1978)

Berne, Eric, *What Do You Do After You Say Hello?* (London: Corgi Books, 1975)

Bianculli, David, *The Platinum Age of Television* (New York: Doubleday, 2016)

Bignell, Jonathan, 'The Police Series', in John Gibbs and Douglas Pye (eds), *Close-Up 03* (London: Wallflower Press, 2009)

Bignell, Jonathan, and Andrew O'Day, *Terry Nation* (Manchester: Manchester University Press, 2004)

Bloom, Harold, 'Foreword', in John Burt (ed.), *The Collected Poems of Robert Penn Warren* (Baton Rouge, LA: Louisiana State University Press, 1998)

Blotner, Joseph, *Robert Penn Warren* (New York: Random House, 1997)

Bochco, Steven, *Truth Is a Total Defense* (self-published, 2016)

Boyd, Brian, *On the Origin of Stories* (Cambridge, MA: Belknap Press of Harvard University Press, 2009)

Brooks, Cleanth, R. W. B. Lewis and Robert Penn Warren, *American Literature: The Makers and the Making, Book B, 1826–1861* (New York: St. Martin's Press, 1973)

Brooks, Cleanth, R. W. B. Lewis and Robert Penn Warren, *American*

Literature: The Makers and the Making, Book C, 1861–1914 (New York: St. Martin's Press, 1973)
Brooks, Cleanth, R. W. B. Lewis and Robert Penn Warren, *American Literature: The Makers and the Making, Book D, 1914 to the Present* (New York: St. Martin's Press, 1974)
Burt, John (ed.), *The Collected Poems of Robert Penn Warren* (Baton Rouge, LA: Louisiana State University Press, 1998)
Butler, Jeremy, *Television Style* (New York: Routledge, 2010)
Caldwell, John Thornton, *Production Culture* (Durham, NC: Duke University Press, 2008)
Caldwell, John Thornton, *Televisuality* (New Brunswick, NJ: Rutgers University Press, 1995)
Cavell, Stanley, 'The Fact of Television', in *Themes Out of School: Effects and Causes* (Chicago: University of Chicago Press, 1984)
Cavell, Stanley, *Little Did I Know* (Stanford, CA: Stanford University Press, 2010)
Cavell, Stanley, *The World Viewed: Enlarged Edition* (Cambridge, MA: Harvard University Press, 1979)
Collini, Stefan, *Common Reading* (Oxford: Oxford University Press, 2008)
Cronin, Gloria L., and Ben Siegel (eds), *Conversations with Robert Penn Warren* (Jackson, MI: University of Mississippi Press, 2005)
Currey, Mason, *Daily Rituals* (New York: Knopf, 2013)
Delbanco, Andrew, *Melville: His World and Work* (London: Picador, 2006)
Donoghue, Denis, *Arts without Mystery* (London: BBC Books, 1983)
Douglas, Pamela, *Writing the TV Drama Series* (Los Angeles: Michael Wiese Productions, 2007)
Dutton, Denis, *The Art Instinct* (London: Bloomsbury, 2010)
Edgerton, Gary, *The Columbia History of American Television* (New York: Columbia University Press, 2009)
Empson, William, *Using Biography* (Cambridge, MA: Harvard University Press, 1984)
Enright, Anne, 'The Genesis of Blame', *London Review of Books* 40.5 (8 March 2018)
Faulkner, William, 'Banquet Speech', 10 December 1950, www.nobelprize.org/nobel_prizes/literature/laureates/1949/faulkner-speech.html (accessed 29 April 2019)
Fechner, Gustav, *The Little Book of Life after Death* (Cambridge: Little Brown, 1904)
Fiedler, Leslie, *Love and Death in the American Novel*, rev. edn (New York: Stein and Day, 1966)
Fiedler, Leslie, *What Was Literature? Class Culture and Mass Society* (New York: Simon and Schuster, 1982)
Frankfurt, Harry, 'Identification and Wholeheartedness', in Ferdinand David Shoeman (ed.), *Responsibility, Character, and the Emotions: New*

Essays in Moral Psychology (Cambridge: Cambridge University Press, 1987)
Frankfurt, Harry, *Necessity, Volition, and Love* (Cambridge: Cambridge University Press, 1999)
Fried, Michael, *Why Photography Matters as Art as Never Before* (New Haven, CT: Yale University Press, 2008)
Frye, Northrop, *Words with Power* (Toronto: University of Toronto Press, 2008)
Furedi, Frank, *Power of Reading* (London: Bloomsbury, 2015)
Gaut, Berys, *A Philosophy of Cinematic Art* (Cambridge: Cambridge University Press, 2010)
Grimshaw, Jr, James A. (ed.), *Cleanth Brooks and Robert Penn Warren: A Literary Correspondence* (Columbia, MO: University of Missouri Press, 1998)
Guyer, Paul, *Kant* (New York: Routledge, 2007)
Hark, Ina Rae, *Deadwood* (Detroit, MI: Wayne State University Press, 2012)
Holt, Jennifer, 'Vertical Vision: Deregulation, Industrial Economy and Prime-Time Design', in Mark Jancovitch and James Lyons (eds), *Quality Popular Television* (London: BFI, 2003)
Hotaling, Edward, *They're Off: Horseracing at Saratoga* (Syracuse, NY: Syracuse University Press, 1995)
Hungerford, Amy, *Postmodern Belief: American Literature and Religion since 1960* (Princeton, NJ: Princeton University Press, 2010)
Jacobs, Jason, *Body Trauma TV: The New Hospital Dramas* (London: BFI, 2003)
Jacobs, Jason, *Deadwood* (Basingstoke: Palgrave/BFI, 2012)
Jacobs, Jason, 'Issues of Judgment and Value in Television Studies', *International Journal of Cultural Studies* 4.4 (2001)
James, Clive, *Play All: A Bingewatcher's Notebook* (New Haven, CT: Yale University Press, 2016)
James, William, *Habit* (New York: Henry Holt, 1914)
Jones, John, *Dostoevsky* (Oxford: Clarendon Press, 1983)
Kant, Immanuel, *Critique of Judgement* [1790], trans. Werner S. Pluhar (Indianapolis, IN: Hackett Publishing, 1987)
Kennedy, Angus, *Culture Wars* (Exeter: Imprint Academic, 2014)
Klevan, Andrew, 'Notes on Teaching Film Style', in John Gibbs and Douglas Pye (eds), *Style and Meaning: Studies in the Detailed Analysis of Film* (Manchester: Manchester University Press, 2005)
Kristeva, Julia, *Black Sun* (New York: Columbia University Press, 1989)
Kunitz, Stanley, 'Reflections', introduction to *The Collected Poems* (New York: W. W. Norton, 2000)
Lasch, Christopher, *Haven in a Heartless World: The Family Besieged* (New York: W. W. Norton, 1977)
Lasch, Christopher, *The Minimal Self* (New York: W. W. Norton, 1984)

Lavery, David (ed.), *Reading Deadwood: A Western to Swear By* (London: I. B. Tauris, 2006)

Lewis, R. W. B, 'Afterword', in James A. Grimshaw, Jr (ed.), *Cleanth Brooks and Robert Penn Warren: A Literary Correspondence* (Columbia, MO: University of Missouri Press, 1998)

Lewis, R. W. B., *Edith Wharton* (New York: Fromm International Publishing, 1993)

Lury, Karen, 'A Response to John Corner', *Screen* 48.3 (2007)

Martin, Brett, *Difficult Men: Behind the Scenes of a Creative Revolution: From The Sopranos and The Wire to Mad Men and Breaking Bad* (London: Penguin, 2014)

Maycock, A. L., *Nicholas Ferrar of Little Gidding* (Grand Rapids, MI: William B. Eerdmans, 1980 [1938])

McCarthy, Cormac, *Blood Meridian* (New York: Random House, 1985)

McGurl, Mark, *The Program Era: Postwar Fiction and the Rise of Creative Writing* (Cambridge, MA: Harvard University Press, 2009)

Melville, Herman, *Billy Budd, Sailor* (Harmondsworth: Penguin, 1985)

Michaels, Walter Benn, *The Shape of the Signifier* (Princeton, NJ: Princeton University Press, 2006)

Milch, David, *Deadwood: Tales of the Black Hills* (New York: Bloomsbury, 2006)

Milch, David, and Bill Clark, *True Blue: The Real Stories Behind NYPD Blue*, rev. edn (New York: Avon Books, 1997)

Newcomb, Horace, and Robert S. Alley, *The Producer's Medium: Conversations with Creators of American TV* (Oxford: Oxford University Press, 1983)

Parker, Watson, *Deadwood: The Golden Years* (Lincoln, NE: University of Nebraska Press, 1981)

Perkins, V. F., *Film as Film: Understanding and Judging Movies* (London: Penguin, 1972)

Pippin, Robert, *After the Beautiful: Hegel and the Philosophy of Pictorial Modernism* (Chicago: University of Chicago Press, 2015)

Pound, Ezra, *A B C of Reading* (New York: New Directions, 2010)

Pound, Ezra, 'T. S. Eliot', in *Literary Essays* (New York: New Directions, 1968)

Ricks, Christopher, 'Literary Principles as Against Theory', in *Essays in Appreciation* (Oxford: Clarendon Press, 1996)

Robillard, Douglas (ed.), *The Poems of Herman Melville* (Kent, OH: Kent State University Press, 2000)

Rosen, Charles, *Romantic Poets, Critics, and Other Madmen* (Cambridge, MA: Harvard University Press, 1998)

Scruton, Roger, *Gentle Regrets* (London: Bloomsbury, 2006)

Shields, David, *Remote* (Madison, WI: University of Wisconsin Press, 2003 [1996])

Sontag, Susan, *Illness as Metaphor* (London: Picador, 2001)

Stasi, Paul, and Jennifer Grieman (eds), *The Last Western: Deadwood and the End of American Empire* (New York: Bloomsbury, 2013)
Thomasson, Amie L., 'Fictional Characters and Literary Practices', *British Journal of Aesthetics* 43.2 (2003)
Thorburn, David, 'David Milch's Depraved Saints', *in media res*, 27 April 2012, http://mediacommons.org/imr/2012/04/27/david-milchs-depraved-saints (accessed 29 April 2019)
Toles, George, 'Dipping into Omniscience with Willa Cather: Authorial Knowledge as Love', in Susan Wolf and Christopher Grau (eds), *Understanding Love: Philosophy, Film, and Fiction* (Oxford: Oxford University Press, 2014)
Toles, George, 'Trying to Remember Clementine', in Christopher Grau (ed.), *Eternal Sunshine of the Spotless Mind* (London: Routledge, 2009)
Toles, George, 'Writing about Performance', in Alex Clayton and Andrew Klevan (eds), *The Language and Style of Film Criticism* (London: Routledge, 2011)
Warren, Robert Penn, *A Place to Come To* (New York: Random House, 1977)
Warren, Robert Penn (ed.), *Selected Poems of Herman Melville* (Boston, MA: David R. Godine, 2004)
Wilson, George, *Narration in Light: Studies in Cinematic Point of View* (Baltimore, MD: Johns Hopkins University Press, 1986)
Vest, Jason P., *The Wire, Deadwood, Homicide, and NYPD Blue: Violence is Power* (Santa Barbara, CA: Praeger, 2011)

Index